Advancing Doctoral Leadership Education Through Technology

We dedicate this book to learning as it is the one constant in change.
Laura Hyatt and Stuart Allen

Advancing Doctoral Leadership Education Through Technology

Edited by

Laura Hyatt

Professor, Department of Organizational Leadership, University of La Verne, California, USA

Stuart Allen

Professor, Department of Organizational Leadership, Robert Morris University, Pennsylvania, USA

Edward Elgar
PUBLISHING

Cheltenham, UK • Northampton, MA, USA

Published by
Edward Elgar Publishing Limited
The Lypiatts
15 Lansdown Road
Cheltenham
Glos GL50 2JA
UK

Edward Elgar Publishing, Inc.
William Pratt House
9 Dewey Court
Northampton
Massachusetts 01060
USA

A catalogue record for this book
is available from the British Library

Library of Congress Control Number: 2018954365

This book is available electronically in the **Elgar**online
Business subject collection
DOI 10.4337/9781786437020

Printed on elemental chlorine free (ECF)
recycled paper containing 30% Post-Consumer Waste

ISBN 978 1 78643 701 3 (cased)
ISBN 978 1 78643 702 0 (eBook)

Typeset by Servis Filmsetting Ltd, Stockport, Cheshire
Printed and bound in the USA

Contents

PART III   DELIVERY: ACROSS DISCIPLINES, COURSES
           AND BORDERS

Figures

Tables

About the editors

Laura Hyatt is a Professor at the University of La Verne, CA, USA where she served as Department Chair and teaches in the Organizational Leadership Doctoral program. She is an associate of an international think-tank, participated as an advisor to the Office of the Assistant Secretary for Planning and Evaluation at the Department of Health and Human Services in Washington, DC, and was appointed to a White House Policy Conference by the President of the United States. Prior to teaching, she was Vice President of Education for a production company and part of a collaborative effort that won several awards in the entertainment industry. Dr Hyatt has published books, book chapters, journal articles, serves on editorial boards for peer-reviewed journals, and has developed contemporary research methods utilized by researchers in the US and in Europe including the *Dynamic Narrative Approach* and the *Case Story* research method. Dr Hyatt has received recognition and grants for her research, which focuses on the intersections of learning, neuroscience, change, and the powerful climates created by our convergent stories as individuals, organizations and communities.

Stuart Allen is a Professor of Organizational Leadership at Robert Morris University in Pittsburgh, PA, USA. He currently teaches research in the Doctor of Science in Information Systems and Communications program and previously taught for the Organizational Leadership Doctoral program at the University of La Verne. Dr Allen is an active researcher and author in leadership, leadership education, adult learning, online learning, non-profit leadership, workplace pluralism and diversity, and post-traumatic stress in the workplace. He has received multiple grants related to leadership education. He is originally from South Africa where he worked as an industrial psychologist, CEO, board chair, trainer, coach, consultant and entrepreneur. Stuart has published articles in journals such as the *SA Journal of Industrial Psychology*, *International Journal of Management Education*, *Journal of Leadership Educators* and *Journal of Management Inquiry*, as well as chapters in various books, and a handbook on leadership. He is an editorial board member for the *International Journal of Organizational Analysis* and has received awards for his doctoral teaching and journal review work.

About the contributors

We wish to express our deep appreciation to the accomplished group of contributors to this book.

Elisabeth E. Bennett is Associate Teaching Professor of Organizational Leadership Studies at Northeastern University, Boston, MA, USA. Dr Bennett's research includes virtual human resource development, technology, organizational culture, and informal learning. She co-edited two Advances in Developing Human Resources issues on virtual HRD as well as writing book chapters and articles on the subject. Dr Bennett previously was Director of Education Research and Development at the Western Campus of Tufts University School of Medicine, and has worked in financial services, manufacturing, and university-based continuing education. She served on the board of the Academy of Human Resource Development and presently is a member of the editorial boards for *Human Resource Development Quarterly*, *Adult Education Quarterly*, *Advances in Developing Human Resources* and *New Horizons in Adult Education and Human Resource Development*.

Stephanie J. Blackmon is an Assistant Professor of Higher Education in the School of Education at William & Mary School of Education, Williamsburg, VA, USA. Her research area is teaching and learning, with a current emphasis on technology integration in various higher education, professional development and adult learning contexts. She has conducted studies on instructors' and students' experiences with three-dimensional virtual worlds, massive open online courses (MOOCs), and various learning management systems (traditional and non-traditional). She is also the co-editor of the *New Directions for Institutional Research* special issue 'MOOCs and Higher Education: Implications for Institutional Research'.

Sara Brierton is the Online Learning Specialist for Wake County Public Schools in North Carolina, the 15th largest school district in the United States. She is working to improve and expand professional learning for K-12 teachers. For Dr Brierton, online professional learning offers large districts the opportunities for growth, development and connection that are hard to achieve via traditional methods. She is particularly interested in fostering quality online discussions, online community, and conveying individuality and personality in the online environment.

Cynthia J. Brown is an Associate Professor at the University of West Georgia (UWG) Tanner Health System School of Nursing, USA and currently teaches in a one hundred percent online Master's and EdD program. Her research interests include qualitative methodologies, self-care of health care professionals, and caring and engagement in the online environment. She completed a postdoctoral clinical research fellowship in complementary and alternative therapies, enjoys facilitating online student Caring Groups and *Caring Connections*, an interactive site for all master's students at UWG. Dr Brown has published in scholarly, peer-reviewed journals, presented at local, national and international conferences, and holds certifications both as a nursing educator and as an advanced practice holistic nurse. She received a 'Best of the West' faculty of the year award at UWG in 2016.

Jackie Bruce is a leadership educator and faculty member in the Department of Agricultural and Human Sciences at NC State University, USA. Jackie teaches courses in leadership development, advises undergraduate and graduate students, serves as the Co-Coordinator of the Leadership and Social Justice Program in Agricultural Sciences, is an Equal Opportunity Institute Graduate Scholar, an LGBT Center Advocate, and is a member of the College of Ag and Life Sciences Diversity Council. Jackie is particularly interested in the intersectionality of leadership and social justice work, and how we can better develop more inclusive and just educational environments.

William Cain is Assistant Director for the CEPSE/COE Design Studio in the College of Education at Michigan State University, USA. He received his PhD in Educational Psychology and Educational Technology from Michigan State University. His interests focus on the cognitive, affective and kinesthetic experiences of teachers and students in technology-rich learning environments. He has published his scholarship in educational research journals such as *International Journal of Designs for Learning* and *TechTrends*, and has presented his work at both national and international educational conferences. Dr Cain is currently co-Chair of the Creativity SIG and past Chair of the Teaching and Learning with Emerging Technologies SIG for the Society of Information Technology in Education. He is a three-time recipient of the AT&T Award for Excellence for his work in online, blended and synchronous hybrid course designs.

Leslie Dinauer is a Professor and Program Chair of the Doctor of Management program at the University of Maryland University College, USA. Her international teaching includes work in Taipei and Jakarta. She is currently Treasurer for the Executive DBA Council, which seeks to foster excellence and innovation in executive doctoral degree programs worldwide. Dr Dinauer's research interests focus on pedagogical issues, particularly in the online environment. She is on the conference committee of University of Wisconsin Distance Teaching and Learning as well as the European Conference on Research Methodology for Business and Management Studies. Dr Dinauer is a member of Sigma Xi, The Scientific Research Society, the American Statistical Association and the Academy of Management. She has published articles in journals such as *Human Communication Research* and the *Journal of Public Policy & Marketing*.

Katja Einola holds the position of a Post-doctoral Researcher at the School of Economics and Management, Lund University, Sweden. She earned her PhD at Turku School of Economics, Finland in 2017 with a dissertation studying how successful teams form and evolve over time. Her Master's degree is from *Ecole des Hautes Etudes Commerciales* in Montreal, Canada. Her research interests span multiple methods and focus on global teams, leadership, research methods, and management education. Katja has twenty years of professional, consulting and management experience in small and large multinational firms spanning three continents mainly in tourism and telecommunications. She has been involved in teaching on all levels and is fluent in six languages.

Margaret Gorman is an Assistant Professor at Northeastern University, Boston, MA, USA where she served as faculty co-lead for the EdD at the Southeastern Regional Campus, Vice Chair of Academic Program Committee for College of Professional Studies, and teaches in the Organizational Leadership Doctoral Program. Prior to joining Northeastern University, she spent 22 years at George Washington University in various academic roles, to include faculty director of the Executive Leadership Doctoral Program and Center for the Study of Learning and Teaching in the Human Organizational Studies Program. Her research interests focus on organizational learning, complexity leadership and change. Dr Gorman has published various book chapters, to include 'Elliott Jaques: Father Time and Requisite Organizations' in Szabla et al. (eds) *The Palgrave Handbook of Organizational Change Thinkers* (2016) and 'Lessons from the Land of Oz: An Empirical Case Study of a US Financial Services Firm amidst Transformational Change, Effort and Leaderships' Roles in Fostering Knowledge Creation Capability' in Alegre et al. (eds) *Shedding New Lights on Organizational Learning, Knowledge and Capabilities* (2014).

Danah Henriksen is an Assistant Professor of Educational Leadership and Innovation at Arizona State University, USA. She received her PhD in Educational Psychology and Educational Technology from Michigan

State University. Her interests focus on creativity, thinking skills, and design thinking for education. Her scholarship has been published in peer-reviewed journals such as *Teachers College Record*, *Thinking Skills and Creativity*, *Journal of Technology & Teacher Education* and *Educational Technology*, as well as practitioner venues such as *Phi Delta Kappan* and *Educational Leadership*. She is co-Chair of the Creativity SIG for the Society of Information Technology in Education. Dr Henriksen teaches varied topics, in educational psychology, research methods, systems change, leadership, design thinking, and educational technology. She has been a recipient of the AT&T Award for Excellence, for pedagogical innovation in the design and teaching of hybrid doctoral education.

Emmanuel Jean-Francois is an Associate Professor of Comparative and International Education at Ohio University, USA. He is the Coordinator of the Doctoral program in Educational Administration/Leadership, as well as the doctoral specialization in Comparative and International Educational Leadership. His most recent books include: *Perspectives in Transnational Higher Education* (2016), *Building Global Education with a Local Perspective: An Introduction to Global Higher Education* (2015), *Financial Sustainability for Nonprofit Organizations* (2014), *Trans-Cultural Blended Learning and Teaching in Post-Secondary Education* (2012) and *Global Education on Trial by U.S. College Professors* (2010). Dr Jean-Francois is the Editor-in-Chief of the peer-reviewed journal *The African Symposium*, the Chair of the African Educational Research Network (AERN), and the Past-President of the Transnational Education and Learning Society (TELS).

Surinder Kahai is an Associate Professor and a Fellow at the Center for Leadership Studies at Binghamton University, State University of New York (SUNY), USA. He has a program of research that spans over 25 years and attempts to understand how information and communication technologies mediate leadership, collaborative work, and learning. His work has been funded by the National Science Foundation and UNISYS. Dr Kahai has disseminated his research findings through numerous research papers, many of which have appeared in prestigious journals and have been presented at selective conferences. He has employed his research to coach many business leaders and university teachers about how IT can mediate what they do and influence their performance. Dr Kahai has won numerous awards for his teaching, including the statewide SUNY Chancellor's Award for Excellence in Teaching.

Jim Martin is an Assistant Professor in the Interdisciplinary Leadership Doctoral Program at Creighton University in Omaha, NE, USA. He is also the Assistant Director of the program. He holds a PhD in political science with a specialization in comparative politics from Florida State University (2013), and an MA in international relations from Creighton University (2006). Dr Martin's research interests include the study of government performance, the effects of immigration on political parties, and SoTL work that includes the study of trust in educational institutions from a social network perspective. Dr Martin has presented at numerous national scholarly conferences and his work has been published in a variety of interdisciplinary journals and venues.

Jennifer Moss Breen is an Associate Professor at Creighton University, NE, USA where she serves as Program Director and faculty member in the Interdisciplinary Leadership Doctoral Program. She is an associate for the global research and consultancy group (Global Leadership Initiatives), serves as the senior editor for the Information Age Publishing Group Book Series 'Running with Scissors: Leading in Complexity', and is a principal owner of the Center for Strategic Leadership Development and Planning. Prior to joining Creighton University, she was the inaugural program director for Bellevue University's PhD in Human Capital Management program. Research interests focus on leadership humility, leadership in medical education, leader resilience and interdisciplinary leadership. Dr Moss Breen has published several book chapters and journal articles, and presented over 60 conference and professional sessions.

Ronald E. Riggio is the Henry R. Kravis Professor of Leadership and Organizational Psychology and former Director of the Kravis Leadership Institute at Claremont McKenna College, CA, USA. Dr Riggio is a leadership scholar with more than a dozen authored or edited books and more than 150 articles/book chapters. His books include: *Transformational Leadership* (with Bernard M. Bass), *Leadership Studies: The Dialogue of Disciplines* (with Michael Harvey), and edited books, *The Practice of Leadership* and *The Art of Followership*. His research interests are in leadership, organizational communication, and social competence. He is part of the Fullerton Longitudinal Study, examining leadership development across the lifespan (from one year of age and through middle adulthood). Besides research on leadership development, he has been actively involved in training young (and not so young) leaders.

Sean Robinson is an Associate Professor of Higher Education Leadership at Morgan State University, in Baltimore, MD, USA. Sean has over 25 years of experience on university campuses in both academic affairs and student affairs. His teaching interests include higher education administration, policy, and legal issues; organizational behavior and theory; student development theory; and qualitative research methodology. His primary research interest is related to identity development and sexual orientation/ gender expression within university and college environments, with a particular interest in the ways in which culture and climate impact the professional experiences of LGBTQ faculty and staff. His secondary research relates to the mentoring and socialization experiences of minority graduate students, with a particular interest in doctoral student socialization at minority serving institutions.

Delene Volkert is an Assistant Professor and the Director of the Doctorate in Nursing Education program at the University of West Georgia, Tanner Health System School of Nursing, USA. She currently teaches in the one hundred percent online EdD program. Her research interests include quantitative methodologies, persistence and attrition of doctoral nursing students, and the support needs of doctoral nursing students. She completed a PhD in Nursing Education from the University of Nevada, Las Vegas in 2016. While a student, she received the Tony and Renee Marlon Charitable Foundation Nursing fellowship and the Outstanding PhD Student award from the UNLV School of Nursing. Dr Volkert has presented at state, regional, national and international conferences, has published in scholarly, peer-reviewed journals, and holds a national certification as a nurse educator. In 2017 Dr Volkert earned the Best International Presentation Award at the RCSI Nursing Research Conference in Dublin, Ireland.

Bruce E. Winston is a Professor of Business and Leadership and the Program Director for the PhD in Organizational Leadership program in the School of Business and Leadership at Regent University, VA, USA. Dr Winston has served at the School of Business and Leadership and its predecessor schools: The School of Business and the School of Leadership as both an Associate Dean and as Dean. During his administrative tenure at the predecessor schools, he was instrumental in developing and launching online education programs. Dr Winston's research interests include servant leadership, person–organization fit, person–job fit, and values-based leadership.

Peter Zettinig is an Adjunct Professor in International Business at the University of Turku, Finland. He has previously worked as Senior Lecturer and International Business Program Director at Victoria University of Wellington in New Zealand, where he also received a degree in Higher Education Teaching and Learning. Peter's research interests revolve around core strategic issues in international business and are published in peer-reviewed journals such as *Organizational Dynamics, Foresight, Thunderbird International Business Review, European Management Journal, Journal of*

Cross-Cultural Management, *Critical Perspectives of International Business*, *European Journal of Innovation Management* and *Competitiveness Review*, among others. Peter leads a number of industry projects, many related to shipbuilding and shipping industries and for the Finnish State's Export Credit Agency. To date Peter has supervised over a dozen doctoral candidates (in Finland, New Zealand and Australia).

Foreword

There is no doubt that technology is changing the teaching and learning of leadership, as well as the practice of leadership. Higher education has historically been very slow to change and adapt to new technology, as compared to competitive businesses. In higher education, technology is often integrated at a snail's pace, and some educators are not motivated to keep up with the latest technological innovations. Hopefully, this is all changing, as educators realize the critical role that technology plays in both the delivery of leadership education and as a tool in the future lives of leadership students.

This book is primarily about doctoral education in technology-mediated programs in leadership (although I will argue that the lessons apply well to classroom-based education). A skeptic might say that learning leadership in a virtual, technology-driven setting is inconsistent with the goals of learning to lead and with what we know about leader effectiveness. However, as you will see when reading about e-leadership and global leadership education and practice, today's leaders need to be technologically savvy and capable in order to lead effectively.

As a professor who has spent 90 percent of my teaching time in traditional classroom settings, I realize the strengths and limitations of face-to-face instruction. The 10 percent of the time that I have spent teaching virtually was enough to convince me of two things: (1) distance education done right is much more challenging for the faculty member than in-class teaching; (2) teaching online effectively requires the instructor to be even more well-versed in theories and concepts of education and learning. In short, there are important lessons to be learned for education of all forms by understanding more about teaching through technology.

Regarding the challenges of teaching effectively online, my colleagues who teach online courses tell me (as well as my own experience with online courses), that it takes more work to do a good job. For instance, in a classroom you can often sense from students' comments, and their nonverbal cues, when they are getting it and when they are not. In online teaching, you need to constantly anticipate, to view the learning from the students' perspectives, and figure out ways to 'check in' with students regularly. It takes more work to figure out strategies to engage and stimulate them when you are not face to face. When online education is asynchronous, and students are distributed across time zones, professors are more 'on-call'. It is hard to compartmentalize your teaching into specific days and hours.

As far as being aware of theories of learning, online instructors, like classroom instructors, need to consider the best ways to deliver content for retention, to motivate students and to assess learning. Programs with an online component offer an opportunity and an incentive to explore cutting-edge technologies to better engage students and enhance their learning. For instance, gaming platforms and simulations offer opportunities to both learn about leadership and to develop leadership skills. Smartphone apps are being developed to enhance learning and leadership development on a daily, ongoing basis. These forms of technology also allow the opportunity for ongoing assessment of student learning, as well as pacing learning to the individual needs of students.

As I read through this book, I began to think about the role that technology plays in my own work – not so much my teaching, because I am typically in a classroom setting. Instead, I focused on how I conduct research and writing today when working with collaborators. Nearly always, our connections are technology mediated. In recent years I have written papers with co-authors who are scattered across the globe, and we never meet face to face during the entire process. Last year, I co-organized a conference with two colleagues – one on the East Coast, the other a hundred miles away. All of the year-long organization of the event was done virtually, through email, videoconferencing, shared electronic documents, and the like. We are now producing a book from the proceedings, but the only time that we interacted face to face was during the two-day conference! This is an example of how technology is transforming leadership and scholarship and changing the landscape that doctoral graduates will enter in the future.

This collection offers a variety of examples, experiences and techniques for advancing doctoral education in leadership using technology. There are lessons here for the design of online courses, the strengths and weaknesses of different technological modalities, tips for teaching specific online courses (for example, statistics, research methods), and ideas for the design and creation of online and hybrid doctoral programs in leadership. Moreover, the issues that are discussed, such as the levels and forms of 'connectedness' between professor and student (as well as student-to-student connections and team projects), the delivery of course readings and content, synchronous vs. asynchronous communication, workload, and grading and evaluation, are concerns in every type of postgraduate and graduate education, not just online education. Although I suspect that the primary readers of this book will be those who are involved in teaching or administering online and hybrid graduate programs in the study of leadership, every professor, whether she or he is working in a classroom-based, or primarily in virtual environments, or in a hybrid of both, could benefit from reading this book. Doctoral students engaged in completing their dissertations and research projects will also find a wealth of information related to higher education teaching, learning, and technology. Clearly, leveraging technology is the future of education. Graduate education in leadership is a particularly important form of education. In many ways, it models other 'professional' programs, in that many graduates of leadership programs will become practicing, professional leaders. Indeed, many students of leadership in graduate programs are already practicing leaders, and technology makes further education possible for them. Moreover, much of leadership today requires familiarity with technology, and an ability to use that technology to lead – to inspire, to clarify, to motivate, and to connect with followers. For those of us in leadership education, and for those who aspire to be more effective leaders in our high-tech world, this book is essential.

Ronald E. Riggio, PhD

Henry R. Kravis Professor of Leadership and Organizational Psychology, Claremont McKenna College, CA, USA

Acknowledgements

We would like to acknowledge the contributors to this book. You are an accomplished group who generously shared your expertise and precious knowledge.

We extend our appreciation to Ron Riggio for writing the foreword and for seeing the potential in a collaborative text like this to share ideas and experiences across doctoral programs, furthering scholarship and inquiry into this topic.

This book benefited greatly from the sound guidance and support of our Executive Editor, Alan Sturmer, at Edward Elgar Publishing. We also want to thank the reviewers and the team at Edward Elgar who edited the book. We appreciate your time, effort and valuable input.

Developing an interest in doctoral leadership education through technology does not happen by chance. Numerous examples of great professors and experience in teaching courses have spurred our interest in the potential of technology to support learners as they earn a doctorate. It would be impossible to thank all the faculty, students, staff and administrators who we have learned from and who have raised valuable questions about doctoral teaching practices. However, we each extend some special thanks below.

Laura is grateful to her family and friends, especially Dave and Molly who encouraged her writing, challenged her to try new things, and provided unconditional love. She also appreciates all the teachers, mentors and colleagues along the way who sparked her curiosity and fueled her imagination. Laura is thankful for the opportunity to collaborate with Stuart, acknowledging that our shared values, curiosity, and interest in teaching and learning resulted in an enjoyable endeavor.

Stuart wishes to thank his parents for seeding his curiosity about computers and technology. He thanks Dr Karen Ortlepp for encouraging his interest in teaching and setting a great example of higher education instruction in the days before online education. Stuart would also like to thank his wife Danielle for being an ever patient sounding board for ideas. The faculty at Regent University were an inspiration and great support during his early journeys into online learning. Stuart is also grateful to Laura for being a great partner in this important project.

PART I

Discovery: introduction and context

1. Introduction

Laura Hyatt and Stuart Allen

The growing number of programs and the more recent inclusion of leadership courses within varied postgraduate disciplines provide evidence of rising interest in doctoral leadership education over the past 15 years. Technology plays a significant role in doctoral leadership studies, providing a channel for teaching, learning, research and administrative processes. Existing and new programs seek to leverage technology-mediated learning, especially through the internet, in order to provide access, convenience and enriched learning, and to develop new pathways to achieve a doctorate. In this context, technology applied in doctoral leadership studies requires further exploration and serves to benefit students and society through innovative programs and learning designs. It is a fruitful time to ask questions about the benefits, challenges and needed solutions to prepare for the future design and delivery of postgraduate leadership education. This includes examining how new and changing technologies will impact doctoral students, faculty and the university milieu.

Much of the education and technology literature addresses K-12 or higher education in general. In the recent decade there has been exponential growth in the use of technology for teaching and learning in graduate and postgraduate education. While some research has been published relative to technology and graduate courses, less focuses on technology and postgraduate education. There is also a paucity of writings specific to technology-mediated doctoral leadership studies. Various aspects are similar in both graduate and postgraduate education such as critical thinking expressed through digital assignments or products, while others are unique to the degree level. For instance, during the course of a doctoral program in leadership, students gain knowledge, but they also undergo a metamorphosis of identity as they become doctors (Danby and Lee, 2012). The technology-mediated doctorate adds unique nuances to this identity, including the development of technology competence and the ability to work and lead virtually. While technology-mediated learning has impacted all professions and areas of study (Vaughan et al., 2013), for doctoral leadership programs the benefits of technology-mediated learning are not just conveniences such as reduced time on the physical campus, but also include the awareness and skill in working and leading in various technology-mediated contexts. Leading through technology-mediated communication is an increasingly relevant skill in globalized and technology-dependent organizations.

CONTEXT

The technology-mediated learning environment is no longer just a context in which students engage in learning about leadership, but also one in which they learn to lead in technology-mediated environments. Knowledge objects, enactments and products (Danby and Lee, 2012) of postgraduate work (for example conversations, writing and presentations) are also transformed in the technology-mediated programs. The ability to facilitate a conversation late at night with diverse and geographically distributed colleagues who are tired from their professional day at work is a unique enactment of advanced learning. This evolution aligns with the emergence of e-leadership (Avolio et al., 2014). Coordinating work, communicating, researching, networking and presenting are some of the many areas of technologically transformed enactments that were once practiced only in face-to-face classrooms. Adult learning principles (Knowles et al., 2015) are especially relevant for the postgraduate student as the technology-mediated learning context provides numerous opportunities to tailor learning experiences suited to working adult professionals. Leveraging new technology to match the needs of adult learners is one of the challenges faculty face.

Universities in the US and internationally continue to develop, revise and expand the number of doctoral leadership programs. Along with the growth in leadership programs, the number of leadership courses incorporated in diverse postgraduate fields has also increased. In addition to programs that are specific to the discipline of leadership, courses in leadership are included in the fields of business and management, communication, education, entertainment and arts, healthcare, information systems and technology management, non-profit, public policy and government, science and engineering, and numerous other social science and professional doctoral degrees. Advances in technology provide a vehicle to deliver content and information to a wide array of learners. With more than two decades of experience in delivering doctoral leadership education through technology, it is a fertile time to examine what has been learned and to explore future possibilities.

One prime example that entreats examination is the variation of terms and definitions associated with technology-mediated teaching and learning. Two terms, blended and hybrid, are used interchangeably by some institutions, while other institutions argue that these terms are not synonymous. To confound matters further, there are varied definitions attached to each of these terms. For instance, Garrison and Vaughan (2008) describe blended learning as: 'The basic principle [of blended learning] is that face-to-face oral communication and online written communication are optimally integrated such that the strengths of each are blended into a unique learning experience congruent with the context and intended educational purpose' (p. 42). Still, other authors attribute percentages of time necessary for a course to be considered as blended learning: 'blended courses are defined as those that combine in-class and online instruction with 30% to 70% online content' (King and Arnold, 2012, p. 1), whereas Allen and Seaman (2004) write: 'Blended education courses are defined as having between 30% and 80% of the course content delivered online' (p. 4). Our examination of doctoral leadership programs that increasingly include technology-mediated learning and communication shows that multiple different labels are used.

CONTENT

The intent of this book is to generate a dialogue about emerging technology-mediated doctoral leadership education including current challenges, potential solutions and future possibilities. An accomplished group of authors contributed to the contents of this book which are distributed in three sections: Part I: Discovery: introduction and context; Part II: Design: learning applications; and Part III: Delivery: across disciplines, courses and borders. The following are brief introductions to the peer-reviewed chapters included in *Advancing Doctoral Leadership Education Through Technology*.

Part I: Discovery: Introduction and Context

Chapter 1: Introduction by Laura Hyatt and Stuart Allen

Technology plays a significant role in doctoral leadership education providing a channel for teaching, learning, research and administrative practices. In this context, technology applied in doctoral leadership studies requires further exploration and serves to benefit students and society through innovative programs and learning designs. This chapter familiarizes the reader with the content and structure of the book. This is followed by an introduction to each of the chapters and their respective authors. The recent shifts in doctoral education and technology invite a conversation about pedagogical philosophies, processes and policies to consider regarding learning environments and practices that will facilitate the future of postgraduate leadership education.

Chapter 2: E-leadership: an essential part of doctoral leadership education by Surinder Kahai

It is important to include e-leadership in doctoral leadership studies. Learning about e-leadership will contribute to students' development as future leaders, teachers and researchers. In addition to being comfortable with the content of e-leadership in order to be able to deliver it in the classroom as future academics or as leaders in organizations, doctoral students will need to be capable of thinking about the dynamic relationship between technology and leadership in order to make it more relevant. Mere acquaintance with e-leadership will not suffice and inclusion of this topic in students' studies will help them to develop a deeper understanding of e-leadership. Future doctoral research in e-leadership is also discussed.

Chapter 3: Into the new: a creatively focused and technology fluent (CFTF) mindset for emerging doctoral contexts by Danah Henriksen and William Cain

To develop creative leaders in online and hybrid contexts, programs and coursework must provide learning opportunities using the creative and technological affordances of the medium, while also maintaining the strengths of existing scholarly norms. The chapter authors reason that online and hybrid doctoral programs require a creatively focused and technologically fluent mindset on the part of faculty instructors and other program stakeholders. The authors also describe the context for change in emerging opportunities for online and hybrid doctoral studies, and propose a creative and flexible mindset for instructors, designers and developers in such programs. This chapter covers theoretical foundations in creative thinking, openness, and willingness to experiment or engage with the new.

Part II: Design: Learning Applications

Chapter 4: Beyond cybernation: technology and teaching in doctoral educational leadership by Stephanie J. Blackmon

This chapter focuses specifically on three currently used technologies in doctoral educational leadership classrooms: social media, blogs and virtual worlds. A major premise of this chapter is that the relationship between technology and its users is dialogical. Furthermore, these exchanges are value laden. Therefore, the examples of technology provided in this chapter will move beyond cybernation and not only address the complex exchange that occurs when educational leadership instructors and students employ various technologies (the unidirectional relationship of user to technology), but also address ways to mitigate that complex exchange.

Chapter 5: Selecting and implementing technology in support of doctoral curriculum and program management by Bruce E. Winston

This chapter presents the challenges of scoping, aligning, acquiring and implementing educational technology to meet hybrid and online doctoral leadership program needs from the program administrator's perspective. Program administrators need to select, implement and train faculty and staff on the right technical systems that meet students, faculty and staff needs, and align with the university's goals and objectives. The right technical systems are those that provide benefits for the recruitment and retention of students, efficient operations, and quality improvement. To accomplish this, it is essential that program administrators follow strategic foresight principles of scanning, forecasting, trend analysis, cost–benefit analysis, training, and performance appraisal – before and after implementing new technology and evaluating upgrade requirements.

Chapter 6: Informal and experiential learning in virtually mediated organizational leadership doctoral studies by Elisabeth E. Bennett and Margaret Gorman

Informed by virtual human resource development (VHRD), this chapter discusses informal and experiential aspects of doctoral leadership programs that dovetail scholarship and practice, as well as the question of transferring learning from the doctorate to the organizational context. The chapter includes discussion of leadership in practice, the relationship between virtual doctoral studies and such constructs as virtual teams, course design that incorporates experiential components, and maintains that empirical research in the doctoral program is a highly experiential learning encounter that transforms the individual leader and potentially transforms how organizations solve future problems.

Part III: Delivery: Across Disciplines, Courses and Borders

Chapter 7: Online doctoral programs: a call for caring educators by Cynthia J. Brown and Delene Volkert

As doctoral programs evolve into online settings, how can educators best support students? The online format may be a course or program that has a hybrid structure with some online and some face-to-face aspects, or courses and programs that are completely online. In this chapter, nursing faculty discuss caring, highlighting caring communication between students in the course, between faculty and students, and between faculty, particularly those co-teaching a course. Case studies and the experience of the authors are intertwined throughout the chapter to provide the reader with examples of caring communication in the online, doctoral education setting.

Chapter 8: Social media identity in doctoral leadership education: SMILE by Jackie Bruce and Sara Brierton
This chapter looks at three general leadership arenas: the self, groups and teams, and organizations. Within these arenas, the chapter discusses the key components of leadership and explores the development and role of a social media identity (SMI) in each case. The priority is to help students determine their SMI needs. The authors present an approach to formulate a Social Media Identity in Leadership Education (SMILE). It is appropriate in the world of 'like', 'share', and 'retweet' that a SMILE has a place. Enhancing and improving work, professional relationships, and sense of self through social media is a goal for doctoral leadership students and practicing leaders.

Chapter 9: Beating anxiety and building community: best practices for teaching doctoral research methods and statistics online by Leslie Dinauer
This chapter shares some of the insight that emerged from the experience of teaching statistics including the appreciation for the role of each student's individual orientation to the material, to the classroom – both affectively and cognitively – and to the faculty. The chapter addresses the need to deliberately build a statistics course within an online doctoral program, as opposed to allowing instructors to simply reproduce the face-to-face coursework. Next, statistical anxiety is examined as a fundamental force to be conquered within the classroom, followed by the best practices that emerge from these understandings.

Chapter 10: Teaching leadership research courses online at the doctoral level: why we do it and how it works by Jennifer Moss Breen and Jim Martin
This chapter shares practices, challenges and ideas concerning teaching leadership online at the doctoral level. Specifically, the chapter addresses the process of implementing a series of reforms for teaching critical thinking skills in online research courses. The authors discuss how to ensure that students get the same experience across multiple sections of a course, and that academic expectations for full-time and adjunct faculty are aligned. This chapter offers a broad overview of online teaching and provides practical, hands-on tips for those new to teaching in the online environment.

Chapter 11: A technology-based glocal perspective for teaching in doctoral educational leadership programs by Emmanuel Jean-Francois

The evolution of globalization, as well as other factors such as rapid technological changes, demographic shifts, migration, new forms of communication and interactions, and environmental and social challenges have served as drivers fostering the demand for new skills and competencies expected from university graduates by employers and other stakeholders. The purpose of this chapter is to articulate a technology-based glocal perspective for teaching doctoral educational leadership programs. This chapter is informed by the transnational and glocal education frameworks, and includes key insights for practitioners to contribute to glocal teaching and learning in leadership education through technology.

Chapter 12: Integrating doctoral research and teaching with technology: a case from a Finnish business school by Peter Zettinig and Katja Einola

Education is becoming a field where universities fight for the best students and sometimes existence, and PhD students compete against each other for scarce jobs. In such an environment, how do educators build a relevant doctoral training program to prepare a future generation of educators and researchers capable of conducting meaningful social research and finding their place in the volatile job market? In this chapter, faculty from Finland discuss how the use of technology-mediated communication enabled them to turn a master's level international strategy course into a shared laboratory that combined completion of doctoral research, teaching, course design and coordination, and assisted students to acquire practical leadership skills.

Chapter 13: E-mentoring in a technology mediated world: implications for doctoral leadership education by Sean Robinson

The purpose of this chapter is to explore the role of mentoring within online doctoral leadership education, with attention directed to the benefits and role of e-mentoring as a way to help aspiring leaders (doctoral students) develop the necessary skills and mindset for effective leadership. Given the shifting landscape of communication processes coupled with the exponentially changing world of computers and technology, considering the role of e-mentoring for leadership development within doctoral education is timely and needed.

GENERATING A DIALOGUE

Whether focusing on pedagogical philosophies, processes or policies, discovering priorities in research related to technology-mediated learning environments will facilitate better programs and beneficial learning for postgraduate leadership students. While not entirely unique, leadership students represent varied professional disciplines and will experience new challenges as technologies evolve that can be better understood and considered in curriculum and program design. The need for global competence is increasingly relevant as faculty often employ technology to teach students across borders, multiple time zones, cultures and environments. In addition, students in postgraduate leadership studies compete for attention with many other activities that place demands on working adults, where technology can encourage curiosity and learning.

This book is about questions rather than answers. It is intended to share ideas and spark conversations among doctoral faculty, administrators and students about how the future design of doctoral leadership studies would best serve students and the organizations they will lead. Research indicates that leadership occurs in relationship with others (Cunliffe and Eriksen, 2011; Gergen, 2009; Hosking, 2007; Uhl-Bien, 2006). While technology has increased efficiencies, how might we use technology to develop the way we lead and improve organizational relationships? What teaching and learning tools would be useful now? And in the future? How will technology impact the future design of research and dissertations? The increasing role of technology-mediated learning also has implications for academic leadership and policy, introducing unique challenges for higher education administrators. The aforementioned issues are among many topics this book explores, making the contents valuable to doctoral faculty, chairs and directors, administrators, higher education researchers, and students engaged in learning and research in higher education and leadership programs.

REFERENCES

Allen, I.E. and J. Seaman (2004). *Entering the mainstream: The quality and extent of online education in the United States, 2003 and 2004*. Sloan Center for OnLine Education (SCOLE). Needham, MA: Sloan-C, accessed at: http://www.sloan-c.org.

Avolio, B.J., J.J. Sosik, S.S. Kahai and B. Baker (2014). E-leadership: Re-examining transformations in leadership source and transmission. *The Leadership Quarterly*, **25**(1), 105–31.

Cunliffe, A.L. and M. Eriksen (2011). Relational leadership. *Human Relations*, **64**(11), 1425–49.

Danby, S. and A. Lee (2012). Researching doctoral pedagogy close up: Design and action in two doctoral programmes. *Australian Universities Review*, **54**(1), 19–28.

Garrison, D.R. and N. Vaughan (2008). *Blended learning in higher education: Framework, principles, and guidelines*. San Francisco, CA: Jossey-Bass.

Gergen, K.J. (2009). *Relational being: Beyond self and community*. New York, NY: Oxford University Press.

Hosking, D.M. (2007). Organizing, leadership and skillful process. *Journal of Management Studies*, **25**(2), 147–66.

King, S.E. and K.C. Arnold (2012). Blended learning environments in higher education: A case study of how professors make it happen. *Mid-Western Educational Researcher*, **25**(1/2), 44–59.

Knowles, M., E. Holton and R. Swanson (2015). *The adult learner: The definitive classic in adult education and human resource development* (8th edn). Abingdon: Routledge.

Uhl-Bien, M. (2006). Relational leadership theory: Exploring the social processes of leadership and organizing. *Leadership Quarterly*, **17**(6), 654–76.

Vaughan, N.D., M. Cleveland-Innes and D.R. Garrison (2013). *Teaching in blended learning environments: Creating and sustaining communities of inquiry*. Alberta, CA: Athabasca University Press.

2. E-leadership: an essential part of doctoral leadership education

Surinder Kahai

The human race is witnessing a major transformation in the use and form of information technology (IT) right in front of our eyes. During a recent trip to India, I could not help but notice a huge rush of people at the store of a mobile service operator where I had gone to purchase a wireless data plan for my computer. People were upgrading to faster, beefier data plans for their smartphones, which continue to grab even greater attention every day. Like for other consumers in the rest of the world, the consumption of information by Indians was being encouraged in no small part by the falling price of computing. Just as semiconductor companies struggle to bring down computing costs by keeping Moore's Law going (Waldrop, 2016), cloud computing is chipping in by enabling consolidation of computing infrastructure and services and the accompanying economies of scale (Hashem et al., 2015). Cloud computing is also helping us enjoy mobile computing's promise of access to our information as well as processing and storage capacities irrespective of where we might be. In this scenario that we are witnessing, how we interact with, perceive and influence others is not remaining the same. Work is changing. In fact, rapid advances in artificial intelligence (AI) and increasing automation of work by IT in general are fueling the question of what work will remain for us in the future (Manyika, 2017).

Can the topic of leadership endure these changes? Can the practice and research of leadership proceed as if it is business as usual? I do not believe so. To the extent that information and its processing are bases for a leader's power, changes in who has access to information, what kind of information is collected and processed, and where it is being used will inevitably lead to changes in leadership (Avolio and Kahai, 2003). For instance, an ordinary citizen carrying a cellphone can become an unheralded hero and affect a company's reputation by recording and sharing a video of how it mistreats its customers. Avolio et al. (2014) argue that the changing IT scenario is changing the source of leadership, how leadership is transmitted and received, and the context that embeds leadership. An inspiring leader, for example, may transmit positivity via social media. The leader's positivity may be received and interpreted by thousands of individuals who then transmit the effects in both electronic and non-electronic interactions they have with others. Depending on whether the constituents believe in the leader's authenticity and message, the leader's positivity may go viral or just become diminished.

Kahai et al. (2017) provide further support for why the practice and research of leadership cannot proceed as if it is business as usual. The authors argue that while the requirements for leader benevolence, competence and caring are intact in today's IT-rich environment, as are those for building high-quality relationships with followers and engaging them, other aspects of leadership are changing. Specifically, the fundamental human processes by which leaders engage others and influence them are changing because they are mediated significantly by IT today. For instance, though humans tend to be unaware of their egocentricity and tend to be overconfident about being interpreted correctly when communicating with others, electronic communication escalates this overconfidence (Kruger et al., 2005), potentially altering the effort a leader puts into influencing others. Kahai et al. (2017) further argue that certain leadership behaviors and the tactics for displaying them may become more critical as IT changes the nature of work. IT is driving more work to become virtual, for instance. As more work is being done in multicultural virtual teams with high diversity in how time is viewed and acted upon, temporal leadership which can manage this diversity (Mohammed and Nadkarni, 2011) is becoming more important. According to Kahai et al. (2017), IT may also affect leadership by enhancing or substituting for leadership. Uber's platform, for instance, substitutes for leaders who would normally supervise the drivers. It does so by sending certain types of emails and alerts to drivers that attempt to motivate them to work at the weekends and discourage them from logging off when demand is high (Rosenblat and Stark, 2016).

Thus, with IT influencing how leadership is exercised today, the practice and research of leadership cannot proceed as if it is business as usual. IT needs to be a part of thinking about leadership.

E-LEADERSHIP AS A TOPIC OF STUDY IN DOCTORAL EDUCATION

IT is not some fixed medium that is affecting leadership. It is shaped by the culture, the system of performance measurement and rewards, and the knowledge, skills and attitudes of users within the context in which it is used – all of which are influenced by leadership (Avolio et al., 2014;

Avolio et al., 2001). Thus, while IT affects leadership, it is affected in turn by leadership. E-leadership is a topic of study that focuses on this dynamic between IT and leadership – how IT affects leadership, how leadership affects IT, and the adaption of leadership to the IT-dominated reality faced today. In their attempt to capture this rich and complex dynamic between IT and leadership, Avolio et al. (2014) define e-leadership as 'a social influence process embedded in both proximal and distal contexts mediated by AIT [Advanced Information Technology] that can produce a change in attitudes, feelings, thinking, behavior, and performance' (p. 107).

Is it relevant for doctoral leadership students to include e-leadership in their studies? The answer to this question is 'yes' and there are several arguments that can be made in support of this answer. First, doctoral leadership students need to be knowledgeable about different aspects of leadership. As argued above, e-leadership is becoming an increasingly integral part of leadership. For the sake of completeness in their education, doctoral leadership students must include e-leadership in their studies. Learning about e-leadership will contribute to their development as future teachers and researchers of this topic. In addition to being comfortable with the content of e-leadership in order to be able to deliver it in the classroom as future academics, doctoral students will need to be capable of thinking about the dynamics between IT and leadership in their leadership research in order to make it more relevant. Mere acquaintance with e-leadership will not suffice and only inclusion of this topic in their studies would help them develop in this way.

Second, doctoral leadership students are likely to become practitioners of leadership in the future. They will practice leadership in one or more of the following ways, which are likely to involve mediation by IT and, hence, e-leadership: (1) as leaders for their students when they teach – they may deliver their material online or interact with their students electronically; (2) as a member of the academic community, such as when they hold a formal position (for example, editor, associate editor, program chair) or when they are engaged in a practice-oriented discourse with their peers; (3) as a member of the professional human relations community; and (4) as someone called upon to fulfill a leadership role within administration (for example, as a dean, or a head of department). Third, they might be called upon as consultants or advisors to develop leadership capabilities of practitioners. They will be expected to be knowledgeable about e-leadership in this role not only because it is an important aspect of leadership (as described earlier) but also because when one considers e-leadership broadly as the dynamic between IT and leadership, it also entails technology-based development of leaders (Kahai, 2012). Training and development of practitioners is increasingly taking place via IT over distance in the form of games, simulations, virtual reality and plain electronic delivery of content.

HOW IT SHAPES LEADERSHIP

When one surveys work by scholars on the topic of IT's effect on leadership, a range of views can be found. For some scholars, IT does not change leadership. They argue that leaders still have to be competent, caring and benevolent and they still need to relate to and personally engage with others (Champy, 2010; Sutton, 2010). For others, IT mutes leadership. Purvanova and Bono (2009) argue that computer-mediated transformational leadership and leader–member exchange may suffer due to attenuation of emotions. Avolio and Kahai (2003) argue that IT alters leadership by changing how information, an important basis of influence and power, is acquired, stored, interpreted and disseminated. Kahai et al. (2004) question whether participative leadership would be able to influence participation when a team uses a Group Support System (GSS), which can substitute for the leader by encouraging participation. They also question whether a GSS neutralizes a directive leader by conflicting with the leader's style. Another viewpoint argues that digitization might improve leadership effectiveness. Reeves et al. (2008) illustrate how a virtual team's technology can help someone emerge or be more effective as a leader.

The seemingly contradictory viewpoints can be reconciled using Yammarino et al.'s (2001) integrative leadership model, which describes five focus areas in leadership research. The first, fundamental human processes, refers to the psychological and related processes that enable leadership and it covers cognitive and emotional processes, interpersonal attraction, communication, and the norms, values and culture of collectives. The second, leadership core processes, focuses on the behaviors for exercising leadership (for example, charisma, transformational leadership, empowerment, providing task and relationship functions to groups, and supervision or management). The third, leadership outcomes, covers the leadership tactics of putting together leadership core processes, which include, for example, team building, delegation, and participation in decision-making. The fourth, second-level leadership outcomes, refers to the immediate outcomes of leadership core processes, including performance, satisfaction, absenteeism, engagement of followers, and leader–follower relationships. The fifth, substitutes for leadership, refers to leadership enhancers, neutralizers and replacements.

Scholars claiming that leadership remains unchanged are focusing on a leader's behaviors or qualities and second-level outcomes. They are accurate in that leaders still need to display behaviors that reflect benevolence, competence and caring and seek outcomes like high level of follower engagement and high-quality leader–follower relationships, but they ignore other areas in Yammarino et al.'s (2001) model. They ignore IT's effect on fundamental human processes (for example, transmission of non-verbal cues) that enable leaders to display certain behaviors and qualities and relate to their followers. They fail to realize that leaders have to change to overcome challenges and benefit from opportunities created by IT. Certain leadership behaviors or qualities, such as temporal leadership aimed at scheduling deadlines, synchronizing team member behaviors, and allocating temporal resources (Mohammed and Nadkarni, 2011), as well as the tactics for displaying them may need to be scaled up as more work becomes virtual. At the same time, tactics such as top-down leadership may need to be toned down with greater deployment of IT (Hitt and Brynjolfsson, 1997). Those who believe that leadership is unchanged may also be missing the point that in a world being made increasingly complex by IT, the locus of leadership may be shifting from individuals to emergent and dynamic interactions among various stakeholders (Bennett et al., 2014; Uhl-Bien et al., 2007). Scholars who argue that leadership is changing focus on how IT changes fundamental human processes by altering cognition, emotions and communication, as well as the norms, values and culture of collectives. Scholars who question the relevance of traditional leadership behaviors in an increasingly digitized world are generally focusing on neutralizers and substitutes. They question whether leadership core processes, such as supervision, charisma or empowerment, are impactful in the presence of IT, which can potentially neutralize or substitute for leader behaviors. Scholars who point to IT helping in the emergence or strengthening of leaders are focusing on IT as an enhancer.

Thus, the range of views presented by different scholars complement each other to suggest that in the emerging IT-dominated context leadership cannot be expected to remain the same. Leaders need to understand this new context and how it makes a difference for them. In organizations, the evolution of IT-supported work has followed that of IT networks. Local area networks (LANs) enabled the development of GSS to support same-place meetings. LANs gave way to the larger internet, which allowed organizations to tap into remote human resources and create virtual teams. The internet also evolved from a network in which powerful entities, such as businesses, provided much of the content, to one that enabled anyone to contribute via social media. With the emergence of a more egalitarian internet, organizations turned their attention to online communities in which external stakeholders, such as customers with whom they share an interest, are influencing them in unprecedented ways. More recently, IT networks have evolved into powerful computing platforms, giving rise to what is known as cloud computing. Today, it is possible to access highly scalable, always on processing and storage capabilities from something as simple as a smartphone. Cloud computing is changing the nature of work by enabling computing from anywhere and advances in artificial intelligence, among other things. As more of people's daily activities are conducted on cloud computing networks, the pendulum of power is swinging back in favor of companies that are turning the digital footprints left on cloud computing networks into predictions of what individuals will like or do, sometimes even before those preferences are developed or actions are taken. Companies now have the ability to influence individuals' thoughts and behavior like never before. The following summarizes the changing pattern of leadership in the four stages of evolution of IT networks.

Leadership in Same-Place IT-Supported Meetings

Studies (for example, Kahai et al., 1997; Sosik et al., 1997) indicate that a leader's core processes and tactics (transformational vs. transactional and participative vs. directive behaviors) are impactful in GSS settings. However, while anonymity provided by a GSS may enhance the effects of transformational leadership that rely on increased group salience, it can replace transformational leadership for outcomes such as idea flexibility (Sosik et al., 1998). Transactional leadership may lose its potency and directive leadership may be seen as information rather than as controlling in anonymity's presence (Kahai et al., 1997; Sosik et al., 1997). Statistical feedback provided by a GSS may neutralize a leader by conflicting with the leader (Hiltz et al., 1991). Certain fundamental processes, such as a collective's culture, do not change. When the GSS enables identification, the leader is viewed in a culturally-consistent way, as seen in the maintenance of the leader's higher status (Lim et al., 1994).

Leadership in Virtual Teams

Changes in fundamental human processes caused by technology are thought to be responsible for some of the findings about virtual team leadership. For instance, while certain personality variables (for example, extraversion and emotional stability) predict emergent transformational leaders in face-to-face teams, they fail to do so in virtual teams, probably due to the loss of non-verbal cues in virtual teams (Balthazard et al., 2009). In the absence of non-verbal cues, the human processes behind making sense of others and their situation come to rely on textual information and related meta-information. On the other hand, some studies suggest that the challenges in group processes due to virtuality may create a situation in which certain core leadership processes and tactics (for example, shared leadership) have an even larger impact by compensating for these challenges (Hill and Bartol, 2016). Evidence also suggests that virtuality may strengthen the mechanisms underlying core leadership processes such as inspirational leadership (Joshi et al., 2009).

Research findings suggest that virtual team leaders need a variety of skills, some that are shared with traditional team leaders and others that are not (Roy, 2012). Those that are shared with leaders of traditional teams, though with greater importance due to challenges imposed by virtuality, include being able to: create an open and supportive environment, establish trust, embrace diversity, foster a team spirit, motivate team members, and defuse the frustrations of team members as part of relationship-building skills. Virtual team leaders, like those of traditional teams, also need to possess emotional intelligence and be able to lead by example. What is new in virtual teams is the requirement that a leader possess the technical ability to use a variety of communication media, including video-conferencing, instant messaging (IM) and email. Ineptness with IT might negatively impact leadership effectiveness in a virtual context. Enabling understanding of and sensitivity to different cultures within the team is another requirement that virtual team leaders may face to avoid conflict or misunderstandings stemming from cultural differences.

When leading virtual knowledge networks, which consist of cooperative intra- and inter-organizational relationships, leaders face the challenge of dealing with conflict (Jarvenpaa and Tanriverdi, 2003). Conflict over rewards allocation is common in such networks due to the nature of knowledge and knowledge work. Jarvenpaa and Tanriverdi (2003) argue that to minimize conflict, leaders need to shift from being firm-centric to network-centric and focus on building trust and relationships. Leaders may have to be transformational and offer a compelling vision to others in the network to inspire them to rise above 'what's in it for my firm' mindset.

Leadership in the Age of Social Media

Empirical research on what social applications mean for leadership is largely restricted to traditional electronic media such as email, discussion boards and instant messaging instead of contemporary social media such as Facebook and Twitter. While social applications can easily help a leader shape the fundamental cognitive and emotional processes of others and build social capital, they can also help those with a more compelling message neutralize a formal or existing leader's power and rise. Indeed, in online communities, which bring together people with a common interest, leadership is likely to be emergent and informal. It is others who recognize someone to be a leader (Johnson et al., 2015). Formal hierarchies are rare and governance tends to be bottom-up; those in formal leadership positions are not necessarily seen as leaders (Johnson et al., 2015).

In online communities, it is the mediated, text-based interactions that render leadership as different. In the absence of multiple channels that help convey information in traditional settings to predict leadership emergence, it is the quality and quantity of text communication in online communities that end up predicting leadership emergence (Huffaker, 2010). A leader has to engage in core leadership processes and tactics via the written message (Zhu et al., 2012). Beyond the written message, it is the leader's visible actions that become the influence tactic (Eseryel and Eseryel, 2013). The nature of an online community's work, such as that of a 'collab' community, can neutralize leadership (Luther and Bruckman, 2008).

A popular thought that emerged in the wake of the Arab Spring, Occupy Wall Street and other protest movements during 2010 and 2011 is that social media are enabling citizen-inspired, grassroots-based social movements without a galvanizing figure who mobilizes all and spurs action (Gerbaudo, 2014). Leaders who provide the glue to hold the participants together in traditional social movements are no longer considered to be necessary for enabling and sustaining technology-enabled social movements. Instead, like-minded people are enabled by social media to come together, share their thoughts and frustrations, and coordinate joint action.

In this vein, Bennett et al. (2014) concluded from an analysis of tweets related to the Occupy movement that it is small transactions or networking micro-operations of individual participants (for example, tweets, retweets, posting links, adding multiple hashtags) that enable them to weave together different networks into a larger network and create coherence and rationality in actions. According to the authors, connective action enabled by technology-based social media ends up substituting for collective action that is inspired by a leader in traditional social movements.

Gerbaudo (2014), however, argues that the picture of individually inspired actions aggregating to a larger movement provided by Bennett et al. (2014) is incomplete and that there is a collective phenomenon in the form of a common identity and culture as well as collective leadership associated with the technology-enabled movement. To be sure, Gerbaudo (2014) argues, there is no one leader as in traditional movements, but leadership is certainly present as are leadership functions, although they are now enabled by the meaning associated with technology's use. There are digital vanguards, or a set of individuals often bound together by friendship and comradeship, which initiate and steer relevant internet conversations. They set up a collective space where others come and make their contributions in a way that leads to the formation of a common identity. Common identity also follows when participants use a particular technology and a language that is fully understood only by those 'in the know' or individuals who share their worldview. The common identity and shared culture become a source of coherence otherwise provided by a human leader. In this sense, technology-enabled identity and the culture shared by participants substitute for features of a traditional social movement that would have been facilitated by the movement's leader.

Social media use is not restricted to outside organizational boundaries; it is becoming ubiquitous within organizations too ('How social tools', 2016). According to Richter and Wagner (2014), the use of social media within organizations has implications for leadership development, an aspect of leadership not covered in the Yammarino et al. (2001) model. As more work within organizations occurs via modern social media, leaders need to adapt their influence processes because those that worked for them in settings dominated by older electronic channels such as email will probably no longer be effective. While these applications offer leaders the opportunity to increase their contact and be more social, they also create challenges. Therefore, a number of measures need to be taken to help leaders adapt to the use of social media in organizations. Data from interviews of individuals responsible for social media implementation in their organizations suggests that leaders need to be convinced (engaged and activated) about, sensitized to (shown the impact of and developed for new kinds of leadership with), and coached about (provided assistance to embrace the new tools of and understand emergent use cases of) the new social applications.

Leadership in Cloud Computing Contexts

A host of issues are arising for leadership due to increases in cloud computing. Cloud computing is changing the nature of work by enabling mobile computing powered at the backend by learning from historical data. Rosenblat and Stark's (2016) description of how Uber uses its software platform to manage its drivers illustrates some of the issues arising for leadership with cloud computing. Uber sees itself as having created software that allows its customers – drivers and passengers – to connect with each other. It does not have to treat drivers as employees because the use of technology obviates the need to have any premises where the drivers would have to come and take directions for their work. Uber also claims that it is not managing its drivers, so therefore they cannot be treated as its employees. Its software alerts drivers to opportunities for connections with passengers and it is up to them to accept or reject those offers. By treating drivers as customers, Uber does not have to contribute to their social security. It also skirts the law that would have allowed drivers, if they were treated as employees, to organize and choose a representative to negotiate with Uber.

Though Uber claims that it is not managing its drivers, it uses findings from data to offer suggestions to its drivers that could help them increase their ratings. It also entices the drivers to act in a certain way by offering promotions, which its drivers can access only via the software and by allowing the software to track their behavior. According to Rosenblat and Stark (2016), the software that Uber uses is important for enabling information and, hence, power asymmetries. When the drivers are told of opportunities for connecting with a passenger nearby, they are not informed about where the passenger has to go and, hence, how much they would be paid. There is no person or manager the driver could question and clarify what they would be paid. The software enables disintermediation between Uber's top management and drivers. There is no middle management to give orders or directions or from whom to seek clarification. There are no middle managers to rate the performance of employees – this is done by passengers. The software that Uber uses incentivizes and controls how the drivers behave. It does what would otherwise be done by a leader and, therefore, substitutes for a leader.

Parry et al. (2016) hypothesize a scenario in which machine-based intelligent technology supports or substitutes decision-making by organizational leaders. They present both the positive and negative outcomes of such AI-based decision-making. They expect AI-based decision-making to yield better decisions because of the minimization of irrelevant social constraints during decision-making, discovery of latent patterns from historical data, mitigation of agency problems during decision-making, and separation of unpalatable decisions in the eyes of followers from the human leader(s). The negatives include the inability of AI-based systems to balance quantitative considerations with qualitative considerations, the potential unwillingness of followers to follow such a system, and the inability to hold a human leader accountable for decisions that are made by an AI-based system, especially in situations where the human leader does not hold the power of veto. The authors argue that to make human leaders accountable for decisions made by an AI-based system, they would have to be given the power of veto. However, by doing so, the positive consequences of AI-based decision systems are likely to be compromised. They propose that a 'logged' power of veto might be a way to reconcile the conflicting possibilities of reaping benefits of AI-based decision-making versus holding human leaders accountable.

Future Research on How IT Shapes Leadership

The existing research on how IT shapes leadership is sufficient to show that IT makes a difference for leadership. The surface has barely been scratched in the leadership domains covered above and, thus, there are tremendous opportunities for doctoral students in leadership to make novel contributions to the understanding of how IT can affect leadership. For instance, smartphones have given rise to a potential for research on how back-channel communication affects leadership in same-place meetings. Back-channel communication is that which occurs simultaneously with the main communication but is secondary to it. Such communication has been enabled at Purdue University via 'Hotseat' technology for collaborative 'micro-discussions' in and out of the classroom (Aagard et al., 2010).

An example that illustrates the relationship of back-channel communication enabled by smartphones to leadership is that of the Florida state senator caught receiving 'off the record' texts from a lobbyist in the audience while participating in a committee meeting on property insurance: the texts contained questions to ask the office of insurance regulation (Gomes, 2010). Such an act influences the attributions that the senator's followers will make about the leader. Moreover, these attributions would be different depending on whether or not the followers become aware of the leader being prompted by a lobbyist. Those who become aware are likely to question the ethics of the senator while others might attribute the questioning to the intelligence of the senator. Besides such attributions, back-channel communication of various types enabled by smartphones – between the leader and outsiders, between the leader and those the leader is meeting, between those the leader is meeting and outsiders, or that among those meeting the leader – redraw both the physical boundaries of same-place meetings and of what is socially acceptable in them (Dennis et al., 2010). Such communication can change, among other things, the direction of the leader, the support or challenge for the leader (and, potentially, the emergence of a new leader), the relationships among followers (and, hence, how they might respond to or act towards the leader), the capability of the whole group (and, hence, how the group's leader is perceived), and the formation of coalitions or cliques among those at the meeting (and, hence the conflict for the leader to manage). Future research is needed to clarify these effects.

In virtual teams, research on how leaders can contribute to the development of their teams and the well-being of its members to perform effectively remains an unexplored topic. Virtual teams need a distinct set of skills or competencies to be able to operate virtually (Hertel et al., 2006; Krumm et al., 2016; Schulze et al., 2017). Organizations often provide little help for the development of relevant skills or competence and it is left to team leaders to work with team members to develop them and enable team success. In addition to focusing on the development of skills and competencies of team members, leaders also have to be concerned about the well-being of team members who may feel isolated and lonely due to their dispersion and unfamiliarity with other team members (Gilson et al., 2015). Leaders have to be concerned about the well-being of members of their teams, at the very least because of its potential to impact how team members interact with each other and perform. With increasing deployment of virtual teams, examination of which leadership core processes and tactics help virtual teams develop and how is clearly warranted.

According to Kahai (2012), social networks enabled by social media can be considered as complex systems because they consist of a large number of highly interconnected and constantly changing nodes which make them unpredictable. According to Uhl-Bien et al. (2007), leadership in complex systems lies not only in individual or formal positions but also in the interaction among the system's agents. Research on this possibility in technology-enabled environments has just begun. This was evident in Bennett et al.'s (2014) analysis of tweets related to the Occupy movement. The authors argued that connective actions enabled by tweets, retweets, the posting of links, and the use of multiple hashtags ended up substituting for the collective action and coherence that is normally inspired by a leader in traditional social movements. Gerbaudo (2014), however, argued that the technology-based interactions are not sufficient for coherence; there is a collective phenomenon in the form of a common identity and culture as well as collective leadership associated with the technology-enabled movement. Future research is needed to clarify the role of technology-based transactions within social networks enabled by social media and their potential interaction with the context in substituting for leadership.

As the use of social media increases, both within and outside organizational boundaries, it gives rise to the question of how leaders can be developed for such an environment. The example of leadership in Humans of New York (HONY), a social media site, illustrates how leadership may need to change for social media. HONY's author, Brandon Stanton, writes posts about individuals from different walks of life living in New York city or a place that Mr Stanton may be visiting. Each post includes a story about the featured individual in that person's words. Mr Stanton never issues an explicit call for conversation among HONY's followers. After making a post, he rarely participates in the conversation that HONY's followers engage in. HONY's followers identify with the stories that Mr Stanton posts, which are usually about a personal triumph or challenge, because they see something about their own lives in them. Each of Mr

Stanton's posts is followed by a healthy conversation in the form of an extremely large number of likes and comments. HONY's followers share stories that illustrate the triumphs and travails in their own lives and these stories themselves amass a large number of likes and comments. The followers become leaders, much like Mr Stanton, by triggering conversations.

What is seen in the example of HONY is the emergence of unappointed, informal leaders who have a powerful influence over others. The networking, viral communication and widespread reach enabled by social media makes it likely for someone like Mr Stanton with an appealing vision to be discovered by people from different corners of the world. People connect with this informal leader because they feel an emotional connection to the leader's vision, which he or she is constantly modeling through actions shared via technology. After stimulating action, the leader gets out of the way. The followers, with the help of technology, take it upon themselves to share their thoughts, their interests, and become leaders in their own right. There is no top-down system through which leadership is exercised.

Future research is needed on how leaders like Mr Stanton can be developed. The leadership he models is not only relevant for a context mediated by social applications. Nor is it relevant only for a non-corporate setting. In today's highly complex and dynamic environment, leaders cannot take it all upon themselves to interface with the outside world or even those within their own organization. A leader cannot be at all the places demanding attention. Not only is the pace relentless but the variety of issues is too large for one supreme leader to be able to handle all events in a timely and competent fashion. An emergent, self-organizing system is needed. Others will have to be empowered to rise, respond and engage others to rise too. Smart leaders create conditions for others to emerge as leaders and then get out of the way. They create an emotionally engaging vision that others can relate to readily. They share their vision, model that vision, and stimulate a conversation among their followers. They do not try to control the events. Instead, they become facilitators who remove the barriers and make it easy for others to contribute towards their vision. The followers then take off. Some emerge as leaders themselves. The prevailing view of leadership is that it is concentrated in one or a few people at the top of a hierarchy, either within an organization or an organizational entity such as a business unit, a department, or a team. How people can be prepared or future leaders developed for a world in which they hand over their leadership to unknown others on an emergent basis and without any prior determination, while keeping them aligned with a common vision, is a challenge worthy of future research.

The use of software by a company between itself and an army of human workers to eliminate a layer of management is being practiced not only by

Uber but also by other companies such as 99designs in the visual design industry and Homejoy in the cleaning industry. More companies are likely to follow suit in the future. Moreover, some are warning that even high-level executives might not be immune from the coming onslaught of automation (Fidler, 2015). The Institute for the Future has created a software-based virtual management system called iCEO to automate complex work of many different types (for example, sales, quality assurance, and hiring) by breaking it into small individual tasks (Fidler, 2015). This system then assigns these to workers available through oDesk, Uber, Elance, Amazon's Mechanical Turks, and others. iCEO's creators envision its applications as being endless.

With significant changes in the nature of work and disruption to ranks of leaders just around the corner, doctoral students of leadership cannot proceed with their studies by ignoring the rapid advances of IT and what they mean for the future of leadership. What aspects of leadership will be retained by humans and what will be replaced by IT? This question warrants future research. It will not be an easy question to answer because the capabilities of AI-based IT are advancing rapidly (Ford, 2015). Even the human connection attributed to humans may not remain the domain of humans only, as seen in the movie 'Her' in which the main character develops a relationship with an intelligent computer operating system possessing a human's voice. The software learns and therefore evolves to become increasingly sensitive to the conditions of the movie's main character. Humans often have a tough time reading others, probably because of our biases and other things that may be going on in our lives which burden our sensitivity. Machines do not have such issues. Doctoral students need to be concerned about the future of leadership for another reason. When companies eliminate middle management, they take away a possible path for those aspiring to top positions. This gives rise to another question that needs to be examined by future research: how will individuals be developed to take top positions, where they will have to deal with extremely complex issues and make decisions having a broad set of implications, without the benefit of the experience provided by middle management positions?

The above discussion indicates why it is important for doctoral students of leadership to both initiate and take part in whatever conversations are taking place about the future of managerial work and leadership. Parry et al. (2016) attempted to initiate such a conversation with their work, which was discussed earlier. Parry et al.'s work is not without limitations. It makes several assumptions whose relaxation offers opportunities for future research. The authors assume a simple model of an organization. They assume an organization as a hierarchical entity with the leader at the apex. The authors assume that much of a leader's decision-making would be related to visioning without getting into the details of the visioning process or what kinds of vision might be produced. They fail to consider that visioning may be more emotional than cognitive in nature. There are other issues to be considered too. These include, for instance, the displacement of the human worker when AI systems are used and the deployment of Uber-like systems that allow organizations not to hire traditional employees and still use humans for work. Despite these limiting assumptions, the work of Parry et al. is important in that, as they have stated, it has started a conversation focused on the question of what will become of the humanity that society expects leaders and organizations to display in the face of greater replacement of human activity by IT.

HOW LEADERSHIP SHAPES IT

Due to IT spreading into almost every sphere of people's lives today, both inside and outside organizations, leaders are expected to play a more active role in shaping IT via its initiation, implementation, and assimilation and management. With industries standing to be disrupted by innovative IT applications, CEOs and other business leaders today are expected to develop a deeper knowledge of IT and incorporate IT-based innovations in their processes and products (Mims, 2017). The following section discusses the role that leaders are expected to play during the initiation, implementation, and assimilation and management of IT.

Leadership for Initiating IT

IT deployment in organizations begins with advocating its use. Since IT is utilized to solve some organizational problems or to take advantage of an opportunity, it is an organizational leader who generally promotes or is expected to promote IT use. Such a leader also has to work with the IT department when making a case for IT use. Bassellier et al. (2003) refer to a leader's advocating of IT use and working with the IT department as championship of IT. They found that IT competence, made up of IT-related knowledge (which, among other things, includes knowledge of applications of IT) and experience of a leader with IT projects and management, accounted for 34 percent of the variance in leaders' intentions to champion IT. Stuart et al. (2009) found partial support for this model with school leaders. They found that the intentions of school leaders to champion information and communication technology (ICT) are influenced by their knowledge of ICT but not their experience with ICT projects and management. Beath's (1991) study on IT champions offers another perspective. She observed that successful IT champions value support from the IT department in the form of: (a) assistance in developing information to help sell their IT vision; (b) flexibility in the implementation process; and (c) legitimation of their ideas for using IT.

The above discussion lends support to the encouragement in the popular press for leaders to develop deeper knowledge of IT and its applications so that they are able to think about how to incorporate IT-based innovations in their processes and products (for example, Mims, 2017). Stuart et al.'s (2009) finding that ICT use by school leaders predicted their ICT knowledge suggests that leaders themselves need to be more prolific users of IT in order to increase their personal knowledge of IT and their willingness to initiate IT in their organizations. The above discussion also suggests that leaders may need to be transformational in order to encourage the IT unit to transcend its self-interests and work closely with them (Beath, 1991).

Leadership for Implementing IT

After a decision has been made to deploy IT, an organization goes through its implementation. IT implementation is a complex social phenomenon that requires effective leadership. Ke and Wei (2008) argue that enterprise resource planning (ERP) implementation success requires a culture of learning and development, participative decision-making, support and collaboration, power sharing, communication, and tolerance for conflict and risk. They further argue that it is the responsibility of leaders to create such a culture. Literature provides some support for this line of thinking. Sarker and Lee (2003) found that strong and committed leadership, existing at various levels in the organization, is necessary for ERP implementation success. Wang et al. (2005) report that charismatic behavior of the ERP project leader predicted the cohesiveness and overall performance of the project team. The importance of charismatic project leadership was also found by Neufeld et al. (2007) who reported that such leadership during IT implementation influenced the many antecedents to use the IT being implemented. Thite (2000) found that a combination of transformational and technical leadership of IT leaders augmented their transactional leadership to influence project success.

The above results should not be considered to imply that it is only IT leaders who should be concerned about their leadership during the implementation of IT. Successful IT implementation requires complementary changes in several parts of an organization and it is the responsibility of leaders to bring about these changes. Hitt and Brynjolfsson (1997) argue that complementary changes in the leadership, rewards, and location of decision-making authority are required within the organization to ensure gains from IT investments. They found that IT deployment tends to be accompanied by more decentralized decision-making, teamwork and knowledge work. Leaders need to alter their core leadership processes and leadership tactics to adapt to this new context. Greater empowerment, delegation, participation in decision-making and emphasis on team building will be required. With a greater shift to knowledge work, measurement of work and, hence, making rewards contingent on the level of work performed become challenging. In such a situation, leaders have to motivate performance by helping workers align their goals with those of the organization. Leaders will have to practice inspirational leadership and follow high quality goal-setting processes to help organizational workers share the organization's vision and internalize its interests (Hertel et al., 2004; Hitt and Brynjolfsson, 1997).

Leadership for Assimilation and Management of IT

Past research has been quite unequivocal on the importance of senior leadership support for successful application of IT (for example, Jarvenpaa and Ives, 1991; Oz and Sosik, 2000). This support may take the form of a senior leader's involvement, whereby the leader considers IT to be important and sends the right signals about its use to the organization, and participation, whereby the leader takes part in IT planning, development and implementation. Such participation prevents abandonment of expensive long-term IT projects (Oz and Sosik, 2000). Chatterjee et al. (2002) found that senior management can affect IT's assimilation by manipulating institutional structures of signification, legitimization and domination. By offering a vision of the organization and how IT fits into that vision, leaders provide meaning to others and help them understand the significance of IT. Leaders legitimize IT by discussing opportunities and risks with the application of IT and by acting as role models; leaders become role models by believing in IT, participating in IT strategy and projects, and using IT. By creating mandates and policies regarding IT adoption and use, leaders regulate IT-related behavior and manipulate structures of domination.

   To be sure, IT leaders have an important role to play in engaging leaders not only for assimilation and management of IT but also for initiation and implementation of IT. Eom et al. (2015) found that transformational Chief Information Officers (CIOs) promote mechanisms that help IT and business units develop shared domain knowledge. These mechanisms, in turn, enable strategic IT–business alignment both directly and indirectly. They do so indirectly by first influencing mechanisms that allow IT and business units to integrate their specialized knowledge in the production of the business's products and services. These knowledge integration mechanisms then lead to strategic IT–business alignment when mechanisms to develop shared domain knowledge occur at relatively low frequency.

Future Research on How Leadership Shapes IT

As discussed above, past research suggests that it is critical for leaders to have knowledge of IT, what it is capable of, and how to harness its capabilities. Such knowledge motivates leaders to champion IT. Future research could examine if there are any leader qualities or traits that make it more likely for them to acquire such knowledge and be IT champions. Bennis (2013) offers some direction in this regard. He argues that power in society comes from the absorption of uncertainty about various stakeholder groups. Those who are able to capitalize on the sense-making enabled by information and communication technologies in a digital world will be more powerful. Leaders need to be aware of the power of IT and what it enables. They need to embrace and harness the transparency that comes with IT. To be able to do so, Bennis claims that leaders need adaptive capacity. Adaptive capacity arises from resilience or the ability to rebound from difficulty or adversity and come back effectively, openness to the new or the willingness to try new things and the ability to learn from failures and mistakes, and an optimistic sense of can do and can try. Research on the relationship of leader qualities or traits, such as adaptive capacity, to knowledge of IT, what it is capable of, and how to harness its capabilities is very sparse at the moment (for example, Stuart et al., 2009).

Any IT offers a range of affordances or possibilities for use and leaders play a significant role in how those possibilities are exercised. When I help managers think about using social media, a common reaction is 'You have convinced me that I should use social media. Which one should I start with first?' I respond by suggesting email, adding, 'Though email is not social media like Facebook, you can make it social if you wish. It depends on how you use it.' To be sure, social media offer features that make it easier to be social. For instance, the 'like' or 'reactions' feature in Facebook makes it easy for someone to communicate their reaction to a post; in the absence of such a feature, email communication lacks such responsiveness that helps sustain or develop social relationships. Indeed, though HONY has been around for a while, it was only after it moved to Facebook that it really took off. This discussion, nevertheless, prompts the question of whether and how different leader behaviors or styles influence which affordances of IT get exercised within organizations. Future research should examine this question because IT assimilation remains challenging (Mu et al., 2015) and examination of the relationship between different leader behaviors or styles and how each gets used would be beneficial for increasing the returns from IT investments.

One could broaden the question about the relationship of different leader behaviors or styles to IT affordances that get exercised to examine the suitability of different leadership styles for different aspects of IT deployment including initiating IT, implementing IT, and assimilation and management of IT. Since it is not just IT leaders but also business leaders who need to participate in the deployment of IT, the suitability of leadership of both IT and business leaders could be examined. Moreover, since IT deployment may require complementary changes in leadership, future research should examine whether leaders are able to change their leadership styles or behaviors successfully. Whether they are able to or not would have implications for whether organizations should develop their existing leaders or replace them when IT deployment necessitates complementary changes in leadership.

There is a need for research on the relationship of leadership to broader implications, including those at societal, national and global levels, of IT deployment and use. By demonstrating the viability of the iCEO software, the Institute for the Future has alerted managers to the possibility that their work and not just that of blue-collar service workers and office managers can be replaced. What course of action should leaders take in such an environment? Should they favor maximization of shareholder returns or should they favor the workers within their company and work for their well-being even if doing so reduces shareholder returns? Are leader qualities or traits likely to be related to the course a company takes or are market forces likely to dominate? These are a sample of questions that future research could look at.

The iCEO software system does not aim to replace the human worker – it simply aims to shift the work from within a company's boundary to outside. AI software, on the other hand, does away with the cost of the human worker, while promising speed and precision unmatched by any human. In his compelling book *Rise of the Robots: Technology and the Threat of a Jobless Future*, Martin Ford (2015) warns of social upheaval that the increasing and widespread automation is likely to lead to. According to Ford, AI is advancing simultaneously in multiple fields; no field, including those involving creative endeavors, is immune from automation due to AI. This is likely to cause a simultaneous disruption to employment in multiple sectors of the economy. When technology advanced and automated work previously, it did so in one or a few industrial sectors. Disruptions to employment in one sector of the economy would be accompanied by movement of workers from that sector to other sectors that were still robust or growing due to advancements in technology. Ford argues that such opportunities will vanish when AI disrupts employment throughout the economy, potentially giving rise to social unrest when people face a jobless future. Potential implications of AI use are not just restricted to nature of work and number of workers to be employed in the future; they are also related to the issue of human dignity. Rosenberg and Markoff (2016) report that the extent of advancement in AI is such that scientists and engineers are only about a decade away from successfully building weapon systems capable of making autonomous decisions to attack enemy positions and equipment and kill enemy soldiers. They add that it is not easy to decide in favor of sending machines to war because doing so raises the question of whether being killed by a machine is a greater violation of human dignity than if the killing is done by another human.

Much of the discussion so far on how leaders shape IT has implicitly assumed that leaders have the goal of optimizing organizational performance. But there is an increasing potential for leaders to shape IT deployment and use to manipulate others. For instance, researchers have shown that it is possible to estimate personalities from their digital footprint, such as what they like on Facebook (Youyou et al., 2015). This can enable unprecedented influence and control over others not by profiling them demographically, which only provides rough estimates of their tendencies and behaviors, but by profiling them on the basis of their psychological make-up, which leads to more accurate estimates of their tendencies and behaviors. An analytics-based marketing company, Cambridge Analytica, has been credited with playing a significant role in Donald Trump's victory and the vote for Brexit (Cadwalladr, 2017; Grassegger and Krogerus, 2017). It is claimed that the company targeted voters with different 'emotional triggers' via Facebook and face-to-face campaigning on the basis of their personality profiles gleaned from their Facebook likes and offline data. While such claims have been controversial (Confessore and Hakim, 2017), they do suggest the potential of 'big data' to reshape politics. Previously, organizations would analyze data and learn from it to influence people's shopping behavior. People accepted manipulation of their thoughts probably because by and large its effects were largely restricted to the relationship with that company. Today, it seems that individuals and organizations may be in a position to control national referendums and the elections of public servants at high enough levels to influence the fate of nations and the world.

The above discussion provides a taste of AI's potential for widespread and ethical implications. Given this potential, it is clear that leaders would need help to determine where they should draw boundaries in the division of labor between humans and machines and in the consequences they seek with the use of IT. To help leaders make reasonable judgments, conversations among various stakeholders, including futurists, policy makers, organizational and military leaders, and academics in various fields, including leadership, philosophy and computer science will have to take place. Much like Parry et al. (2016), doctoral students of leadership could help initiate or contribute to such conversations through their research.

CONCLUSIONS

At a simple level, the proliferation of IT is bringing about several information-related changes which, in turn, are influencing leadership. Changes are evident in access to information and media, channels of communication, flow and dissemination of information, storage of information, and interpretation of information (Avolio and Kahai, 2003; Kahai, 2012). Moreover, the nature of work, management and leadership are changing with significant advances in the capabilities of AI-based IT. I have tried to argue that in such an environment, leadership is not remaining the same as before and neither should the practice and research of leadership. Through their research and practice of leadership, doctoral students of leadership can play a major role in initiating, participating in, and modeling conversations that are needed to understand and influence leadership in an age dominated by IT. In the absence of such conversations, leaders will resort to default choices about how they lead others and how they deploy IT with the focus mainly on immediate gains for oneself and the organization one may be working for. The impact of IT, however, even when focusing on individuals and the organizations they are members of, is likely to be much broader. This demands attention of leaders. This demands that scholars and educators be in a position to convince leaders. And nothing but research on e-leadership, something that I encourage doctoral students of leadership to do more of, would be more convincing.

REFERENCES

Aagard, H., K. Bowen and L. Olesova (2010). Hotseat: Opening the backchannel in large lectures. *Educause Quarterly*, **33**(3), 2.

Avolio, B.J. and S.S. Kahai (2003). Adding the 'E' to e-leadership: How it may impact your leadership. *Organizational Dynamics*, **31**(4), 325–38.

Avolio, B.J., S. Kahai and G.E. Dodge (2001). E-leadership: Implications for theory, research, and practice. *The Leadership Quarterly*, **11**(4), 615–68.

Avolio, B.J., J.J. Sosik, S.S. Kahai and B. Baker (2014). E-leadership: Re-examining transformations in leadership source and transmission. *The Leadership Quarterly*, **25**(1), 105–31.

Balthazard, P.A., D.A. Waldman and J.E. Warren (2009). Predictors of the emergence of transformational leadership in virtual decision teams. *The Leadership Quarterly*, **20**(5), 651–63.

Bassellier, G., I. Benbasat and B.H. Reich (2003). The influence of business managers' IT competence on championing IT. *Information Systems Research*, **14**(4), 317–36.

Beath, C.M. (1991). Supporting the information technology champion. *MIS Quarterly*, **15**(3), 355–72.

Bennett, W.L., A. Segerberg and S. Walker (2014). Organization in the crowd: Peer production in large-scale networked protests. *Information, Communication & Society*, **17**(2), 232–60.

Bennis, W. (2013). Leadership in a digital world: Embracing transparency and adaptive capacity. *MIS Quarterly*, **37**(2), 635–6.

Cadwalladr, C. (2017). The great British robbery: How our democracy was hijacked. *The Guardian*, 7 May. Accessed at https://www.theguardian.com/technology/2017/may/07/the-great-british-brexit-robbery-hijacked-democracy.

Champy, J. (2010). Does leadership change in a web 2.0 world? *HBR Blog Network*, 4 May. Accessed at http://blogs.hbr.org/imagining-the-future-of-leadership/2010/05/does-leadership-change-in-a-we.html.

Chatterjee, D., R. Grewal and V. Sambamurthy (2002). Shaping up for e-commerce: Institutional enablers of the organizational assimilation of web technologies. *MIS Quarterly*, **12**(2), 65–89.

Confessore, N. and D. Hakim (2017). Data firm says 'secret sauce' aided Trump: Many scoff. *The New York Times*, 6 March. Accessed at https://www.nytimes.com/2017/03/06/us/politics/cambridge-analytica.html.

Dennis, A.R., J.A. Rennecker and S. Hansen (2010). Invisible whispering: Restructuring collaborative decision making with instant messaging. *Decision Sciences*, **41**(4), 845–86.

Eom, M., S. Kahai and A. Yayla (2015). Investigation of how IT leadership impacts IT–business alignment through shared domain knowledge and knowledge integration. AMCIS 2015 Proceedings. Accessed 31 August 2017 at http://aisel.aisnet.org/amcis2015/HumanCapital/GeneralPresentations/7/.

Eseryel, U.Y. and D. Eseryel (2013). Action-embedded transformational leadership in self-managing global information systems development teams. *The Journal of Strategic Information Systems*, **22**(2), 103–20.

Fidler, D. (2015). Here's how managers can be replaced by software. *Harvard Business Review*, 21 April. Accessed at https://hbr.org/2015/04/heres-how-managers-can-be-replaced-by-software.

Ford, M. (2015). *Rise of the robots: Technology and the threat of a jobless future*. New York, NY: Basic Books.

Gerbaudo, P. (2014). The persistence of collectivity in digital protest. *Information, Communication & Society*, **17**(2), 264–8.

Gilson, L.L., M.T. Maynard, N.C.J. Young, M. Vartiainen and M. Hakonen (2015). Virtual teams research 10 years, 10 themes, and 10 opportunities. *Journal of Management*, **41**(5), 1313–37.

Gomes, T. (2010). Do smart phones thwart public records laws? *NPR Around the Nation*, 14 February. Accessed at http://www.npr.org/templates/story/story.php?storyId=123573568.

Grassegger, H. and M. Krogerus (2017). The data that turned the world upside down. *Motherboard*, 28 January. Accessed at https://motherboard.vice.com/en_us/article/mg9vvn/how-our-likes-helped-trump-win.

Hashem, I.A.T., I. Yaqoob, N.B. Anuar, S. Mokhtar, A. Gani and S.U. Khan (2015). The rise of 'big data' on cloud computing: Review and open research issues. *Information Systems*, **47**, 98–115.

Hertel, G., U. Konradt and B. Orlikowski (2004). Managing distance by interdependence: Goal setting, task interdependence, and team-based rewards in virtual teams. *European Journal of Work and Organizational Psychology*, **13**(1), 1–28.

Hertel, G., U. Konradt and K. Voss (2006). Competencies for virtual teamwork: Development and validation of a web-based selection tool for members of distributed teams. *European Journal of Work and Organizational Psychology*, **15**(4), 477–504.

Hill, N.S. and K.M. Bartol (2016). Empowering leadership and effective collaboration in geographically dispersed teams. *Personnel Psychology*, **69**(1), 159–98.

Hiltz, S.R., K. Johnson and M. Turoff (1991). Group decision support: The effects of designated human leaders and statistical feedback in computerized conferences. *Journal of Management Information Systems*, **8**(2), 81–108.

Hitt, L.M. and E. Brynjolfsson (1997). Information technology and internal firm organization: An exploratory analysis. *Journal of Management Information Systems*, **14**(2), 81–101.

How social tools can reshape the organization (2016, May). Accessed at http://www.mckinsey.com/business-functions/digital-mckinsey/our-insights/how-social-tools-can-reshape-the-organization.

Huffaker, D. (2010). Dimensions of leadership and social influence in online communities. *Human Communication Research*, **36**(4), 593–617.

Jarvenpaa, S.L. and B. Ives (1991). Executive involvement and participation in the management of information technology. *MIS Quarterly*, **15**(2), 205–27.

Jarvenpaa, S.L. and H. Tanriverdi (2003). Leading virtual knowledge networks. *Organizational Dynamics*, **31**(4), 403–12.

Johnson, S.L., H. Safadi and S. Faraj (2015). The emergence of online community leadership. *Information Systems Research*, **26**(1), 165–87.

Joshi, A., M.B. Lazarova and H. Liao (2009). Getting everyone on board: The role of inspirational leadership in geographically dispersed teams. *Organization Science*, **20**(1), 240–52.

Kahai, S.S. (2012). Leading in a digital age: What's different, issues raised, and what we know. In M.C. Blight and R.E. Riggio (eds), *Exploring Distance in Leader–Follower Relationships: When Near is Far and Far is Near* (pp. 63–108). New York, NY: Routledge.

Kahai, S., B. Avolio and J. Sosik (2017). E-leadership. In G. Hertel, D. Stone, R. Johnson and J. Passmore (eds), *The Wiley Blackwell Handbook of the Psychology of the Internet at Work* (pp. 285–314). Chichester: John Wiley & Sons.

Kahai, S.S., J.J. Sosik and B.J. Avolio (1997). Effects of leadership style and problem structure on work group process and outcomes in an electronic meeting system environment. *Personnel Psychology*, **50**(1), 121–46.

Kahai, S.S., J.J. Sosik and B.J. Avolio (2004). Effects of participative and directive leadership in electronic groups. *Group & Organization Management*, **29**(1), 67–105.

Ke, W. and K.K. Wei (2008). Organizational culture and leadership in ERP implementation. *Decision Support Systems*, **45**(2), 208–18.

Kruger, J., N. Epley, J. Parker and Z.W. Ng (2005). Egocentrism over e-mail: Can we communicate as well as we think? *Journal of Personality and Social Psychology*, **89**(6), 925–36.

Krumm, S., J. Kanthak, K. Hartmann and G. Hertel (2016). What does it take to be a virtual team player? The knowledge, skills, abilities, and other characteristics required in virtual teams. *Human Performance*, **29**(2), 123–42.

Lim, L.H., K.S. Raman and K.K. Wei (1994). Interacting effects of GDSS and leadership. *Decision Support Systems*, **12**(3), 199–211.

Luther, K. and A. Bruckman (2008). Leadership in online creative collaboration. In *Proceedings of the 2008 ACM Conference on Computer Supported Cooperative Work* (pp. 343–52). New York, NY: ACM.

Manyika, J. (2017). *Technology, jobs, and the future of work*. May. Accessed at http://www.mckinsey.com/global-themes/employment-and-growth/technology-jo bs-and-the-future-of-work.

Mims, C. (2017). Wall Street to CEOs: Disrupt your industry, or else. *The Wall Street Journal*, 26 May. Accessed at https://www.wsj.com/articles/wall-street-to-ceos-the-future-is-now-1495791003.

Mohammed, S. and S. Nadkarni (2011). Temporal diversity and team performance: The moderating role of team temporal leadership. *Academy of Management Journal*, **54**(3), 489–508.

Mu, E., L.J. Kirsch and B.S. Butler (2015). The assimilation of enterprise information system: An interpretation systems perspective. *Information & Management*, **52**(3), 359–70.

Neufeld, D.J., L. Dong and C. Higgins (2007). Charismatic leadership and user acceptance of information technology. *European Journal of Information Systems*, **16**(4), 494–510.

Oz, E. and J.J. Sosik (2000). Why information systems projects are abandoned: A leadership and communication theory and exploratory study. *The Journal of Computer Information Systems*, **41**(1), 66–78.

Parry, K., M. Cohen and S. Bhattacharya (2016). Rise of the machines: A critical consideration of automated leadership decision making in organizations. *Group & Organization Management*, **41**(5), 571–94.

Purvanova, R.K. and J.E. Bono (2009). Transformational leadership in context: Face-to-face and virtual teams. *The Leadership Quarterly*, **20**(3), 343–57.

Reeves, B., T.W. Malone and T. O'Driscoll (2008). Leadership's online labs. *Harvard Business Review*, **86**(5), 58–66.

Richter, A. and D. Wagner (2014). Leadership 2.0: Engaging and supporting leaders in the transition towards a networked organization. In *Proceedings of the 2014 47th Hawaii International Conference on System Sciences* (pp. 574–83). Washington, DC: IEEE Computer Society.

Rosenberg, M. and J. Markoff (2016). The Pentagon's 'Terminator conundrum': Robots that could kill on their own. *The New York Times*, 25 October. Accessed at https://www.nytimes.com/2016/10/26/us/pentagon-artificial-intelligence-termi nator.html.

Rosenblat, A. and L. Stark (2016). Algorithmic labor and information asymmetries: A case study of Uber's drivers. *International Journal of Communication*, **10**(2016), 3758–84. Accessed at http://ijoc.org/index.php/ijoc/article/view/4892.

Roy, S.R. (2012). Digital mastery: The skills needed for effective virtual leadership. *International Journal of e-Collaboration*, **8**(3), 56–66.

Sarker, S. and A.S. Lee (2003). Using a case study to test the role of three key social enablers in ERP implementation. *Information & Management*, **40**(8), 813–29.

Schulze, J., M. Schultze, S.G. West and S. Krumm (2017). The knowledge, skills, abilities, and other characteristics required for face-to-face versus computer-mediated communication: Similar or distinct constructs? *Journal of Business and Psychology*, **32**(3), 283–300.

Sosik, J.J., B.J. Avolio and S.S. Kahai (1997). Effects of leadership style and anonymity on group potency and effectiveness in a group decision support system environment. *Journal of Applied Psychology*, **82**(1), 89–103.

Sosik, J.J., S.S. Kahai and B.J. Avolio (1998). Transformational leadership and dimensions of creativity: Motivating idea generation in computer-mediated groups. *Creativity Research Journal*, **11**(2), 111–21.

Stuart, L.H., A.M. Mills and U. Remus (2009). School leaders, ICT competence and championing innovations. *Computers & Education*, **53**(3), 733–41.

Sutton, R. (2010). What every new generation of bosses has to learn. *HBR Blog Network*, 9 June. Accessed at http://blogs.hbr.org/cs/2010/06/good_bosses_ have_a_passion_for.html.

Thite, M. (2000). Leadership styles in information technology projects. *International Journal of Project Management*, **18**(4), 235–41.

Uhl-Bien, M., R. Marion and B. McKelvey (2007). Complexity leadership theory: Shifting leadership from the industrial age to the knowledge era. *The Leadership Quarterly*, **18**(4), 298–318.

Waldrop, M.M. (2016). The chips are down for Moore's law. *Nature*, **530**(7589), 144–7.

Wang, E., H.W. Chou and J. Jiang (2005). The impacts of charismatic leadership style on team cohesiveness and overall performance during ERP implementation. *International Journal of Project Management*, **23**(3), 173–80.

Yammarino, F.J., F. Dansereau and C.J. Kennedy (2001). Viewing leadership through an elephant's eye: A multiple-level multidimensional approach to leadership. *Organizational Dynamics*, **29**(3), 149–63.

Youyou, W., M. Kosinski and D. Stillwell (2015). Computer-based personality judgments are more accurate than those made by humans. *Proceedings of the National Academy of Sciences*, **112**(4), 1036–40.

Zhu, H., R. Kraut and A. Kittur (2012). Effectiveness of shared leadership in online communities. In *Proceedings of the ACM 2012 Conference on Computer Supported Cooperative Work* (pp. 407–16). New York, NY: ACM.

3. Into the new: a creatively focused and technology fluent (CFTF) mindset for emerging doctoral contexts

Danah Henriksen and William Cain

INTRODUCTION

The need for creativity and innovation in higher education is increasingly important (Dill and Van Vught, 2010). As the world transforms through digital technologies, globalization and economic change, there are opportunities to rethink higher education structures in online or hybrid doctoral learning (Henriksen et al., 2014). Such opportunities, however, require consideration of the foundations of doctoral studies, a creative rethinking of learning aligned with this, and attention to the advantages and constraints of online and hybrid contexts.

Doctoral studies aim to create scholarly leaders in academia or other professional domains. This involves teaching students how to conduct systemic inquiry, interpret and disseminate research, creatively lead change, engage in broader discourse, and innovate to create new knowledge and structures. To develop creative leaders in online and hybrid contexts, programs and coursework must provide learning opportunities using the creative and technological affordances of the medium, while also maintaining the strengths of existing scholarly norms.

In this chapter, we argue that online and hybrid doctoral programs require a creatively focused and technologically fluent mindset on the part of faculty instructors and other program stakeholders. We describe the context for change in emerging opportunities for online and hybrid doctoral studies, and propose a creative and flexible mindset for instructors, designers and developers in such programs. This chapter covers theoretical foundations in creative thinking, openness, and willingness to experiment or engage with the new. Such a mindset must be grounded in: a knowledge of the discipline and of teaching with technology (Mishra and

Koehler, 2006); a desire to promote creativity in instructors' own teaching and in their students' thinking (Lilly and Bramwell-Rejskind, 2004); and a willingness to explore within new techno-pedagogical spaces.

Creativity and technology-fluency are emphasized in discussions of 21st-century leadership skills (Mishra et al., 2016). After describing this mindset, we share examples of how this has played out across two different online and hybrid doctoral programs: the Educational Psychology and Educational Technology PhD program at Michigan State University (hybrid), and the Educational Leadership and Innovation EdD program at Arizona State University (online).

EMERGING CONTEXTS PUSHING EDUCATORS FORWARD: SHIFTING PRACTICES OF DOCTORAL EDUCATION

Online education has flourished and become a mainstream practice in higher education. Yet the overwhelming majority of online or hybrid programs were initially in undergraduate or master's programs, with comparatively few doctoral offerings (Ghezzi, 2007). Doctoral learning has traditionally been based on in-person, apprenticeship-like models in which advisors pass on the values, norms and rules of the academy in focused or one-on-one interactions or research and teaching experiences. In its nascent stages, online learning was frequently dismissed as lacking the affordances to support the types of in-depth, rigorous, personal interactions that fit with the traditional doctoral model.

In the last two decades, however, universities have gradually started to implement doctoral programs that make use of online and hybrid modalities (Picciano, 2017). Critics may question whether online technologies and practices can fully address the complexity of doctoral learning. These are valid questions, but not because online modalities are a poor fit for doctoral studies. Rather, these questions should arise in *any* new construction or instantiation of learning, be it online or in person, as instructors should continuously consider how elements of coursework provide learning experiences that connect with pedagogical goals.

Goals of Doctoral Education: Linking Theory, Research and Practice

Pedagogical strategies vary, but there is a common purpose across doctoral programs in education – the development and training of educational leaders, scholars and researchers. This purpose is expressed through domain-level competencies: fluency in understanding and

applying theory; intensive training in research methodologies; identifying valid and researchable problems and questions for impact; and the ability to communicate and disseminate ideas (Brown, 1966; 1991; Levine, 2005; 2007). The goal is to produce researchers for the academy or practice who can inform the field.

Universities traditionally aim at generating and disseminating new knowledge, yet observers cite a disconnect in translating research into actual educational practice (Bradley, 1999; Damrosch, 1995; Levine, 2007). This has been a longstanding criticism and ongoing concern in higher education (Brown, 1966; Levine, 2005; Robinson, 2014). On the one hand, academics in 'ivory towers' are viewed as disconnected from the everyday life of classrooms and practice (Lovitts, 2001). On the other, practitioners are criticized for not employing the most effective research-based strategies (Perry and Imig, 2008; Sullivan, 2005). This disconnect between theory and practice may be where the demand and opportunities for online or hybrid doctoral programs have entered.

Often, traditional or face-to-face programs cannot meet the needs of expert practitioners who might otherwise be suited to doctoral studies. Online or hybrid programs offer opportunities for such students to enrich the field. Practitioners pursuing doctoral studies are uniquely poised to overcome the theory–practice disconnect using their hard-won expertise to notice trends, issues and questions non-practitioners might overlook. Steeped in professional insights, these expert practitioners may only lack the methodological and theoretical tools to investigate and inform (Perry and Imig, 2008). This is where online and hybrid contexts allow students to become drivers of educational change and scholarship. With the evolution of technologies that break down barriers of time and space (for example, enhanced telepresence, digital platforms for real-time collaboration), new pathways for training and development can be enacted for doctoral students across local, national and international contexts.

Every medium for learning comes with affordances and constraints. Scholars have noted that online or hybrid settings are not inherently better or worse than traditional face-to-face settings; they are simply different (Mishra et al., 2007; Knight, 2013). Yet in many cases, faculty, instructors and course developers are so accustomed to traditional settings that they assume face-to-face is superior and that students benefit more there (Mitchell et al., 2015). Much research on teaching, however, tells us that assumptions about students, complacency about customs, or failure to flexibly revisit teaching practices ultimately leads to pedagogical obsolescence, regardless of context (Davies et al., 2014).

For new online and hybrid doctoral programs to expand and be successful, faculty, program developers, course designers and other stakeholders

need a mindset for creativity, flexibility, technology-fluency (not necessarily expertise), and openness for the new. This is characterized here as a 'creatively flexible and technologically fluent' mindset (or CFTF mindset). While such habits of mind are essential to good teaching in any modality, they are particularly essential for new and technologically-rich contexts, such as online or hybrid doctoral studies. It is important to examine the scholarly underpinnings of creativity in teaching and learning, then consider it as a lens for teaching, learning and curriculum development in online or hybrid doctoral settings.

CREATIVITY AS A MINDSET FOR TEACHING AND LEARNING

The value of creativity in teaching is central to developing learning experiences that are engaging and effective (Henriksen and Mishra, 2015). Creativity, however, is a broad construct and a vast area of research. So it is important to consider what a mindset for creativity means, and how creativity is defined.

Most research defines creativity as having several core components. First, a creative idea, process or product is *novel* – it brings something into play that either did not exist before, or is relatively new for its context. Cropley (2003) asserts, however, that a novel idea with no potential use cannot be taken as 'creative', because novelty does not guarantee that something will be *effective* (Amabile, 1996; Oldham and Cummings, 1996; Zhou and George, 2001). Creative outcomes (for example, ideas, processes or products) must be also 'effective' – or useful, logical, understandable or of some value to others. A final characteristic, according to Sternberg and O'Hara (1999), involves 'task appropriateness'. Creative outcomes are sensitive to the context or domain within which they are created. Mishra and Koehler (2008) term this third construct '*wholeness*' – the contextual aspects of creative work, or how well it fits into that work's specific purpose. Around these three constructs of novelty, effectiveness and wholeness (NEW), creativity fits well with what instructors aim to do in teaching (Henriksen et al., 2015).

The problem of creating learning experiences that are novel (relatively so, in an instantiation of a course), effective and whole in online or hybrid doctoral studies is that the contexts are so new that instructors often do not fully understand what the goals, settings, outcomes or challenges look like. Evolving contexts change frequently and instructors may deal with uncertainty and unknowns. This is why there is value in focusing on a mindset that corresponds with creative thinking, rather than chasing a target of novelty, effectiveness and wholeness, or seeking perfect creativity. Henriksen and Mishra (2015) provide evidence that good creative teaching is related to instructor mindset and beliefs. If instructors start by understanding and aiming for creative and flexible teaching mindsets, doctoral-level educators are better positioned to identify new and better ways to teach their students in online and hybrid contexts.

Aspects of Creativity in Mindset and Teaching

From a psychological perspective, much creativity research has focused on traits or personality characteristics that tend to be associated with creative individuals. For example, the most commonly known and utilized measure of creativity thinking, the Torrance Test, was designed to help psychological researchers understand how different thinking tendencies and problem-solving skills arise in constellations of personality or thinking traits, directed at measuring creativity (Torrance and Horng, 1980). Flexibility and fluency are key aspects of this common measure (among other components) – as creative people can flexibly move between categories and contexts, and fluently come up with alternatives and ideas.

Other scholars focused on psychological traits associated with creativity, frequently note the value of flexibility, open-mindedness, tolerance for ambiguity, intellectual risk-taking and willingness to 'play' (to play with ideas or details, or tinker with plans and designs) (Baer and Oldham, 2006; Prabhu et al., 2008; Silvia et al., 2009). Karwowski (2014) notes the importance of mindset, since viewing creativity as malleable and open to change and growth is important to applying it. Working to adopt and practice habits of mind such as flexibility, or openness to experience, directly influences such habits in terms of problem-solving skill growth and performance – an idea that is often discussed in terms of growth mindset (Dweck, 2006).

Characteristics and habits of mind like flexibility, open-mindedness, willingness to try new things and intellectual risk-taking, seem to relate and overlap in a mindset that connects to creativity. These may be phrased or framed differently in different areas of scholarship, but the relationships between them and creative thinking seem clear (Amabile, 2012). Amabile (1983) emphasizes that this does not guarantee that people with these traits are 'creative', nor does it give us a clear formula or constellation of personality traits for creativity. But it does give a sense of habits of mind that are helpful with situations or goals impacted by creative thinking.

Elements of a CFTF (Creatively Focused and Technology Fluent) Mindset

These habits of mind for a creative mindset also play out in teaching contexts. Even with the challenges of standardization and the pressures of evolving demands in higher education, there is increasing recognition that creative thinking is central to meeting the challenges (Freedman, 2007; Zhao, 2012). It is particularly relevant in emerging contexts, where everything is still being defined and practices materialize along the way, or must be figured out in situ. In responding to these demands, both scholars and practitioners have discussed the 21st-century importance of emphasizing creativity and problem-solving skills in teaching, or program and curriculum development. As Cropley (2003) asserted:

> [Education] cannot limit itself to the transmission of set contents, techniques and values, since these will soon be useless to living a full life, but must also promote flexibility, openness for the new, the ability to adapt or see new ways of doing things, and courage in the face of the unexpected, in other words, creativity. (p. 136)

The focus here involves a creative mindset for teachers. But educational researchers have consistently and historically noted creativity as a broader goal for everyone, especially learners (Cropley, 2003; Fasko, 2001; Hickey, 2001; Lilly and Bramwell-Rejskind, 2004; Renzulli, 1992). Creative teachers have a marked impact on the development of their students' own creative thinking skills, as well as enjoyment and success in learning (Amabile, 1996).

In a study of some of the most effective teachers in the United States, Henriksen (2011) and Henriksen and Mishra (2015) showed how successful teachers integrate a mindset for creativity in practice. The award-winning teachers they studied describe creativity not as a process or skill separate from other thought processes, but as an integrated openness in thinking. The defining characteristics of a creative teaching mindset are intellectual risk-taking, open-mindedness, and an openness for the new – habits of mind supported by existing creativity literature. As one teacher characterized it in their study: 'You are just always open to things, always looking for new ways of thinking in the classroom. Always keeping that open ear and that open eye to look for new ways. I don't think we can expect to just stand and deliver, and close our classroom doors' (Henriksen, 2011, p. 72).

While existing work on teacher creativity examines K-12 settings, these broader principles apply across contexts to higher education as well. In fact, the ideas apply wherever people are thinking and learning. Davidovitch and Milgram (2006) investigated creative thinking as a predictor of teacher effectiveness among college-level instructors, finding a significant, clear correlation between creative thinking and instructor effectiveness. Based on their findings, they suggest the potential benefits of instructional professional development built around creative thinking, and including creativity in evaluations of faculty.

Gibson (2010) brings this issue into higher education contexts as she critiques the status quo of conventional university teaching. She reflects on the fact that 'for many years, the higher education enterprise has been criticised for dampening creativity rather than fostering it', and suggests that higher education should reconsider how it innovates through teaching and technology, 'if they hope to graduate the future leaders of twenty-first century society' (p. 607).

This topic of instructional mindset and creativity is of heightened interest in online or hybrid doctoral education. In these contexts, instructors seek to innovate in the design and delivery of student learning, and to develop the next generation of educational thinkers and leaders.

Technology-fluency as a component of mindset
The creative mindset naturally fosters a willingness to engage with the new, or with different technologies to find effective ways to teach content and engage students. The previously mentioned notion of 'technology-fluency' is not about technology expertise or in-depth knowledge but rather about approaching technology in ways that serve the content and context for student learning and experience. This relates to the theory of Technological Pedagogical Content Knowledge (TPACK). TPACK is a framework that addresses teachers' awareness and knowledge of technology integration for teaching. Mishra and Koehler (2006) build on Shulman's (1986) foundational work, which proposed Pedagogical Content Knowledge as a way to define the relationship between knowledge of subject matter and pedagogical knowledge about teaching. The TPACK framework weaves in technology, to challenge the conventional separation of these areas in teacher professional development and practice.

Central to the notion of CFTF mindset is that instructors must have a fluidity of approach as they weave between content, pedagogy and technology. Technology-fluency does not mean expertise or deep knowledge of technology – that would be an unreasonable goal for most instructors, whose expertise lies within their content area. Rather, it means that as teachers work in new settings where the opportunities and constraints of digital technologies are front and center, they must have a mindset that appreciates the fluid intersection of pedagogy and content, and how technology can best mediate this.

Given the creativity components of flexibility and openness for the new, instructors must be aware of how they might find a viable approach to the content through different technological means. In hybrid or online doctoral contexts, instructors must be willing to experiment with new approaches to communicating and teaching in digital spaces. All instructors will not use this mindset to fit the same mold. Instead, as suggested by both creative practice and technology-fluency, instructors retain their own unique styles and ways of thinking about the content. Then when paired with these broad mindset traits, they can introduce their own teaching approaches and style in ways that suit who they are already, and bring that forward in new contexts.

Translating the existing ideas, goals and norms of doctoral education into the new contexts of online and hybrid education is a complex endeavor. There are no clear right or wrong ways to do this, only a range of possibilities. To help the reader consider how this might play out, we share some examples from online and hybrid doctoral programs at two institutions that we have been involved in: the Michigan State University hybrid PhD program in Educational Psychology and Educational Technology (EPET), and the Arizona State University online EdD program in Educational Leadership and Innovation.

EXAMPLE FROM THE FIELD: THE MICHIGAN STATE UNIVERSITY HYBRID PHD IN EDUCATIONAL PSYCHOLOGY AND EDUCATIONAL TECHNOLOGY

The EPET hybrid doctoral program is an example of a program with a clear mandate to be open and creative with the use of new and emerging technologies. To illustrate, we review the program's origins, and take a closer look at two examples of hybrid course design. The goal is to show how risk-taking, innovation, openness and creativity shaped the EPET program and, in turn, shaped the faculty and students within the program.

Origins of a Hybrid Doctoral Program

The idea for the EPET Hybrid program actually came from another program: MSU's online Master of Arts in Educational Technology (MAET). Attracting in-service teachers from around the country who want to further their professional training but need the flexibility of an online program, MAET is designed to give in-service teachers knowledge and experience in using a variety of technology-enhanced strategies for teaching and learning. Though almost entirely online, MAET courses emphasize hands-on design experiences in areas like universal designs for learning (UDL), website creation, and digital media literacy, scholarship and pedagogy.

Extending MAET's model to doctoral education seemed initially straightforward. EPET courses were transitioned to online lessons and modules and the first cohort of students enrolled in the EPET Hybrid program in 2010. The first year seemed to go well, yet Hybrid students and faculty feedback gave pause for concern. Faculty found themselves teaching the same courses twice in a single semester, with face-to-face course design for on-campus students and an online, web-based design for the hybrids. Instructors were frustrated and felt that duplicating their efforts was inefficient and time-consuming. The Hybrid students, while responding well to the online format, longed to develop a deeper connection and sense of enculturation with the on-campus EPET professors and students.

Retooling the program seemed daunting. But these two perspectives converged at a time when synchronous web-based communications tools like Skype and Google Hangouts were evolving and maturing, allowing the creation of a new form of online doctoral learning experience – the *synchronous hybrid course*.

Synchronous hybrid (or 'blended synchronous') courses are based on the idea that a class can be taught with both face-to-face and online students present. The goal is to achieve comparable learning experiences for all students, while allowing instructors to teach with preferred pedagogical strategies. For example, an instructor may use an alternating class design in which students gather for seminar-type discussions for part of the class but then break into small groups for collaboration. Effective synchronous hybrid course designs must ensure students stay connected at all times, but with appropriate levels of presence that fit the different class activities (for example, small group work, seminar discussions, whole-class lectures).

Rethinking the EPET program to include synchronous hybrid courses meant exploring how instructors could teach effectively to both physically present and remote students simultaneously, using technologies that were only recently invented. In relation to a CFTF mindset, it also meant creatively rethinking traditional pedagogical strategies to leverage new technologies for new kinds of learning interactions.

To consider CFTF in online doctoral programs, we review examples of actual course designs from the EPET program.

A Motivation and Learning Course in a Hybrid PhD Context

Preparing to teach his course on motivation and learning in 2010, Dr Cary Roseth had a clear idea of what a synchronous hybrid course design should look like. The question was, how to make it happen? Roseth's research broadly focuses on how the presence of others can influence learning, motivation and achievement, so he envisioned class sessions that featured small group collaboration and whole class discussions. Roseth had used this type of course design effectively before with face-to-face students – he felt he only needed to find the right technology and configuration to make it synchronous hybrid.

Since its first synchronous hybrid iteration, CEP 910 – Motivation has been the subject of several research articles and conference presentations (Roseth et al., 2013; Henriksen et al., 2014; Bell et al. 2014). Within EPET, the course has become an exemplar of the CFTF mindset and a testing ground for refining and rethinking synchronous hybrid designs. With the help of the Design Studio (EPET's in-house instructional technology support and research group), Roseth, and later his colleague Dr Lisa Linnenbrink-Garcia, have tinkered and experimented with multiple technologies in many configurations and classroom settings. They have moved from using a 'single-camera-pointed-at-the-students-and-instructor' approach to using a 'virtual flex' classroom with student stations for conducting multiple web conferencing sessions at once. The latest iteration of the course (see Cain and Bell, 2017) is a design for continuous presence with both people and content. It features a carefully structured combination of multiple web conferencing student stations, screen-sharing apps, and shared digital platforms (RealtimeBoard, Google Docs) for collaboratively embodied content.

As noted in Cain and Bell (2017), the course has also become a pioneering case study in robotic telepresence for student-centered learning and instruction. Robotic telepresence enables hybrid students to remotely 'pilot' fully mobile devices with audio-visual capabilities around the classroom to participate in the different course activities. Interviews with students and instructors on this course show enthusiasm for using robotic telepresence devices in class. For students, the devices give greater physical presence and allow them to show discernible attention to people and content in the classroom. For instructors, robotic telepresence devices become visual markers, making it easier to stay connected with remote students in lectures and whole-class discussions. Most of all, the use of robotic telepresence has given both EPET instructors and students opportunities to explore new forms of learning and instruction with technologies that transcend earlier limitations of time and distance.

CEP 910 is an example of CFTF mindset, a willingness to create new models within and around techno-pedagogical parameters. Drs Roseth and Linnenbrink-Garcia have continuously sought to refine their model of a synchronous hybrid class by 'twisting the knobs' of the technology configurations they use. The course has also been a model of technology leadership, breaking new ground in the use of emerging technologies for other faculty members to observe as they consider their own course designs.

A Course about Design in Education: Evolving Existing Content into the New

Dr Punya Mishra faced a similar situation – how best to enact a synchronous hybrid course design – when he taught a design thinking course in Fall 2012. The course focused on exploring, understanding and applying design thinking as a learning process in education. Both Dr Mishra and his co-instructor Dr Danah Henriksen had taught this course before but never using a synchronous hybrid design.

Initially, Mishra and Henriksen taught the first class sessions like those in Roseth's motivation course. Class sessions were structured so that students and instructors could interact in both whole class presentation-discussions and in small project groups; hybrid students used web-based videoconferencing to interact with the rest of the class during discussions. But what they saw happening in small-group interactions began to draw their attention.

The course design and assignments originally called for students to use predetermined tools and technologies for communicating and collaborating in small groups, typically with two physically present students and two telepresent (Hybrid) students. These tools included GotoMeeting for videoconferencing and Etherpad for collaborative documents (digital documents that multiple people on multiple devices can work on together in real-time). But during the fourth class, Drs Mishra and Henriksen had what could be called a creative pedagogical insight, and made a swift turn in approach. The course was about design as a field of study and how design thinking could be applied to learning and instruction from pedagogical and technological perspectives. So they asked themselves: why are we mandating how students should communicate with each other? If the course was really about design thinking, then having the students design their own communication was essential hands-on practice.

The results (described in Cain and Henriksen, 2013) were customized small-group interactions based on the technological and collaborative needs of students, not the instructors. For example, some student groups wanted to use the full range of videoconferencing capabilities (seeing, hearing and screen sharing with each other) when collaborating on projects. Other students found they only needed audio, so they would connect with videoconferencing but turn their cameras off. Still other groups found rich collaboration was possible simply by interacting through Etherpad and later through Google Docs. This open approach to tools and technologies also expanded to a line of creative assignments that students undertook in the course. In creating podcasts of interviews with designers, visual representations and designs of learning experiences, and photo essays about concepts, students were free to choose their technologies without mandate.

Our goal is to highlight the creativity unleashed by a combination of pedagogical insight, openness and flexibility. Before the shift to customization, students were constrained by technologies prescribed, but the emergent nature of interactions and design work suffered. Once customization became par-for-the-course, students were free to experiment and develop strategies that fit needs. Contrasting creative styles and mindsets, Drs Roseth and Linnenbrink-Garcia continued to refine their motivation course design within constraints they defined for themselves through research, whereas Drs Mishra and Henriksen adapted their design to fit the spirit of the course content. While neither of the courses or instructors lay claim to perfect teaching or groundbreaking creativity, their openness to create and experiment demonstrates a CFTF mindset. This has now spread to much of the EPET program, with many courses having significant hybrid enrollment.

One course in particular – Mind, Social Media, and Society taught by Dr Christine Greenhow – featured 14 Hybrid students using a mix of robotic telepresence and videoconferencing. It was the first EPET course with a synchronous hybrid design that had more telepresent students than physically present students. Moreover, the concept of synchronous hybrid interaction using robots and other technologies had become commonplace in other EPET activities, such as research group meetings and dissertation defenses. This did not happen overnight, nor did it occur without hiccups along the way. Still, this type of techno-pedagogical diffusion through doctoral programs is best supported when faculty members adopt creative, flexible and open mindsets towards technology-fluency in educational practices.

EXAMPLE FROM THE FIELD: THE ARIZONA STATE UNIVERSITY (ASU) ONLINE EDD IN EDUCATIONAL LEADERSHIP AND INNOVATION

Arizona State University's Doctor of Education (EdD) degree in Educational Leadership and Innovation (ELID) in the Mary Lou Fulton Teachers College was originally developed as a traditional, face-to-face program implemented in 2006. Since its inception, it has been considered a 'flagship' program for the Teachers College at the university. ELID is a cohort-based (20–25 per cohort), three-year program, with students initially taking courses around theory, research methodologies and scholarly approaches to practice, before moving into dissertation work. Students engage in course content over the first year-and-a-half that builds up knowledge of theory, research and practice. But they do so in contextualized ways, to understand real-world educational problems and their own problem of practice through a lens of scholarly thinking. During the second year, students are put into Leader Scholar Communities (LSCs), which function as small-group cohorts (5–7 students) within their larger overall cohort. LSCs are assigned a faculty member who serves as dissertation advisor to each student in the group. In LSCs each student advances research around their problem of practice individually, but with the support of their peer-group and faculty chair.

This program is a Carnegie Project in the Educational Doctorate (CPED) affiliated program; several graduates have won the CPED Outstanding Dissertation Award, while others have attained professional recognition, exemplified in state and regional awards. This, in addition to a strong completion rate in the face-to-face version (86 percent completion, and higher for those who complete their first year), has made the program highly successful. Given ASU's goal of making learning more accessible, there was an interest in expanding the program. In bringing the program into online settings through admitting two fully online cohorts per year (in addition to the continued once-a-year face-to-face cohort), the program could grow beyond the Phoenix metro area to students nationally and internationally. In the Fall of 2015, the first cohort of students was admitted to an online program version. Additionally, the program is supported by an instructional design team and an online technology studio (an ASU online teaching support structure that undergirds and addresses needs for online courses) at university and college levels.

Since this online program is still in nascent stages, some aspects or courses are still unfolding and developing along the way. So the ASU discussion is limited in scope to one example, as we do not yet have a comprehensive sense of every course or program outcome.

Systems Change and Leadership: A First Course for EdD Students

Systems Change and Leadership is one of the first courses taken by EdD students in this program. It had previously been designed and taught by other faculty in a face-to-face version. It was redeveloped for the first online cohort in Fall 2015 and taught since in every regular semester. The content focuses on education as a system, to look at the embedded nature of educational challenges. Students are new, and just starting to think

about their problem of practice, to understand that it is embedded in a system that influences the nature of the problem, solutions and outcomes.

Converting the course to an online format, Dr Henriksen aimed to figure out the best ways to translate the content to an online medium. The course was primarily asynchronous due to the variability of time zones and the students' professional work schedules. However, virtual synchronous office hours are offered via video conferencing, as well as flexible office hours (scheduled at students' requests). Given the need to build community and give students opportunities for collaboration and in-depth discourse, the course also includes small group work in addition to individual assignments, and varied discussion structures each week. For small group projects, Dr Henriksen decided that students should have freedom in how they communicated and collaborated in groups, allowing them to fluidly complete projects via a mixture of synchronous and asynchronous communications using technologies that suit their purpose (things like Skype, Google Hangouts, Vidyo, Google Docs, and basic email communications are common). This also pushed them, as professional leaders, to figure out how to communicate with collaborators across time and physical boundaries.

In redeveloping the content and coursework, it was necessary to work creatively around the medium's constraints and also take advantage of the affordances. For some of the coursework, this meant using a CFTF mindset to find new ways to do the same assignment, based on a more independent and flexible context. In other cases, it meant coming up with brand new assignments that cover content but take advantage of the technological medium. Small aspects of the course or pedagogical goals required elements of rethinking. It is important to know that creativity is not always about dramatic change (though sometimes that happens too). But as Hofstadter (2008) notes, creative thinking is often about twisting existing knobs rather than landmark changes.

For example, in one assignment from the face-to-face session, students conducted weekly observations of educational sites and wrote a weekly journal document of these observations. Students enjoyed this because it offered opportunities to practice informal research observations. Once the course moved online, however, students could not all observe similar local sites. Yet having different students in different locations presented opportunities for more diverse site observations, as well as sharing across contexts. So the assignment was adjusted so that students could choose (over five weeks) five different sites of their own (physical or virtual), in which some type of learning or educational system was present. Rather than simply turning in a journal at the end, each student was required to create their own blog site, which they updated weekly with site observations

and scholarly reflections about connections to systems thinking and course content.

The type of diversity of sites across the US and internationally expanded, to include not only school sites, but also sports practices, ballet classes, museums, libraries, college campuses or virtual sites. More importantly, using blog sites for journaling meant that students could share and read each other's work, and make their writing and thinking more visible in a public forum online. This is important for budding scholars, and practitioners aiming to become influential. Initially the instructional design team resisted the idea of moving the assignment onto a blog, as EdD students were not technology-focused practitioners. But they were convinced by the fact that learning should be visible and public, as Shulman (1999) noted, 'Learning is least useful when it is private and hidden; it is most powerful when it becomes public and communal' (p. 11).

As online students and lifelong learners, fluency with basic technologies was important from day one. Students confessed that they were initially hesitant, because setting up a blog site was 'one more step to have to do, when it could just be a written assignment for the instructor'. But given time, students overwhelmingly commented that they felt empowered by sharing their work in a more public space and viewed themselves as authors with an audience. A few small changes pushed forward by an online creative rethinking added up to significant benefits.

As a more significant overhaul, one key part of the course had been reading a book by Sutton and Rao (2016), with small groups presenting in class about different chapters. In thinking about the pedagogical goals – deep reading of a text and collaboration to communicate key takeaways – the online space presented an opportunity. A new assignment was developed in lieu of standard presentations. Small groups, assigned their chapter readings, worked collaboratively to build a multi-modal text, to share key ideas and takeaways from the book, and practical applications and implications. In doing this as a multi-modal text (via Google Docs or other relevant technology applications), they were able to reflect ideas and make connections with relevant online resources (videos, images and other media), creating rich, visual and shareable projects. This met the initial goals and built on them, offering an opportunity for simple creativity to enrich the content and communicate it to others in interesting, compelling ways.

The CFTF Mindset in Practice in the ASU Example

This example showcases elements from the ASU ELID program, not as perfect creativity or unassailable practices, but to illustrate the importance

of a CFTF mindset. Such a mindset targets creativity as an approach, not just a product or outcome. The mix of both small and larger changes that occur when programs move toward rigorous doctoral learning online means that instructors and program designers must be willing to question and experiment (asking, 'What does this look like if we rethink it in a new context?' or 'What tweaks or complete shifts are needed?'), to explore and move flexibly to engage new learning spaces and technologies, and as all creative teachers do, work from student-centered perspectives with an eye for innovation. As the examples above demonstrate, the results can be significant, yet any committed instructor can achieve this through the CFTF mindset.

CONCLUSIONS

Scholars note a need for more attention to creativity and innovation in higher education settings (Gibson, 2010). We suggest that online and hybrid doctoral programs are front and center as potential hubs for creativity, given the nature of their context as relatively new and undefined spaces of innovation in technology-rich contexts. The core of doctoral programs remains unchanged, with its focus on developing educational leaders and scholars through focus on methodological rigor and use or development of theory. But new contexts of online or hybrid learning have opened up access to doctoral learning, allowing more inquiry-driven practitioners into these spaces. This means there are opportunities to expand the scope of programs, and work with practitioner leaders who can impact contexts on the ground. There is a dialectic tension here, where new technologies drive new contexts, but new contexts also drive the need for creativity in how we mediate learning.

This chapter suggests that instructors, course designers and other stakeholders in online or hybrid doctoral contexts should adopt a CFTF mindset for creativity and technology-fluency. Support for this position is based on existing scholarship around creativity and technology – involving habits of mind for openness, flexibility, a willingness to try new things, and a technology-fluency in teaching.

The broadness of this mindset means there are limitless ways to apply it, and much diversity of application based on instructor style, pedagogical goals and other situational factors. The examples here suggest how everyday instruction can make small or large changes to engage with the new in online or hybrid settings. Through this we hope that more stakeholders will be ready to engage creatively with new doctoral learning contexts – stepping boldly into the new.

REFERENCES

Amabile, T.M. (1983). *The social psychology of creativity.* New York, NY: Springer-Verlag.

Amabile, T.M. (1996). *Creativity in context.* Boulder, CO: Westview Press Harper Collins Publishers.

Amabile, T.M. (2012). *Componential theory of creativity.* Boston, MA: Harvard Business School.

Baer, M. and G.R. Oldham (2006). The curvilinear relation between experienced creative time pressure and creativity: moderating effects of openness to experience and support for creativity. *Journal of Applied Psychology*, **91**(4), 963–70.

Bell, J., S. Sawaya and W. Cain (2014). Synchromodal classes: Designing for shared learning experiences between face-to-face and online students. *International Journal of Designs for Learning*, **5**(1).

Bradley, A. (1999). Educating the educators. *Education Week*, **19**(2), 38–40.

Brown, L.D. (1966). *Doctoral graduates in education. An inquiry into their motives, aspirations, and perceptions of the program.* Bloomington, IN: Indiana University.

Brown, L.D. (1991). A perspective on the PhD–EdD discussion in schools of education. Paper presented at the American Educational Research Association.

Cain, W. and J. Bell (2017). Navigating between different forms of embodiment in a synchronous hybrid doctoral course. In *Proceedings of the 2017 CHI Conference Extended Abstracts on Human Factors in Computing Systems* (pp. 925–32). New York, NY: ACM.

Cain, W. and D. Henriksen (2013). Pedagogy and situational creativity in synchronous hybrid learning: Descriptions of three models. Paper presented at annual meeting of *Society for Informational Technology and Educational Technology Conference* (SITE), New Orleans.

Cropley, A.J (2003). *Creativity in education & learning.* Bodmin: Routledge Falmer.

Damrosch, D. (1995). *We scholars: Changing the culture of the university.* Cambridge, MA: Harvard University Press.

Davidovitch, N. and R.M. Milgram (2006). Creative thinking as a predictor of teacher effectiveness in higher education. *Creativity Research Journal*, **18**(3), 385–90.

Davies, D., D. Jindal-Snape, R. Digby, A. Howe, C. Collier and P. Hay (2014). The roles and development needs of teachers to promote creativity: A systematic review of literature. *Teaching and Teacher Education*, **41**, 34–41.

Dill, D.D. and F.A. Van Vught (2010). *National innovation and the academic research enterprise: Public policy in global perspective.* Baltimore, MD: Johns Hopkins University Press.

Dweck, C.S. (2006). *Mindset: The new psychology of success.* New York, NY: Random House Incorporated.

Fasko, D.J. (2001). Education and creativity. *Creativity Research Journal*, **13**(3 & 4), 317–27.

Freedman, K. (2007). Artmaking/troublemaking: Creativity, policy, and leadership in art education. *Studies in Art Education: A Journal of Issues and Research*, **48**(2), 204–17.

Ghezzi, P. (2007). The online doctorate: Flexible, but credible? *School Administrator*, **64**(7), 30–35.

Gibson, R. (2010). The 'art' of creative teaching: Implications for higher education. *Teaching in Higher Education*, **15**(5), 607–13.

Henriksen, D. (2011). *We teach who we are: Creativity and trans-disciplinary thinking in the practices of accomplished teachers.* Doctoral dissertation, Michigan State University.

Henriksen, D. and P. Mishra (2015). We teach who we are. *Teachers College Record*, **117**(7), 1–46.

Henriksen, D., P. Mishra and R. Mehta (2015). Novel, Effective, Whole: Toward a NEW framework for evaluations of creative products. *Journal of Technology and Teacher Education*, **23**(3), 455–78.

Henriksen, D., P. Mishra, C. Greenhow, W. Cain and C. Roseth (2014). A tale of two courses: Innovation in the hybrid/online doctoral program at Michigan State University. *TechTrends*, **58**(4), 45–53.

Hickey, M.G. (2001). Creativity goes to school: Observing creative teachers in action. Paper presented at the annual meeting of the American Educational Research Association, Montreal, Canada.

Hofstadter, D. (2008). *Metamagical themas: Questing for the essence of mind and pattern.* New York, NY: Basic Books.

Karwowski, M. (2014). Creative mindsets: Measurement, correlates, consequences. *Psychology of Aesthetics, Creativity, and the Arts*, **8**(1), 62–70.

Knight, J. (2013). The changing landscape of higher education internationalisation: For better or worse? *Perspectives: Policy and Practice in Higher Education*, **17**(3), 84–90.

Levine, A. (2005). *Educating school leaders.* New York, NY: The Education Schools Project.

Levine, A. (2007). *Educating researchers.* New York, NY: The Education Schools Project.

Lilly, F.R. and G.F. Bramwell-Rejskind (2004). The dynamics of creative teaching. *The Journal of Creative Behavior*, **38**(2), 102–24.

Lovitts, B.E. (2001). *Leaving the ivory tower: The causes and consequences of departure from doctoral study.* Lanham, MD: Rowman & Littlefield.

Mishra, P. and M.J. Koehler (2006). Technological pedagogical content knowledge: A framework for teacher knowledge. *Teachers College Record*, **108**(6), 1017.

Mishra, P. and M.J. Koehler (2008). Introducing technological pedagogical content knowledge. Paper presented at the annual meeting of the American Educational Research Association (pp. 1–16).

Mishra, P., L. Peruski and M. Koehler (2007). Developing technological pedagogical content knowledge (TPCK) through teaching online. In *Proceedings of the Society for Information Technology & Teacher Education International Conference*, **2007**(1), 2208–13.

Mishra, P., D. Henriksen, L.O. Boltz and C. Richardson (2016). E-leadership and teacher development using ICT. In R. Huang, Kinshuk and J.K. Price (eds), *ICT in Education in Global Context* (pp. 249–66). Berlin and Heidelberg: Springer.

Mitchell, L.D., J.D. Parlamis and S.A. Claiborne (2015). Overcoming faculty avoidance of online education: From resistance to support to active participation. *Journal of Management Education*, **39**(3), 350–71.

Oldham, G.R. and A. Cummings (1996). Employee creativity: Personal and contextual factors at work. *Academy of Management Journal*, **39**(3), 607–34.

Perry, J.A. and D.G. Imig (2008). A stewardship of practice in education. *Change: The Magazine of Higher Learning*, **40**(6), 42–9.

Picciano, A.G. (2017). *Online education policy and practice: The past, present, and future of the digital university.* New York, NY: Taylor & Francis.

Prabhu, V., C. Sutton and W. Sauser (2008). Creativity and certain personality traits: Understanding the mediating effect of intrinsic motivation. *Creativity Research Journal*, **20**(1), 53–66.

Renzulli, J.S. (1992). A general theory for the development of creative productivity through the pursuit of ideal acts of learning. *Gifted Child Quarterly*, **36**(4), 170–82.

Robinson, V.M. (2014). Reducing the research–practice gap through problem-based methodology. In A.D. Reid, E.P. Hart and M.A. Peters (eds), *A companion to research in education* (pp. 341–52). Dordrecht: Springer.

Roseth, C., M. Akcaoglu and A. Zellner (2013). Blending synchronous face-to-face and computer-supported cooperative learning in a hybrid doctoral seminar. *TechTrends*, **57**(3), 54–9.

Shulman, L.S. (1986). Those who understand: Knowledge growth in teaching. *Educational Researcher*, **15**(2), 4–14.

Shulman, L.S. (1999). Taking learning seriously. *Change: The Magazine of Higher Learning*, **31**(4), 10–17.

Silvia, P.J., E.C. Nusbaum, C. Berg, C. Martin and A. O'Connor (2009). Openness to experience, plasticity, and creativity: Exploring lower-order, high-order, and interactive effects. *Journal of Research in Personality*, **43**(6), 1087–90.

Sternberg, R.J. and L.A. O'Hara (1999). Creativity and intelligence. In R.J. Sternberg (ed.), *Handbook of Creativity* (pp. 251–72). Cambridge: Cambridge University Press.

Sullivan, W. (2005). *Work and integrity* (2nd edn). San Francisco, CA: Jossey-Bass.

Sutton, R.I. and H. Rao (2016). *Scaling up excellence: Getting to more without settling for less*. New York, NY: Random House.

Torrance, E.P. and R.Y. Horng (1980). Creativity and style of learning and thinking characteristics of adaptors and innovators. *Creative Child & Adult Quarterly*, **5**(2), 80–85.

Zhao, Y. (2012). *World class learners: Educating creative and entrepreneurial students*. Thousand Oaks, CA: Corwin Press.

Zhou, J. and J. George (2001). When job dissatisfaction leads to creativity: Encouraging the expression of voice. *Academy of Management Journal*, **44**(4), 682–96.

PART II

Design: learning applications

4. Beyond cybernation: technology and teaching in doctoral educational leadership

Stephanie J. Blackmon

INTRODUCTION

The idea of computer use for automation has been referred to as cybernation, and beyond automating various tasks and occupations with computers are the implications of that transition (Huhtamo, 1999). More specifically, there are power dynamics associated with technology and human interaction or the lack thereof (Huhtamo, 1999). The way technology is integrated into an organization and the type of technology integrated affect the way people interact with each other and their environments. Therefore, technology integration in higher education has implications for multiple areas of academe. From updating software to ensuring Wi-Fi accessibility, institutions have much to consider when adopting even the most basic technologies. Classrooms are often impacted by technology integration, with some classrooms serving as seedbeds for technological innovation. Whether it is through increased inquiries about collaborative tools offered in a learning management system (LMS) or a rallying cry for the lowering of firewalls to access three dimensional virtual worlds (Blackmon, 2015), instructors and students are shifting the way technology functions in classrooms; doctoral educational leadership classrooms are not excluded from these shifts.

Educational leadership courses, which can include K-12 administration, educational technology and higher education administration, have an arguably unique relationship to technology integration because of the leader–learner amalgam. It is not uncommon for doctoral students in general to have careers and hold leadership positions while they are pursuing further education, or to have other responsibilities related to career and family (Gardner, 2009; Offerman, 2011). Researchers have noted that some doctoral students could benefit from more flexible programs or have provided examples of how doctoral students have benefited from the flexibility of technology-enhanced and alternative programs (Martinsuo and Turkulainen, 2011; Servage, 2009). Many doctoral educational leadership students have similar circumstances (Stallone, 2011). For example, a university health and wellness supervisor who is responsible for training others on recognizing students at risk could also be a doctorate of education student who is learning to use the simulation Kognito, which addresses dealing with at-risk students. A number of educational leadership doctoral students are often working in areas of education while also gaining the knowledge and skills, which includes technological competence, to contribute to their growth as educational leaders.

Understanding how technology integration functions in doctoral educational leadership courses can provide useful insights for instructors, students and others involved in educational leadership. This chapter focuses specifically on three currently used technologies in doctoral educational leadership classrooms: social media, blogs, and virtual worlds.

A major premise of this chapter is that the relationship between technology and its users is dialogical. Furthermore, these exchanges are value laden. Therefore, the examples of technology provided in this chapter will move beyond cybernation and not only address the complex exchange that occurs when educational leadership instructors and students employ various technologies (the unidirectional relationship of user to technology), but also address ways to facilitate that complex exchange.

DOCTORAL EDUCATIONAL LEADERSHIP AND TECHNOLOGY CONTEXT

Online and Hybrid Programs

One of the primary ways technology has influenced doctoral educational leadership is through the advent of hybrid and fully online doctoral programs. For example, Ivankova and Stick (2007) discussed students' persistence in a distributed doctoral program in educational leadership. They noted that students could earn PhDs or EdDs via distributed means with little upset to their personal schedules, as parts of the program were delivered through the group functions in the Blackboard LMS and through Lotus Notes (Ivankova and Stick, 2007). They found that graduates of the program reported higher levels of comfort with online learning than study participants who had withdrawn or were inactive in the program; program graduates showed 'increased comfort level[s] . . . when participants rated their learning in the distributed environment as compared to a face-to-face setting' (p. 105). The flexibility that the distributed program provided was important to the students (Ivankova and Stick, 2007). Recent graduates of an online EdD program in educational technology also highlighted flexibility, noting that their online program made it possible for them to remain in their respective locations and maintain employment (Fuller et al., 2014).

Program flexibility was also addressed in Miller and Curry's (2014) work on an online EdD program in educational technology leadership. The program was 'created for individuals who wanted to be educational leaders within their current work positions' (p. 36) and included a yearly, one-week 'face-to-face doctoral seminar' (p. 38). The flexibility was twofold: for doctoral students who worked full time as practitioners and for practitioners who wanted to pursue an educational doctorate but were outside of the university's geographic area (Miller and Curry, 2014). The seminars, however, presented issues for potential international EdD students because of the increase in travel funds to attend sessions and Department of Homeland Security regulations about the requisite amount of face-to-face time for international students (Miller and Curry, 2014). The program also included adjustments and considerations of instructors, as some faculty members had to shift their thinking because the program was not similar to ones they were familiar with or had experienced.

Previous studies have also addressed the changes faculty members make in order to accept and implement fully online or hybrid doctoral programs. For example, Buss et al. (2013) explored the changes faculty members made for what was termed an *innovative* EdD program because of the 'Leader–Scholar Communities', comprised of two faculty members and five students, and the 'hybrid course format', with 'classes meeting face-to-face for 2/3 of the semester and online for 1/3' (p. 62). Faculty reported that their views of research expanded as a result of teaching in the innovative EdD program and how interesting it was to be involved in action research with practitioners. On the other hand, the in-depth involvement in those projects, which were sometimes outside of a faculty member's area of expertise, meant that some faculty were limited in that they were unable to work with other students who had research areas more similar to the faculty members' expertise areas. For the teaching components of the program, faculty members noted that they grew in the area of teaching collaboratively, often planning and debriefing with other instructors. They also mentioned, however, that these efforts were often quite time consuming, as issues faced were sometimes 'messy problems' (Buss et al., 2013, p. 70). Faculty members were excited about the results of the program, but achieving that success was not without its challenges.

Another important aspect of online and hybrid doctoral educational leadership programs is how students apply the experiences and the course content in their careers. As the aforementioned literature indicates, students, faculty and administrators put a lot of time and effort into these doctoral programs. Kumar and Dawson (2013) examined how graduates of a 'professional practice' doctoral program in curriculum and instruction, with a focus on instructional technology, used the material they learned in the program in their respective professions (p. 167). The program included online coursework for two years, 'practice-embedded research' for at least three semesters, and could be done part time (Kumar and Dawson, 2013, p. 167). Nineteen students were interviewed about their experiences with practical application of EdD experiences and concepts, and Kumar and Dawson also reviewed participants' CVs. They found that participants applied program content when sharing content knowledge formally and informally, when making decisions supported by data, and when using new technology as a form of innovation. Some students were so pleased with the LMS from the program that they used it in their respective school districts, while others leveraged their expertise to secure funding to support various technology-related projects. Students also used the research they were exposed to in the program to create opportunities to share what they were learning with others at their schools.

Of course, not all educational leadership doctoral programs are completely online or hybrid, and some programs do not offer online or hybrid courses. However, there are still instances where technology plays a role in courses, either through the LMS or through the integration of technology in more involved ways (for example, online group meetings or video-based assignments). Students also integrate technology into their work in very informal ways (for example OneNote), even when these technologies are not a part of their programs.

Technology Integration

Technology integration can make a difference for course connectivity between students and faculty. Caruthers and Friend (2014), for example, discussed how online areas can function as 'thirdspace', which they defined as 'a socially constructed space built from multiple perceptions, meanings, values, and ideologies of students and instructors' (p. 13). In their study, which included doctoral students who had face-to-face, online, and hybrid courses during their program, they showed the various ways students used online discussion areas as thirdspace. Taylor (2007) also mentioned how online space served as an informal community area for students pursuing a doctorate of education.

Whether faculty members are helping students establish doctoral identities or engaging in critical pedagogy, technology provides a viable way of fostering these programmatic and pedagogical goals. However, technology is not innocuous, as there are implications for the integration of various tools into doctoral educational leadership programs and courses. The next section of this chapter will discuss social media, blogs and virtual worlds and what the use of each could mean for doctoral educational leadership. Because there is much to be gleaned from first exploring how others have used these tools, each section will begin with a general context, move to an education context, and close with recommendations for doctoral educational leadership.

SOCIAL MEDIA

General Context

Social media sites, even ones that are not necessarily designed for educational purposes, can provide an outlet for connecting and sharing work. There are several examples of students in other areas of higher education using social media in education. For example, in a study of how undergraduate students used Facebook, Selwyn (2009) found that students sometimes exchanged practical information related to their courses, and even engaged in 'peer-assisted learning', suggesting various books and articles for other students to read (p. 166). Researchers have found similar interactions via Twitter as well, with Honeycutt and Herring (2009) discussing Twitter's growth as a global 'tool for interpersonal interaction', and a prediction that the tool's use would increase in 'formal collaborative contexts' (pp. 9–10). Their prediction was somewhat confirmed, as Junco et al. (2011) found that Twitter resulted in 'a more rich discussion' of course content (p. 126), and López-Bonilla and López-Bonilla (2013) found that when 132 undergraduates at a university in Spain were asked to collaborate for group projects, 13.2 percent of them elected to do so using Twitter. The remaining students chose to use Facebook (34.1 percent) and Tuenti (52.7 percent) (p. 140).

Education Context

In the aforementioned examples, the study participants have been from areas other than education, and when the focus shifts to education, other uses for and issues with social media arise. For example, in Wandera et al.'s (2016) study of social media and collaboration among cohorts of students in higher educational leadership, organizational leadership and innovation, and educational leadership tracks of an EdD program, they found that more of the 119 students used Blackboard and YouTube (60 percent combined selected 'sometimes' or 'frequently' used), whereas a combined 20 percent of participants used wikis, WebEx/GoToMeeting, Twitter and Instagram 'sometimes' or 'frequently' (p. 127). Many of the EdD students also expressed that their experience as doctoral students was enhanced by social media, and several students found social media cost effective and accessible (Wandera et al., 2016). Overall, however, Wandera et al. (2016) found that students saw social media as an efficient mechanism for idea sharing, but that it had 'no significant impact on academic success' (p. 130). The EdD students' perspectives on social media as a tool for sharing efficiently are consistent with some of the ways other doctoral students and scholars who already hold doctorates use social media (Veletsianos, 2012; Zhu and Procter, 2015).

Although social media platforms are proven mechanisms for sharing and collaborating, there are considerations to keep in mind when using them. For example, Kimmons and Veletsianos (2014) investigated teacher-education students' perspectives on their evolving social media and social networking identities as they moved from the role of student to the role of educator. They found that the teacher-education students were using what Kimmons and Veletsianos term 'acceptable identity fragments (AIF)' (p. 295). The AIF included characteristics students deemed most fitting for their audience. These identities are not fixed, however, and can enhance or encumber other aspects of students' identities, depending on the recipients of the social media self (Kimmons and Veletsianos, 2014). Doctoral students in educational leadership may face similar social media issues. Just as teacher-education students were concerned about how others would view them as future educators, doctoral students in educational leadership often hold positions as teachers or administrators while completing their programs. There is a complexity associated with balancing the social media doctoral *student self* and the social media working *professional self* – not to mention the social media *personal self*.

Addressing this complexity, nevertheless, creates an opportunity to explore how to integrate social media into educational doctoral leadership in a way that acknowledges the challenges associated with its implementation.

Recommendations

Use social media to teach doctoral students about promoting their work
Students who already use social media such as Facebook or Twitter will not be strangers to the status update. A social media tool like Twitter, as the aforementioned studies showed, is an excellent way to make a research-related

status update. Some students may not have large networks just yet, so allowing students to serve as networks for each other could be beneficial. A cohort-based approach to this could be particularly helpful because in addition to allowing doctoral students to extend their networks, they can also see work that matriculated students have done, which could function as inspiration or a peer-related road map through the program for those who need it. Instructors can do something similar with a YouTube channel for the program. Wandera et al. (2016) noted that educational leadership doctoral students in their study benefited from YouTube. Cohorts and programs can share their work with each other and other cohorts via a YouTube channel.

If students have concerns over work being pilfered from social media, as was brought up by students in Zhu and Procter's (2015) study on Twitter, blogs and Facebook, then students could consider sharing more general ideas and tips instead of budding ideas they plan to use for themselves, or limit access to the group or site. The potential audiences for this work could also include administrators of local school systems. If doctoral educational leadership programs created a social media site and purposefully connected with administrators of local or regional programs, the connection could result in outreach opportunities for students as well as faculty.

Use social media as a way to guide digital responsibility
Social media boundary setting and identity construction do not stop once students complete undergraduate programs that used social media or once students complete their doctoral programs (see Veletsianos and Kimmons, 2013). Instructors who choose to employ social media in courses or programs must also understand that what students share for courses could be automatically connected to other aspects of their lives. If those areas somehow conflict or result in a convergence that causes upset between factions of a doctoral student's life (as happened with a faculty member from the Veletsianos and Kimmons 2013 study), the student will be taxed with additional stress and pressure.

Faculty and students should discuss the ways in which students can responsibly engage online. For example, a student might set up an account only affiliated with a course or program – to take advantage of opportunities to share and collaborate, but also to maintain a student space that is separate from the professional or personal space. The student can choose to combine those identities or use information from one or the other at a time of her or his choosing. There is a tremendous amount of value in engaging via the open web and creating dialogue between doctoral students who are in programs and with people who are already occupying the spaces students seek to enter. However, not all students are in the same place personally or professionally, so a conversation about the complexities of identity on social media before establishing or using accounts for courses would be helpful to students.

Evaluation

Evaluating students' contributions to a course via social media can vary based on the medium. For example, Twitter allows fewer characters than other platforms, so students would have different options available for posting on one outlet versus the other. However, students can be instrumental in designing rubrics for their participation via social media. A co-created rubric could also be helpful because students' contributions may be associated with their real names – so having a say in what gets attached to their names could be important to them both personally and professionally. When introducing social media as a part of the course meeting, faculty might locate reputable educational outlets on a particular platform, discuss the characteristics of the posts with students, and provide guidance on what posts are appropriate or helpful for the course. The posts could be used as a form of class participation or as a hybrid session for a course, particularly with activities like Twitter chats where the students must use a particular hashtag (#) and faculty members can access students' participation by accessing the hashtag.

BLOGS

General Context

Weblogs, or blogs, are typically used as a collaborative learning or engagement tool. Ferdig and Trammell (2004) pointed out that blogs are similar to 'online personal journals' (para. 1), but unlike personal journals, blogs are designed to be shared with others. These are spaces for logging thoughts and ideas about the personal, professional or sometimes both. Unlike discussion boards, which are usually associated with a particular course or topic, blogs can address any topic the blogger chooses. Blogs are a form of social media, but in higher education they often function in ways that are unique to the blog medium, which is why they were not included in the Social Media section of this chapter. Williams and Jacobs (2004) noted, for example, that groups and communities may establish blogs as well, which can happen with other forms of social media but certainly not in the same way. According to Ferdig and Trammell (2004), 'Blogs are useful teaching and learning tools because they provide a space for students to reflect and publish their thoughts and understandings' (para. 6). Furthermore, they stated, '[blogs] provide opportunities for feedback and potential scaffolding of new ideas' (para. 6).

Ward and West (2008) suggested blogs could be useful for helping students grow into researchers and scholars and assisting with the doctoral supervision process. They also highlighted the growth and '"breakthrough" learning moments' (Ward and West, 2008, p. 68) doctoral students can have as a result of blogging, a point noted in Ferdig and Trammell (2004). Mortensen and Walker (2002) began blogging as doctoral students, and used their blogs for reasons similar to those later mentioned in Ward and West (2008); however, Mortensen and Walker also saw blogs as mechanisms for 'being part of a discussion which potentially extends beyond the academic community' (p. 250). The blogs helped them establish online personas that were beneficial when attempting to conduct research in and about online spaces. Several years later, however, Walker (2006) provided insight on what it means to blog from the position of the employed academic, instead of the doctoral student seeking employment. The challenges Walker mentioned will prove useful for a more specific discussion of educational leadership doctoral students later in this section.

Education Context

In Ladyshewsky and Gardner's (2008) study of blog use among undergraduates studying physiotherapy, they suggested that pre-service teachers could also use blogs to connect regarding their experiences with teaching in their practicums, after finding that the physiotherapy students had an overall positive experience with blogs. Top (2012) later conducted a study of 50 pre-service teachers' use of blogs in two courses: Web Design and Internet Based Programming. Top (2012) found that the students had 'positive feelings about the collaborative learning and perceived learning' and 'moderate feelings related to sense of community' with blogs in the two courses (p. 27).

Meyer's (2010) study specifically addressed students' experiences with blogs and other tools in a 'doctoral-level' online course on higher education finance (p. 228). Meyer noted that '[a]ll doctoral students in this program are adult, working professionals working full-time at a variety of positions in higher education or organizations that provide educational services to K-12 schools' (p. 228). Students in the course expressed that blogs were easy to use and gave them an opportunity to connect and have community on the internet, with content autonomy (Meyer, 2010). Meyer also used a wiki in the doctoral course, but when students made contributions to the wiki, they were not listed as authors. Wikis allow users to make edits, but their contributions are often combined with the contributions of others and not highlighted according to contributors' names. The students in Meyer's course seemed pleased to see an authorship function as a part of the blog because their names were associated with their contributions (Meyer, 2010). The option to share comments between blogs was disabled for the course, and students mentioned missing that aspect of the blog experience.

Educational leadership doctoral students can experience many of the same benefits with blogs that other students, graduate and undergraduate, have experienced. Ferdig and Trammell (2004) listed four benefits students get from blogging: subject matter expertise; greater sense of 'interest and ownership in learning'; participation opportunities; and various perspectives 'within and outside of the classroom' (Farmer et al., 2008; Ferdig and Trammell, 2004, para. 18), and these are all areas of benefit for doctoral students in educational leadership. Whether training to be researchers or practitioners, educational leadership doctoral students are growing subject matter experts, and blogs can help them cultivate their own expertise as well as connect with others in the field. These interactions provide the various perspectives, participation opportunities and learning ownership opportunities students need. They can establish connections within their programs and cohorts, as well as outside of the institution. There are, however, some challenges associated with implementing blogs.

Walker (2006) discussed how her blog was read and received once she was employed as a faculty member and head of her department. She recounted a story about someone recognizing her from her blog, overhearing a conversation that Walker was having with a friend, and sharing that information with other people. Walker found that even though the blog was only a portion of her identity (an idea that comes up in the Social Media section of this chapter when discussing AIF from Kimmons and Veletsianos, 2014), people thought that they knew her – in toto. Educational leadership doctoral students may have these same challenges not only once they either obtain employment or transition into other positions, but also as they are working and completing their doctoral studies. They, again, will have to balance their student, personal and professional selves.

Recommendations

Incorporating blogs while being mindful of the challenges of their use can be achieved in the following ways.

Discuss online personas

Students may want to maximize their following by connecting their blogs to other forms of social media. For example, once they post on their blogs, those entries can automatically post to their Twitter accounts and show up as a tweet. Students may be fine with this option at first, but will they be fine with what is posted there once they are no longer doctoral students? If students are apprehensive about using their real names for blogs, they can always write pseudonymously (see Walker, 2006) or selectively share information between academic and personal accounts. Students will need to keep in mind, however, that in an effort to maximize the connections outside of their respective programs, they may lose a bit of anonymity when trying to leverage a larger network because people may want to know who they are before subscribing to the blog. Instructors will want to spend time talking with doctoral students about what blogging could mean for their various selves: personal, student and professional. These conversations will also be germane to the students' preparation and continued development as educational leaders who may be responsible for others' use of blogs and other technologies. In fact, the first blog post that educational leadership doctoral students submit can set the stage for what readers can expect (or not expect) from their contributions, and also what they expect (or do not expect) from readers.

Guide comments

Students may need additional instructions on how to provide and receive feedback to or from each other (Halic et al., 2010). This lesson would coincide well with the lesson on online personas because students should be aware that if they choose to share more personal information on their blogs, then that personal information is open for critique. Even though blogs may feel like online diaries (Farmer et al., 2008, p. 133), they are often shared with others and may not provide the same safe space as an online diary.

Know the system limitations

A great deal has been said about the avoidance of disclosing too much, but there are also limitations when students want to disclose more. For example, some blogs limit what bloggers can post when using the free version of their platform. Students may be able to upload photos, but they may not be able to upload videos, which could be limiting. There may also be limitations to LMS-based blogs (for example Blackboard) versus blogs on the open web (for example WordPress). Although LMS-based blogs can be a helpful way to get students started with blogging and allow students to get feedback on their blog posts from classmates, these spaces are often not as streamlined as open web-based blogs and limit students' access to the extended community provided via the open web. Perhaps this is why some institutions provide access to open web-based blogs. However, even if an institution provides an unlimited, open web-based blog account for all of its students, there are sometimes restrictions related to content ownership.

Students may have autonomy over blog content, but do they own that content outright, or does their institution own it because they provided the blog? Discussing these issues with IT or a teaching and learning center before using blogs in educational leadership doctoral programs can help faculty members and students understand the implications of what is posted and prevent students from feeling duped once they have graduated and try to access their information, only to find that they have lost access to the university-sponsored blog account.

Evaluation

As mentioned in the Social Media section, co-constructing rubrics for blog participation can be helpful as well. The same potential is there for students' course comments on the blog to intersect with their personal lives, so they may appreciate input during the rubric-construction process at the beginning of the course. Faculty members can provide guidance on the process, of course, and help students ensure that the blog posts are connected to course objectives, but faculty members can also use blogs for formative assessment. Unlike other forms of social media that require brevity, blogs allow users to post longer entries; they can function as a multimedia, interactive reflection space where the comments provide guidance to help students improve work for upcoming assignments or tasks. Because there is a power dynamic between professors and students, faculty members may want to reserve certain comments for direct student feedback so as not to embarrass a student or sway the comments in a particular direction.

VIRTUAL WORLDS

General Context

Educators around the globe have used virtual worlds in higher education, and these environments have numerous pedagogical benefits (Blackmon, 2015) such as creating greater connections between faculty members and students, providing spaces to challenge traditional notions of authority and expertise, and connecting students to spaces that would be logistically challenging to create or access otherwise. According to Dawley and Dede (2014), virtual worlds are 'immersive simulated environments in which a participant uses an avatar (a digital representation of oneself) to interact with digital agents, artifacts, and contexts' (p. 724).

These virtual environments can also include games; however, not every virtual world is a game or game-based environment. Virtual worlds have been utilized for problem-based learning (PBL) in undergraduate education (Vrellis et al., 2016), as well as adult language learning contexts (Chen, 2016) with good results. Participants in both studies reported positive experiences with virtual worlds (Chen, 2016; Vrellis et al., 2016). These environments have also been used in undergraduate nursing education. For example, Menzel et al. (2014) explored the use of Second Life (SL) to teach nursing students about poverty and social justice. They used the tool to create avatars with various roles (for example, child going to school, adult going to work), and students had to interact with the avatars and learn more about who they were and their experiences.

Education Context

Several texts explored the use of virtual worlds for pre-service teacher preparation. For example, Cho et al. (2015) investigated pre-service teachers' use of the virtual world Second Life to practice role playing as teachers and students. They noted that virtual spaces are helpful for these types of professional practice activities because the stakes (for example, embarrassment from faltering during an exercise or not understanding a particular concept) are lower than when students are practicing in actual classrooms (Cho et al., 2015). Pre-service teachers in Woollard's (2011) text had a similar opportunity, except they were given various tasks to navigate SL themselves. They considered the implications of using a virtual space for their pupils and discussed some of the challenges associated with getting started in SL (Woollard, 2011).

In a doctoral context, Snelson et al. (2017) had similar results in their study on using World of Warcraft (WoW) to teach research methods, specifically qualitative research. The participants were doctoral students who worked as higher education professionals. Using WoW for the research methods course allowed students 'to practice participant observation in a virtual game world, collect and analyze data, interpret literature, and discuss ideas as a research team' (Snelson et al., 2017, p. 1451). The doctoral participants were positive about their experiences with WoW, but like previous studies of undergraduates who used virtual environments, they were concerned about the time it took to learn the WoW space. They also wanted more structure, which the instructor mentioned was a balancing act between prescribing learning opportunities and wanting students to learn through creating and interacting in the WoW environment (Snelson et al., 2017).

Despite the benefits of virtual worlds, the use of these spaces in higher education has been quite inconsistent (Gregory et al., 2015). Some of the reasons for that inconsistency have been for the aforementioned reasons:

time and comfort. For doctoral educational leadership students in particular, learning a system that may be completely unfamiliar to them – not only the workings of the system but also knowledge that a particular system even exists – can be overwhelming to balance with their work in the course and possible employment responsibilities. In the Snelson et al. (2017) study, for example, the participants were all employed in higher education and taking the doctoral research course. Some of the challenges that undergraduate students and faculty faced with the use of virtual worlds were not so different from the challenges faced by educational leadership doctoral students and faculty.

Recommendations

These virtual environments hold promise for preparing doctoral students for various experiences and scenarios they may face professionally, so faculty who want to employ these tools should consider the following.

Use tutorials
Unlike blogs and other forms of social media, virtual worlds are not exactly intuitive or ubiquitous in educational contexts (even though some schools have SL campuses); therefore, faculty should locate virtual world tutorials on YouTube or Lynda.com for their doctoral students to use. These tutorials will take time to find and view, but because virtual worlds can be useful for teaching students about issues related to social justice (see Menzel et al., 2014) or for providing various problem-based scenarios for students to work through (see Vrellis et al., 2016), the process may be worth the time and effort. Just as Menzel et al. (2014) used SL to teach students about equity and justice, educational leadership faculty members can use virtual worlds for the same purpose.

Faculty members can use spaces like OpenSimulator to create their own environments and PBL scenarios. Again, these endeavors also mean additional time (and possibly design costs) for faculty members, but in the case of the scenarios, they may only have to spend the up-front time and potential costs to create them, as scenarios can be re-used for various courses. For example, as noted earlier, some colleges and universities have online campus spaces in Second Life, and these spaces could be used to help higher education administration doctoral students work through various student affairs scenarios. Because SL users can design their own avatars, array them in various ways, and control their movements, the students can learn best practices for training staff on addressing student conduct issues or recognizing when particular infractions have occurred (for example, hazing). Instead of just hearing about the signs of hazing, students could see those signs through avatars and scenarios in a virtual world. Programs like Kognito provide practice scenarios for recognizing students in distress, but virtual worlds like SL and OpenSimulator allow users to create and adapt various spaces, leaving room to address other student-related issues as the faculty member sees fit.

For K-12 administration doctoral students, the space could be useful for helping students prepare for various meetings and duties they will have in their post-graduation positions. Organizing a practice meeting with a group of school superintendents is almost impossible in real life, but in the virtual environment, faculty can use role playing in an immersive virtual world to prepare students for a real-life meeting via a mock virtual meeting. Students would have the same responsibilities they would have if the meeting were real, but the stakes would be much lower. Once these spaces and avatars are created, faculty and students can use them for other courses and activities.

Consider multiple-use and support
Because educational leadership doctoral students are already taxed for time in most cases, faculty members may want to consider using virtual world activities several times throughout the course. This may help alleviate any frustration over students feeling that they spent a lot of time learning a system that they will only use once. Interacting with virtual worlds takes more than just creating an account and starting, so if tutorials help increase students' comfort with the virtual world, then faculty may want to consider using the space periodically as the course continues. Faculty should also consider leveraging networks for support. For example, if others in educational leadership doctoral programs are using the same virtual world or system, then faculty may want to connect with those other programs in the virtual world space – to decrease any isolation they or their students may feel.

These connections can also serve as a way to expand participation in scenarios. For example, educational technology doctoral students can use a virtual world space to practice teaching or training others to use various technologies or concepts. Although students can move between the role of instructor or trainer and participant with others in the course, with participants from other institutions, the students can alternate roles and create an expanded community of practice around educational technology. Students can have these practice opportunities in face-to-face or other online areas as well, but virtual worlds allow users to adjust spaces in ways that may not be possible in real life. Faculty should also consider connecting with IT or a campus teaching and learning center for technological support, as the issues with technology for virtual worlds can be frustrating, even though their overall use can be quite positive for faculty and students (Blackmon, 2014).

Evaluation

Because students may be less familiar with virtual worlds, faculty may need to be a little more prescriptive, at least at first, with rubrics that guide the use of these tools in a course or program. These spaces, like blogs, can be used for formative assessment. For example, students can learn about concepts or theories and apply them in the virtual world. Students would receive feedback on their performance and could use that feedback to improve future work. Depending on the course, however, virtual worlds can also be used for summative feedback. If the culminating project in a course is a presentation or the implementation of a particular practice, then the virtual world could be an excellent space for students to do that work. If students are anxious about or uncomfortable with the technology, however, faculty may want to continue with the spaces for formative assessment and practice only. Faculty will also need to be familiar enough with the systems to differentiate between technological issues and issues with a student's understanding of course material.

CONCLUSION

Technology is a growing part of educational leadership doctoral studies. As faculty members continue to incorporate technology into these courses or deliver programs online, they will also have to understand what the use of these tools means for privacy, personas and time for them and for their students – to move beyond cybernation to understand the implications associated with technology use in higher education.

Several of the aforementioned studies highlighted the benefits of technology use in educational leadership contexts, and those benefits can be many. However, just as educational leaders (and budding educational leaders) shape their use of these various technologies, their lives and interactions are being shaped by those tools as well. Although this interactive exchange does not have to be a bad one, and can in fact be positive in some instances, it is an exchange that must be recognized and addressed for the responsible preparation of educational leadership doctoral students.

REFERENCES

Blackmon, S.J. (2014). Professors and Second Life: Technology problems and reasons for persistence. *International HETL Review*, **4**(5). Accessed at https://www.hetl.org/professors-and-second-life-technology-problems-and-reasons-for-persistence/.

Blackmon, S.J. (2015). The pixelated professor: Faculty in immersive virtual worlds. *International Review of Research in Open and Distributed Learning*, **16**(5). Accessed at http://www.irrodl.org/index.php/irrodl/article/view/1797/3193.

Buss, R.R., D. Zambo, S.R. Painter and D.W. Moore (2013). Examining faculty member changes in an innovative educational doctorate program. *Innovative Higher Education*, **38**, 59–74.

Caruthers, L. and J. Friend (2014). Critical pedagogy in online environments as thirdspace: A narrative analysis of voices of candidates in educational preparatory programs. *Educational Studies*, **50**, 8–35.

Chen, J.C.C. (2016). The crossroads of English language learners, task-based instruction, and 3D multi-user virtual learning in Second Life. *Computers & Education*, **102**, 152–71.

Cho, Y.H., S.Y. Yim and S. Paik (2015). Physical and social presence in 3D virtual role-play for pre-service teachers. *Internet and Higher Education*, **25**, 70–77.

Dawley, L. and C. Dede (2014). Situated learning in virtual worlds and immersive simulations. In J.M. Spector, M.D. Merrill, J. Elen and M.J. Bishop (eds), *Handbook of Research on Educational Communications and Technology* (pp. 723–34). New York: Springer.

Farmer, B., A. Yue and C. Brooks (2008). Using blogging for higher order learning in large cohort university teaching: A case study. *Australasian Journal of Educational Technology*, **24**(2), 123–36.

Ferdig, R.E. and K.D. Trammell (2004). Content delivery in the 'blogosphere'. *THE Journal*, **31**(7), 12–20.

Fuller, J.S., L. Lowder and B. Bachenheimer (2014). Graduates' reflections on an online doctorate in educational technology. *TechTrends*, **58**(4), 73–80.

Gardner, S.K. (2009). Student and faculty attributions of attrition in high and low-completing doctoral programs in the United States. *Higher Education*, **58**, 97–112.

Gregory, S., S. Scutter, L. Jacka, M. McDonald, H. Farley and C. Newman (2015). Barriers and enablers to the use of virtual worlds in higher education: An exploration of educator perceptions, attitudes and experiences. *Educational Technology & Society*, **18**(1), 3–12.

Halic, O., D. Lee, T. Paulus and M. Spence (2010). To blog or not to blog: Student perceptions of blog effectiveness for learning in a college-level course. *Internet and Higher Education*, **13**, 206–13.

Honeycutt, C. and S.C. Herring (2009). *Proceedings of the Forty-Second Hawai'i International Conference on System Sciences* (HICSS-42). Los Alamitos, CA: IEEE Press.

Huhtamo, E. (1999). From cybernation to interaction: A contribution to an archaeology of inter activity. *The Digital Dialectic: New Essays on New Media*, (s 96), 110.

Ivankova, N.V. and S.L. Stick (2007). Students' persistence in a distributed doctoral program in educational leadership in higher education: A mixed methods study. *Research in Higher Education*, **48**(1), 93–135.

Junco, R., G. Heibergert and E. Loken (2011). The effect of Twitter on college student engagement and grades. *Journal of Computer Assisted Learning*, **27**, 119–32.

Kimmons, R. and G. Veletsianos (2014). The fragmented educator 2.0: Social networking sites, acceptable identity fragments, and the identity constellation. *Computers & Education*, **72**, 292–301.

Kumar, S. and K. Dawson (2013). Exploring the impact of a professional practice education doctorate in educational environments. *Studies in Continuing Education*, **35**(2), 165–78.

Ladyshewsky, R.K. and P. Gardner (2008). Peer assisted learning and blogging: A strategy to promote reflective practice during clinical fieldwork. *Australasian Journal of Educational Technology*, **24**(3), 241–57.

López-Bonilla, J.M. and L.M. López-Bonilla (2013). Exploring the relationship between social networks and collaborative learning. *British Journal of Educational Technology*, **44**(5), 139–42.

Martinsuo, M. and V. Turkulainen (2011). Personal commitment, support and progress in doctoral studies. *Studies in Higher Education*, **36**(1), 103–20.

Menzel, N., L.H. Willson and J. Doolen (2014). Effectiveness of a poverty simulation in Second Life®: Changing nursing student attitudes toward poor people. *International Journal of Nursing Education Scholarship*, **11**(1), 1–7.

Meyer, K.A. (2010). A comparison of Web 2.0 tools in a doctoral course. *Internet and Higher Education*, **13**, 226–32.

Miller, C.T. and J.H. Curry (2014). But I don't want to be a professor: The innovations of an online practitioner doctorate focused on educational technology leadership. *The Quarterly Review of Distance Education*, **15**(3), 35–46.

Mortensen, T. and J. Walker (2002). Blogging thoughts: Personal publication as an online research tool. In A. Morrison (ed.), *Researching ICTs in Context* (pp. 249–79). Oslo: InterMedia.

Offerman, M. (2011). Profile of the nontraditional doctoral degree student. *New Directions for Adult and Continuing Education*, **129**, 21–30.

Selwyn, N. (2009). Faceworking: Exploring students' education-related use of Facebook. *Learning, Media and Technology*, **34**(2), 157–74.

Servage, L. (2009). Alternative and professional doctoral programs: What is driving the demand? *Studies in Higher Education*, **34**(7), 765–79.

Snelson, C., C.I. Wertz, K. Onstott and J. Bader (2017). Using World of Warcraft to teach research methods in online doctoral education: A student–instructor duoethnography. *The Qualitative Report*, **22**(5), 1439–56.

Stallone, M.N. (2011). Factors associated with student attrition and retention in an educational leadership doctoral program. *Journal of College Teaching & Learning*, **1**(6), 17–24.

Taylor, A. (2007). Learning to become researching professionals: The case of the doctorate of education. *International Journal of Teaching and Learning in Higher Education*, **19**(2), 154–66.

Top, E. (2012). Blogging as a social medium in undergraduate courses: Sense of community best predictor of perceived learning. *Internet and Higher Education*, **15**, 24–8.

Veletsianos, G. (2012). Higher education scholars' participation and practices on Twitter. *Journal of Computer Assisted Learning*, **28**(4), 336–49.

Veletsianos, G. and R. Kimmons (2013). Scholars and faculty members' lived experiences in online social networks. *Internet and Higher Education*, **16**, 43–50.

Vrellis, I., N.M. Avouris and T. Mikropoulos (2016). Learning outcome, presence and satisfaction from a science activity in Second Life. *Australasian Journal of Educational Technology*, **32**(1), 59–77.

Walker, J. (2006). Blogging from inside the ivory tower. Accessed at http://bora.uib. no/bitstream/handle/1956/1846/?sequence=1.

Wandera, S., N. James-Waldon, D. Bromley and Z. Henry (2016). The influence of social media on collaborative learning in a cohort environment. *Interdisciplinary Journal of e-Skills and Lifelong Learning*, **12**, 123–43.

Ward, M.H. and S. West (2008). Blogging Ph.D. candidature: Revealing the pedagogy. *International Journal of Emerging Technologies and Society*, **6**(1), 60–71.

Williams, J.B. and J. Jacobs (2004). Exploring the use of blogs as learning spaces in the higher education sector. *Australasian Journal of Educational Technology*, **20**(2), 232–47.

Woollard, J. (2011). When 'teaching a class of daemons, dragons and trainee teachers' – learning the pedagogy of the virtual classroom. *Management in Education*, **26**(2), 45–51.

Zhu, Y. and R. Procter (2015). Use of blogs, Twitter and Facebook by UK Ph.D. students for scholarly communication. *Observatorio (OBS*)*, **9**(2), 29–46.

5. Selecting and implementing technology in support of doctoral curriculum and program management

Bruce E. Winston

This chapter presents the challenges of scoping, aligning, acquiring and implementing educational technology to meet hybrid and online doctoral leadership program needs from the program administrator's perspective. Program administrators need to select, implement and train faculty and staff on the right technical systems that meet students, faculty and staff needs, and that align with the university's goals and objectives. The right technical systems are those that provide benefits for the recruitment and retention of students, efficient operations and quality improvement. To accomplish this, program administrators must follow strategic foresight principles of scanning, forecasting, trend analysis, cost–benefit analysis, training, and performance appraisal – before and after implementing new technology and evaluating upgrade requirements.

Online course delivery platforms can benefit students by providing choices in content delivery and faculty–student interaction. Effective technical systems aid instructors with faculty presence and communication immediacy, which are important to student recruitment, retention and success. Aligning technology to the doctoral leadership curriculum ensures the right technologies are in place for students to achieve the desired learning outcomes. Without these technologies, faculty are likely to experience limits in what they can achieve with students or need to expend considerable personal energy working around the limits of the available tools.

Acquiring and integrating new technology is often expensive and due diligence is needed to weigh the costs against the benefits. Benefits may include the attraction and retention of students, increase in faculty capacity (allowing more student credit hours per instructor or effort on other initiates), increasing accuracy of administrative reporting to meet accreditation and government agency reporting, as well as internal reporting that improves administration of the doctoral program. The concept of Adoption and Diffusion of Technology can also help program administrators understand how to help faculty and staff embrace changes to technical systems. Resistance to change can be a form of environmental determinism that can prevent the successful implementation of new technical systems into the program's operation. Together with the concepts mentioned in this overview so far, this chapter closes with a look into the future and suggests potential trends that may reshape the learning environment, content delivery, and faculty–student interaction.

SCOPING

Scoping is the preliminary thinking and documentation of what the technology project should be. In preparing to explore or adopt new technologies a systematic approach is needed to review needs and determine outcomes. This is an essential first step when implementing a project, and the university's IT staff should be able to help, together with input from doctoral program faculty, administration and students. Spending adequate time to present the purpose of the technology adoption clearly can avoid problems after the implementation begins. Being clear about the background is important: what led to the desire for this new technology? What methods or systems are currently in use? Identifying the key personnel from the doctoral program and what role each will take in the adoption of new technology is part of the scoping process. This is more than just sharing the workload, but rather an intentional decision about who the people are that best speak to the current process and examine what goals need to be set and accomplished.

KNOW YOURSELF

Every doctoral program has a personality that reflects the institution's personality and can be described by the organization's cultural artifacts, espoused values and underlying beliefs (Schein, 2010). However, uncovering these deeper beliefs and values can take time and collective introspection. The values and beliefs of the program can help predict how administrators will approach potential new technology. Miles and Snow (1978) posited that firms approach technology change through a mixture of character of engineers, entrepreneurs and administrators and described firms as being one of four types: Prospectors, Analyzers, Reactors or Defenders.

Prospectors tend to be more entrepreneurial than engineering or administrative types and adopt technology as a means of reaching and retaining more students. Internal discussions would include high levels of interest in the student–technology interface and how the new technology improves the students' experiences. Prospectors may adopt technology too quickly and have to deal with problems following the implementation.

Analyzers are more balanced across entrepreneurial, engineering and administrative approaches and seek technology that not only assists in reaching and retaining students but also fits with the existing university's systems and contributes to reducing administrative work. Analyzers usually seek input from across the university and spend more time in performing due diligence tasks before adopting new technology.

Reactors are more administrative than entrepreneurial but may be high in the engineering approach. Reactors will consider new technology after there is considerable evidence from other universities that the new technology works well and is helpful. While reactors may miss market opportunities, they also avoid the risks of adopting and implementing new technology that may not be as helpful as hoped.

Defenders are more engineering than entrepreneurial or administrative types and focus more on stability, thus avoiding change. Defenders tend to be risk averse and prefer to continue present practice rather than change systems or add new technology.

Doctoral program administrators who know their doctoral program's personality and the university's personality can make the appropriate decision of whom to add to review and selection committees, as well as more aptly to interpret the comments and recommendations from other departments. Enrollment management departments may be more entrepreneurial, while IT departments may be more engineering orientated. Knowing the personalities of the departments that will be part of the discussion about new technology will also provide insight with negotiations across the university. Back in the mid-1990s the business school where I was the associate dean was thinking about venturing into an online learning platform. There were few online learning platform choices available then, and only a short list of schools around the US using online learning platforms. Knowing the personalities of the various departments that needed to be engaged allowed me to show the IT department that our school would purchase the necessary computer hardware and software if the IT department could maintain the equipment. Since the school was a prospector, according to Miles and Snow's (1978) types, our school adopted an online platform and had great success with it. However, as time progressed, and the university wanted more of its schools to add online programs, it was found that the platform was not robust enough to handle the increased load. By then there were more learning platforms in the marketplace to choose from. The university created a larger technology adoption group and included more departments in the decision to adopt a more robust system. Implementation went well, and the university moved forward into online education. Knowledge of one's own department, other departments, and the university's personality is an important starting place for introducing or upgrading technologies.

ALIGNING

Aligning technology refers to choosing technology that fits the overall strategic plans of the doctoral program, the school, as well as the university (Roberts et al., 2005). Technology is one part of the foundation needed for the program to achieve its desired future. Doctoral program objectives should be a key consideration when planning for new technology. For example, doctoral program administrators need to report performance achievements to the institution, accrediting bodies, and to both internal and external stakeholders, and therefore it is essential to know how the new technology provides the information and reports needed by administrative employees. Data compatibility with Enterprise Resource Planning systems and other reporting systems will avoid extra work in generating reports. As a further example, if a student advising software system is added, it should be compatible with the curriculum delivery platform so that faculty and advisors can access needed data and communicate advising-related information to each other without having to duplicate data entry and reports to provide student support.

According to Cao and Hoffman (2011) alignment of strategies at the unit level with the enterprise's strategies contributes to overall organizational success. Alignment also means considering the needs of students. Curriculum delivery platforms may have add-ins that review written documents for similarity to existing databases of publications and previous students' work that helps recognize plagiarism, as well as add-ins that review and critique writing grammar and style. When considering new technology, it is important to align with existing systems so that the users can gain the value from the new technology without having to use multiple systems. Submitting a written assignment should be a smooth process whether submitting for a review or a grade. In the past, each of these systems tended to be provided by different vendors where the systems did not communicate with each other, but options are now available for new services to work with existing learning management systems.

Technology is changing the way students receive content via books, such as the VitalSource ebook database system and SpringerLink subscription-based ebook databases. VitalSource books are available at lower costs to students, while SpringerLink ebook databases allow students to access books at no additional cost to the student. There is a cost to university libraries who subscribe to the databases. Electronic books provide improved search and citation features and can be accessed on desktop and mobile systems (VitalSource Bookshelf). As one example, SpringerLink's databases contain 100 000 ebooks (SpringerLink). In addition to electronic books, publishers of traditional bound books offer content support websites where students can review additional content, watch video case studies, use interactive databases and watch video discussions with the textbook authors. All of these elements add to the learning experience and provide students with interaction methods that align with the students' learning styles. In selecting resources for students to use, faculty and administrators would be wise to consider the alignment of these resources with goals of the program and other technologies in use.

IMPLEMENTING EDUCATIONAL TECHNOLOGY

This section provides an example of implementing a new technology whose goal is to reduce students' costs, improve their experience, and maintain exam performance, while meeting accrediting agencies' concerns for academic honesty. Our PhD program was offered online with two on-campus residencies and then required all USA-based students to come to campus to take the comprehensive exams. We allowed proctoring in-country for our international students, due to the costs of travel and the difficulty in getting visas to attend a university in the USA. For two years prior to the new technology project we had heard increasing concerns from our students about the cost of traveling to campus and the disruption to their work and family lives, just to be on campus for one day. The project goal was to locate a new method or innovation that would allow students to have proctored exams while staying at their home or office. This included the need to align with existing technology, provide evidence of the students' academic honesty, maintain the existing frequency of offering the exams every two months, and allow the students flexibility in when they could take the exams given time zone differences around the world.

We knew we would have to use the concepts from Rogers' (1962) adoption and diffusion of technology model in order to make the transition to any new technical system successful. Adoption and diffusion of innovation is explained in more detail later on, but in essence it is the process by which people come to accept, adopt and use new technology by seeing how it is similar to the existing processes, but better, as well as the ease and low cost of acquiring the new technology.

When planning implementation, adequate time is needed to install, test, train and begin use in small steps. Before beginning to test the proctoring system, I worked with the Dean of the school and discussed the software and the two providers that I was aware of. The Dean asked the Director of our university's Center for Teaching and Learning (CTL) to join our discussion. The staff of CTL had already tested one provider's proctoring software for another school at the university and added the provider's representative to the discussion. After a demonstration of the software, we set up a test by the PhD comprehensive exam faculty. We created a 'test' course on our learning platform and added the proctoring software tool to the course. Using a sample test with a pool of comprehensive exam questions, the five comprehensive exam committee members completed the exam and went through all of the upfront tasks that prove who the test taker is and that the test-taking environment is free of books or any aids that would not be allowed in an on-campus testing environment.

Following the test completion, we discussed the experience and what accommodations we may need to provide to students in areas of the world that have limited electricity and internet bandwidth. We also discussed how we should implement the software. I followed up with the Dean and discussed the costs and the suggested implementation plan. We are still in the early stages of the implementation and decided that due to the importance and emotional issues associated with comprehensive exams, we would take a full year to announce and have practice sessions with the new software to help students adjust to and prepare to use the new software. We decided to use the software in the last course of the student's concentration area, where we already had five non-proctored mock comprehensive exams. We will convert two of the mock exams to proctored exams using the software and if we find that students need more than two experiences we will convert one or more of the remaining un-proctored comprehensive exams to use the proctoring software.

Students, at the time of the implementation, had to attend three on-campus residencies but we had recently changed this to two residencies and were near the point of phasing out the third residency. We offered the residencies in each of the three trimesters per year so that we could accommodate three intakes of PhD students per year. We decided to announce the proctoring software at the three residencies between the time of the decision to use software and the actual launch of software for the final comprehensive exams. This allowed us to inform both the second and third-year students at each residency before the launch date.

The last course of the concentration was updated to allow students to learn about the proctoring software, the requirements for a webcam, and the preparation of the physical desktop to remove all unwanted materials. We added training documents and videos to the course, and we added a discussion of the proctoring software to the first live discussion event of the course, which we recorded so that students who could attend the live event could still listen to the presentation and discussion. We are still in the year leading up to the launch.

The case example illustrates how we decided to implement the new system in order to reduce our students' anxiety and help prepare them for the proctored experience. Rushing new technology implementation may result in implementation failure of resistance to change by the stakeholders.

TRAIN, TRAIN AND RETRAIN

Training faculty and staff in how to use the new technology is a vital step in successfully adopting new technology (Boothby et al., 2010). Training should be done in stages that match the needs of the faculty and staff that will use the new technology. Tenison et al. (2016) proposed training in phases to move the trainee through cognitive understanding to autonomous responses. The first stage is introduction and explanation and focuses on the what and the why, but not the how. One of the reasons for resistance to change is the fear of loss of control, according to Oreg (2003). This can be reduced or removed by showing the advantages of the new technology to faculty and staff as well as presenting the reasons for selecting the new technology. Members of the decision committee should present at stage one to outline the problems that led to consideration of the new technology and the advantages of the new technology to faculty, staff and students. All of the members of the committee should present so that the attendees can see that the committee represents and mirrors the overall faculty and staff characteristics to avoid a sense of an 'us versus them' mental model of faculty and staff who will need to learn and adapt to the new technology. In addition, the implementation and training plan should be presented. The stages can be accomplished by small as well as large groups. In large doctoral programs, it may be appropriate for multiple sessions of smaller sized groups in order to maintain an environment that is conducive to hands-on demonstrations and discussion. For example, I recall a new technical system that all program directors would use to enter information into a database that would then generate reports for our regional accrediting agency. The training was repeated in four separate sessions for each phase so that we could all have hands-on practice and ask questions. This helped me and others feel more at ease with the new system.

The first stage is also helpful with the adoption and diffusion of innovation process. Rogers (1962) posited that the adoption and diffusion process is facilitated when new users come to understand what the new technology is, how it is similar or dissimilar to current in-use technology, and what the benefit is to the user.

Stage two of the training should be introductory how-to, hands-on training to reduce another cause of resistance to change: lack of psychological resilience (Oreg, 2003). Change can be stressful. Thus, training should be done in stages so as not to overwhelm the new users of the technology. Stage two training should include real-time applications with the work that faculty and staff do on a daily, weekly and monthly basis. Immediate successful use of the new technology will reduce stress and build confidence, which also adds to the adoption and diffusion of the new technology. One-on-one training should be used in stage two so that the new user can understand the specifics.

Stage three should be used to review lessons learned from stage two and introduce more advanced topics for faculty and staff who may have oversight responsibilities of other faculty and staff. For example, while faculty may need to know how to use a new learning platform, they may not need to know how to build a course if a central office performs curriculum design and construction, but the program directors may need training in how to make modifications to a course.

Stage four should include on-demand, self-paced refresher modules about using the new technology. An example of this is the collection of YouTube.com videos by Blackboard on how to use the Blackboard learning platform. Blackboard created videos for students and faculty that allow students and faculty on-demand access to training to refresh prior knowledge or gain first-time training.

USING PRINCIPLES OF STRATEGIC FORESIGHT

Doctoral program directors should use the principles of strategic foresight (Hines and Bishop, 2015) to remain knowledgeable about trends in technology that are useful for academic universities and to prepare scenarios of what future technical systems might offer. Strategic foresight looks 10–25 years into the future, while future studies focus on 50+ years. I have participated in scanning and foresight activities for the past 15 years while working for my present university. An early example was a university-wide committee exploring the replacement learning platform mentioned earlier in this chapter. Our scanning and forecasting activities led us, as a committee, to foresee the use of mobile smartphones as a means of connecting students with instructors, libraries and academic support services, although at the time of the committee's work these opportunities were yet to be developed by telecommunication companies. We envisioned the use of intelligent agents guiding student activities and virtual online conferences in both synchronous and asynchronous environments. While the future would have arrived whether we created scenarios or not, the strategic foresight activities helped all of us at the university understand what the future may be like and it helped shape our thinking.

A LOOK INTO THE FUTURE

While doctoral program directors do not have to do all of the strategic foresight activities, they should be supportive of the process and broadly share the outcomes of the scenario-building sessions. For example, scanning of mobile computing and communication today shows that speeds and bandwidth using 5G and 6G speeds are not too far away. According to Villas-Boas (2017), current 4G speed is around 55 mega*bits* per second, but 5G will be 500 mega*bytes* per second, or an increase in speed of about 90 times faster. Villa-Boas says that we will be able to 'download a 100GB 4K movie in under four minutes' (para. 3). Consider how much content we can move with 5G; 6G has been proposed to reach speeds of 11 Gigabits per second (Vitorr) or 22 times faster than 5G. With 6G we will have greater global connectivity. The type and amount of content and speed of interaction will be significantly different in the not-too-distant future. A decade ago video conferencing was frequently interrupted by bandwidth failures at low resolutions, while future bandwidths might allow multiple channels of video and other information to be shared, facilitating new approaches to teaching and learning.

Faculty Presence and Communication Immediacy

Faculty presence is the perception by students that the instructors are available to and reachable by the students. Technical systems can, and should, facilitate high levels of perceived faculty presence by students, because perceived faculty presence contributes to student satisfaction and retention (Casey and Kroth, 2013). While Casey and Kroth (2013) posit that faculty training is key for success, to experience presence the technical systems have to be easy to use, intuitive to both faculty and students, and allow both synchronous and asynchronous interaction. Systems such as Blackboard Collaborate, WebEx conferencing and FreeConferenceCall.com are examples of web conferencing systems available at the time of this writing.

Collaborate is part of the Blackboard learning platform and has recently been updated and renamed 'Ultra' to provide a more modern website feel to the online conference presentation program. Blackboard added voice response to threaded discussions, which contributes to higher perceived faculty presence by students.

In my discussions with online instructors the availability and ease of use of the learning platforms' add-ons, such as Collaborate, are the key drivers of regular use by faculty. Doctoral program directors should monitor the use of live and recorded sessions by faculty to ensure that faculty use the tools but do not become bogged down and decrease efficiency or increase the risk of burnout. Faculty workload can be reduced through the use of technology, if used appropriately, which allows more courses, credit hours or other initiatives to be handled by faculty, thus increasing efficiency without adding work hours.

Communication Immediacy

Communication immediacy is similar to perceived presence but focuses on the communication behaviors of faculty (Schutt et al., 2009). Communication immediacy, like presence, contributes to student satisfaction and retention. Technical systems such as social media can create a greater sense of communication immediacy, but like presence it can add to the workload of faculty, thus decreasing efficiency. And, like presence, doctoral program directors need to work with faculty to achieve a balance of effectiveness and efficiency.

Doctoral program directors can set desired response times for faculty that provide satisfaction for students and reasonable workload demands on faculty. Technology, such as mobile hand-held platforms (smartphones) can help with quick responses. Text messages are more efficient, but training is needed for faculty to know how to use the text message and voice response programs.

Knowing What Faculty Do and How They Do It

In my time as a doctoral program director I have regularly conducted time and motion studies to see how long it takes instructors to complete tasks (for example, grading) and to see if we can leverage technology, or methods, to improve the process. We gained efficiencies by standardizing syllabi and online course designs so that all of the courses in a program looked and operated identically. As an added bonus, we found that student satisfaction improved because while we standardized and sped up what our faculty were doing, the students also noticed that they were working through course content and assignments at a faster rate because of the continuity across courses and the readily available content.

As part of our efforts to leverage the technology we found that we could use recorded videos from YouTube.com to augment what our instructors were doing with course content. As we moved away from the instructor being the sole content provider, we gained flexibility in faculty assignments, because instructors took on more of a facilitating role than an expert content-specialist role. Assigning courses to adjuncts, or adding adjuncts to assist with a large enrollment course, was facilitated by the standard designs of the courses.

This does not mean that every doctoral course in every university should be the same. Doctoral programs have a specific market segment of students, and the design of online courses as well as blended and on-campus courses can be designed to fit the psychological and aesthetic needs and wants of the student population. Technology has a key role to play in this mix.

CONCLUSION

This chapter has presented the challenges of scoping, aligning, acquiring and implementing educational technology to meet doctoral leadership program needs from the program administrator's perspective. Program administrators need to select, implement and train faculty and staff in the right technical systems that meet the needs of students, university faculty and staff as well as meeting university goals and objectives. The right technical systems provide a benefit for recruitment and retention of students, efficient operations and quality improvement.

To accomplish this, program administrators must follow strategic foresight principles of scanning, forecasting, trend analysis, cost–benefit analysis, training, and performance appraisal – before and after implementing new technology and evaluation of upgrade requirements.

Course delivery platforms can benefit students by providing choices in content delivery and faculty–student interaction. Effective technical systems can aid instructors with faculty presence and communication immediacy. Aligning technology to the doctoral leadership curriculum ensures the right technologies are in place for students to achieve desired learning outcomes.

The concept of Adoption and Diffusion of Technology can help program administrators understand how to help faculty and staff embrace changes to technical systems. Resistance to change can be a form of environmental determinism that can prevent the successful implementation of new technical systems into the program's operation.

All of this should be accomplished by program administrators in a manner that improves the work experience for all stakeholders through a supportive leadership style that is student-focused, faculty-focused, staff-focused, performance-focused and accreditation-focused.

REFERENCES

Boothby, D., A. Dufour and J. Tang (2010). Technology adoption, training and productivity performance. *Research Policy*, **39**(5), 650–61.

Cao, Q. and J.J. Hoffman (2011). Alignment of virtual enterprise, information technology, and performance: An empirical study. *International Journal of Production Research*, **49**(4), 1127–49.

Casey, R.L. and M. Kroth (2013). Learning to develop presence online: Experienced faculty perspectives. *Journal of Adult Education*, **42**(2), 104–10.

Hines, A. and P. Bishop (2015). *Thinking about the Future: Guidelines for Strategic Foresight Second Edition*. Houston, TX: Hinesight.

Miles, R.E. and C.C. Snow (1978). *Organizational Strategy, Structure, and Process*. New York, NY: McGraw-Hill.

Oreg, S. (2003). Resistance to change: Developing an individual differences measure. *Journal of Applied Psychology*, **88**(4), 680–93.

Roberts, M.L., R.R. Liu and K. Hazard (2005). Strategy, technology and organisational alignment: Key components of CRM success. *Database Marketing & Customer Strategy Management*, **12**(4), 315–26.

Rogers, E.M. (1962). *Diffusion of Innovations* (1st edn). New York, NY: Free Press of Glencoe.

Schein, E.H. (2010). *Organizational Culture and Leadership* (4th edn). San Francisco, CA: Jossey-Bass.

Schutt, M., B.S. Allen and M.A. Laumakis (2009). The effects of instructor immediacy behaviors in online learning environments. *Quarterly Review of Distance Education*, **10**(2), 135–48,

Tenison, C., J.M. Fincham and J.R. Anderson (2016). Phases of learning: How skill acquisition impacts cognitive processing. *Cognitive Psychology*, **87**(June), 1–28.

Villas-Boas, A. (2017). Your internet speeds will be insanely fast when 5G arrives. *Business Insider*. Accessed 3 August 2017 at http://www.businessinsider.com/5g-speed-network-lte-2017-3/#-2.

Websites

SpringerLink. Accessed 3 August 2017 at https://www.springer.com/gp/products/springerlink.

VitalSource Bookshelf. Accessed 3 August 2017 at https://www.vitalsource.com/bookshelf-features.

VITORR. Accessed 3 August 2017 at http://vitorr.com/post-details.php?postid=2615.

6. Informal and experiential learning in virtually mediated organizational leadership doctoral studies

Elisabeth E. Bennett and Margaret Gorman

INTRODUCTION

Technology has forever changed the nature of both education and work in developed and many developing nations. The extent to which civilians have access to technologies, including mobile phones and smart devices, determines a country's technical capacity (Bashir et al., 2015). How societies in general, and organizations in particular, leverage technical capacity depends heavily on leadership and the values in practice. What was once simply entertainment or the domain of technical workers has now become embedded in daily life. The extent to which technology functions in the foreground or background may vary, but there are aspects to technology integration that have become so ubiquitous that one no longer notices the individual technologies but rather focuses on what is accomplished through them.

Sometimes technology remains under the radar until something goes wrong and specialists are called in to fix the complex system of programming and electronics. When it is working well, technology provides unprecedented new access and interactivity, though the field of human resources development (HRD) should be concerned' about unreasonable expectations placed on leaders and employees in a 24/7 world (Thomas, 2014), as well as how the field develops people to thrive in the technology-mediated era fraught with potential miscommunication. Text-based communication, for example, obscures the messaging and emotional intelligence of leaders normally conveyed in person (Graham, 2010). There are new intricacies to the medium and method of leadership due to the capabilities and flaws of technology. Indeed, new leadership theory is grappling with how leadership is enacted when organizational members only know a leader through digital representations or when virtual leaders are fully fictional characters (Boje and Rhodes, 2005; Boje et al., 2013). The work of leaders in developed nations has to a large extent become mediated by technology, as has learning in higher education programs that provide academic credentials for those at the helm of technology-enabled organizations.

Technology intersects with the academic discipline of organizational leadership studies (OLS) in at least two ways. First, academic professionals need to prepare leaders to guide organizations that increasingly incorporate sophisticated technologies, opening new avenues of alternative work strategies (Bennett and Bierema, 2010), virtual organization, and workplace automation. Second, OLS can now educate through these new technologies with significant advantages for preparing leaders for tomorrow's technology-enabled organization. Moreover, learning through online platforms makes education more accessible to leaders in practice because they do not have to relocate and leave their professional work to earn a doctorate. Even more importantly, they can simultaneously blend what they learn in theory with what they learn in practice, opening the door to integrated and experiential application of new concepts and theories.

A handful of higher education institutions are pioneering efforts in online education that leverage learning technologies and experiential learning designed to meet the needs of working adults. For example, field projects can be designed so that learners explore the connection between theories in textbooks and how they model – or potentially fail to explain – phenomena in real practice. This lets learners draw in contextual understandings and consider the limits of theories in the messy environment of practice. In an era of the post-traditional student where educational innovation is essential, professionals now have access to learning any time, from anywhere, and with anyone around the world. Leadership education is becoming truly global. With a plethora of mobile technologies, social media platforms and cloud systems, HRD professionals and educators have more tools to meet different learning styles by designing variety into education systems.

There is no doubt that digital technologies have reshaped professional expectations and modes of work in organizational leadership, and virtual learning opportunities abound in formal settings, such as academic institutions, and informal settings, such as watching free instructional videos on YouTube.com. This chapter addresses the informal and experiential facets of virtual doctoral leadership studies that are increasingly common for executives and leaders who seek to develop professionally with fewer space and time boundaries than traditional doctoral programs. Simultaneity of work and learning in virtual programs presents both advantages and disadvantages to students. Some common disadvantages include limitations for how content is taught, particularly the emphasis on communicating through writing, and the challenge of personalizing virtual learning environments. Informed by virtual human resource development (VHRD), this chapter discusses informal and experiential aspects of doctoral leadership programs that dovetail scholarship and practice, as well as the question of transferring learning from the doctorate to the organizational context. The chapter includes discussion of leadership in practice, the relationship between virtual doctoral studies and such constructs as virtual teams, course design that incorporates experiential components, and argues that empirical research in the doctoral program is a highly experiential learning encounter that transforms the individual leader and potentially transforms how organizations solve future problems.

A SEA CHANGE IN LEADERSHIP EDUCATION

Globalization has been made possible by internet technology (Bennett and McWhorter, 2017a; Burkhardt and Bennett, 2015). The interactive effect of globalization and technology has changed how organizations adapt and innovate, as well as how people learn. New challenges emerge for leaders and HRD professionals as they seek to understand how mobile technology and cloud-based systems reshape flexible working arrangements. HRD professionals and educators must now re-imagine ways to leverage social media, mobile apps, blogs, YouTube TedTalks, and other user-driven content knowledge systems. These new paths provide just-in-time training opportunities that allow adults to engage in peer-to-peer learning using a range of technology platforms provided in the workplace or online doctoral programs. Emerging technologies and the internet, in combination with the changing nature of work, augment pedagogy in distance education. In particular, the shifting expectations of the 21st-century lifelong learner who wants to be actively engaged reconciling unsolved puzzles in practice, leading change, and in shaping the work of the future, are challenging doctoral faculty to re-imagine curriculum design and dissertation processes.

Polysynchronous learning is one such new trend that moves beyond the traditional divide of synchronous–asynchronous learning, which sometimes kept education in a linear, one-way information exchange. Education now has potential for a more dynamic interactive approach. Polysynchronous learning integrates interaction between learners, teachers and learners, and learners with content by mixing face-to-face and online communication that has both synchronous and asynchronous modes (Dalgarno, 2014). It is similar to the blended education that Horn and Staker (2015) believe will disrupt the traditional practices of education, lead to greater personalized learning, and reshape how employees go about learning in the future. Everyone in this paradigm functions as a co-participant actively engaged in co-creating emergent ideas embedded in groupware that supports ongoing interactions and developments. Increasingly, the focus will move beyond what students *know* to what they can *do*, which necessarily makes the connection between knowledge acquisition and application based on competencies.

While higher education enrollment is generally declining, online enrollment has been accelerating since 2002, and this trend is expected to continue for the next three to five years (Poulin and Straut, 2016). The *U.S. News & World Report* identified a growth of 3.9 percent in online learning for non-profits with a record 5.8 million students taking at least one distance learning course in 2014 (Friedman, 2016) and online programs – not schools – are now being ranked using methods that include student engagement, peer reputation, and faculty credentials in their respective fields (for rankings in education where many leadership programs reside, see https://www.usnews.com/education/online-education/articles/education-methodology).

The sea change is no better illustrated than in the purchase of Kaplan University – a for-profit and proprietary institution – by Purdue University (Fain and Seltzer, 2017). Purdue reportedly realized it could not meet its objective for growth in online learning using existing capacity and so dramatically increased capacity through the purchase. Kaplan is in the process of being transformed into a non-profit entity as a result. We anticipate that more universities will have both traditional campuses and somewhat separate administration of virtual campuses as different lines of business, at least at first, which may provide flexibility to grow and contract with the educational market, but may create systems with disparate treatment of faculty if campus leaders look at online education primarily as profit centers with a high number of adjuncts to support costly bricks-and-mortar infrastructure.

Online programs have found a legitimate place in higher education and there is strong growth in online professional degree programs that enhance employability in the ever-changing virtual and global economy that emphasizes knowledge work. These professional programs must value, leverage and potentially overcome a leader's work experiences to create scholar-practitioners who build capacity to lead change through ongoing engagement with problems-of-practice and hands-on experience conducting applied research for evidence-based decision-making. This idea is no better illustrated than the difference between giving leaders a textbook answer versus encouraging thinking tools for them to discover the answer that is right for a given context. This requires teaching metacognitive skills – or thinking about how one thinks – to accompany intuitive knowledge often created through practical experience (Quirk, 2006). Leaders here are encouraged to go beyond gut feeling and contextual knowledge derived from experience alone, and to draw new skills and theories into the everyday.

Online OLS doctoral programs designed to bring together experienced professionals from a cross-section of industries have emerged to create communities of inquiry that collaboratively explore new ways to solve complex problems facing today's organizations. Distinct from earlier distance education programs that were grounded in cognitive-behaviorist pedagogy and focused on received knowledge, newer online doctoral programs, such as Northeastern University's Doctor of Education program in OLS, are grounded in social-constructivist and connectivist pedagogies in which the learner is responsible for seeking, critically examining and applying new knowledge to real-world problems (Anderson and Dron, 2011). Additionally, faculty members become conceptual guides that design experiential learning opportunities for solving practical puzzles that result in new knowledge for advancing practice. Northeastern's doctoral program is designed to be flexible and to an extent self-directed, with seminars that emphasize critical inquiry and reflective discourse amongst scholar-practitioners, including faculty with practical knowledge from industry in addition to academic credentials. In this model, faculty members act as thinking partners and intellectual mentors rather than deliverers of content.

The nature of leadership in practice is another key factor shaping pedagogy and knowledge products in online OLS doctoral programs. While early conceptualizations of leadership were grounded in the Great Man Theory with focus on command and control, views shifted to the notion of shared leadership embodied in the interactions of participants (Schwandt and Szabla, 2007). Leadership has a pragmatic orientation that depends upon feedback from practice, and, thus, OLS doctoral curricula often involve projects conducted in real-world settings. A foundational course at Northeastern is grounded in Raelin's (2016) concept of *Leadership-as-Practice*, which does not emphasize leadership as an individual trait or behavior, but rather how leadership emerges through experience in community as groups fashion their own rules to achieve outcomes. In this course, students are organized into small teams in which they develop a team charter to set rules for communication and collective work, and then evaluate the team process and product based on the leadership-as-practice model. Connectivist pedagogy is congruent with curriculum that embeds coordinated action with negotiated rules, reflective discourse and distributed knowledge (Raelin, 2016).

The changing nature of leadership in practice, the emergence of alternative work arrangements, the world wide web, and explosion of emerging technologies have combined to create the conditions for working adults to shift from passive consumers of education to active collaborators in the creation of learning experiences that advance their adaptive capacity to meet the emerging work of the future. Though online learning may have been resisted in its early days, universities are starting to realize that it is the major growth area of the future that allows stronger presence of international students essential for learning in a globalized world. In fact, the goal of universities to prepare students for future international work has been termed pre-HRD (Burkhardt and Bennett, 2015), with universities recognizing the global work paradigm that leaders will enter. Increasingly, higher education is crossing into HRD where learning is part of a student's career development that will be transferred to a work context, or when leaders work and learn simultaneously. In HRD there is a significant focus on leadership development and many HRD faculty are part of doctor of education programs that offer OLS concentrations. For these reasons, understanding how technology plays a role in the development of leaders through virtually mediated programs is important for OLS, underpinned by a new area of inquiry called virtual HRD (VHRD).

VIRTUAL HRD AS A LENS FOR INTEGRATING ONLINE EDUCATION AND PRACTICE

The question of where HRD begins and higher education ends is an interesting one. The position taken by this chapter is that OLS programs in higher education are a major venue for career development and offer a special kind of HRD when knowledge and skills learned in higher education are applied to the practice setting. While a number of PhD programs continue to train future scholars who drive research in the academy, many other programs focus on scholars in practice who enhance their leadership skills through doctoral study. It is common for these programs to be housed in education schools because of the focus on learning, development and organizational change, and they may take multiple forms, such as weekend executive cohort, hybrid or fully online courses that may include annual residencies at the campus of the credentialing institution. This chapter primarily focuses on the latter. Online programs focus on the development of leaders through virtual coursework and shape them to become scholars in practice settings. The knowledge and skills gained in a formal program are eventually, sometimes immediately, applied to the organizations through learning transfer that can result in organizational learning as well as individual learning (Bennett, 2010), including learning that is embedded in an organization's technical systems and thus form a component of Virtual HRD. Indeed, Langer's (2010) view is that it is not possible for technology-driven organizations to be optimized without organizational learning, and advanced technologies, such as artificial intelligence, are troubling the notion that people learn first prior to organizational learning, as machine learning and artificial intelligence may also embed new knowledge in organizational structures and make decisions before the people in the organizations comprehend it (Bennett and McWhorter, 2017b).

Virtual HRD is a new conceptual area of inquiry in the field of HRD that addresses learning and development in virtual spaces (Bennett, 2010; Bennett and McWhorter, 2014). What makes VHRD new is that it is defined as a virtual environment mediated by rich and sophisticated technologies (Bennett, 2009; 2010; Bennett and Bierema, 2010), rather than focusing on traditional definitions of HRD that are more process driven (McLagan, 1989; Swanson and Arnold, 1996). Process-driven strategies, such as career development and training, are still important and are theorized to occur within the virtual environment. Like polysynchronous education, VHRD recognizes that work and learning have become hybridized where people are both physically and virtually engaged and may move seamlessly between the two.

Defining Virtual HRD

Virtual HRD is framed by organizational culture and knowledge management theories modeled to have a mutual influence over one another as leaders determine relevance and meaning of new information and act on it (Bennett, 2009). Knowledge management and organizational learning are related concepts. Various forms of knowledge managed through technology extend from tacit to explicit (Bennett, 2009; Cho et al., 2009; Polanyi, 1966), and they can be integrated into networking technology where users learn organizational culture and see how values are enacted (Bennett, 2014). The more people interact within technology, the more various professional and cultural values are in play. Online learning platforms are no different; leadership and academic values may be embedded in the content as an explicit, or more often implicit, way of enculturating students to a field. For example, leadership behaviors such as empathy, listening and respect for others are reinforced through case studies that an instructor selects or in the ground rules for group discussions. Increasingly, case examples can be found in short videos of real leaders modeling behaviors. Videos are easily hyperlinked into learning software. Additionally, students represent various cultural and professional backgrounds that have a set of values that may or may not harmonize with those taught in a class, which could create dissonance that must be resolved for learning to occur. Over time, course upon course, scholar-practitioner facets of leadership identity are scaffolded with the aid of technology to achieve the goal of deeper insight.

VHRD is defined as a 'media rich and culturally relevant web environment that strategically improves expertise, performance, innovation, and community-building through formal and informal learning' (Bennett, 2009, p. 364). *Web* in this definition means networked technology rather than solely the internet, most often in the form of a corporate intranet or internal knowledge management system. Increasingly, these knowledge management systems are integrated with the Internet of Things in which more devices are communicating with the aid of internet services as well as internal networks. On some level, learning management systems (LMS) represent VHRD because they have the capacity to tie together multiple technologies and systems, as well as interconnect people to create an environment for leadership development. In fact, some institutions use learning platforms for a rudimentary intranet to provide faculty with behind-the-scenes policies, forms and training resources.

The internet is, of course, connected to VHRD when it is webbed into an organization's network. Organizations are increasingly using internet resources to supplement training resources where the authority of the material can be verified, but the most important and proprietary components of organizational networks are protected by a firewall and not open for public consumption. The outward façade of an organization's public image is overshadowed by the vast, tangled labyrinth of the real organization that can only be seen by members. Online OLS programs also web in external resources, such as publicly available videos and lectures by the very scholars students read in a course, thus bringing content to life. External partners can be incorporated into the internal web, such as LMS vendors through whom academic institutions host online courses. Passwords are used to authenticate faculty and student access to the LMS and the connection appears seamless. In fact, some users may not realize they are leaving the virtual territory of the institution and entering the territory of a vendor when they sign into a course.

VHRD as a Learning Environment

VHRD is defined as an environment that includes multiple channels of learning. Fundamental learning processes in the definition of VHRD are formal and informal learning and these processes support strategic improvement and the organizational mission through expertise development, building community, and improving both individual and group-level performance (Bennett, 2009), which are also central concerns for OLS doctoral programs. Individual levels of learning are precursors for learning at the organizational level (Swanson and Arnold, 1996). While emphasis in OLS is based on formal learning, informal and incidental learning or unexpected learning are highly valuable. This learning often occurs through interaction with peer colleagues and the instructor. According to Marsick and Watkins (1990), informal learning represents a significant majority of learning in any organization, and it is theorized to be the primary learning mode of learning in VHRD. Students learn in unexpected ways through discussion, connecting with fellow students and engaging in experiential field projects. An important question is: how does this learning impact the practice environment?

More research and theoretical work needs to be done on informal learning, particularly where it intersects with technology. Tacit knowledge is an important part of organizational culture (Schein, 2010) and it can be learned through technology, but how it works is a mystery due to the inability to articulate brain processes that remain below the surface of consciousness. Toward theorizing different types of informal learning, Schugurensky (2000) described three forms of informal learning, which Bennett (2011, 2012) developed into four modes on an axis. One axis identifies whether the learning is conscious or unconscious and the second axis is whether learning is intentional or unintentional, creating four modes of learning: (a) self-directed; (b) incidental; (c) tacit; and (d) integrative. People are aware when they learn through self-direction or incidentally because they are conscious of learning. Tacit learning is non-conscious. An example of tacit learning is social and professional values that leaders absorb by observing how things are done in an environment, but the leaders remain unaware that they have adopted new values and habits, although they may become aware if they experience cognitive dissonance or conflict.

The fourth form of informal learning, integrative, is unconscious but intentional; that is, adults are aware they have a problem to solve but the solution requires non-conscious, behind-the-scenes processing. They may experience a mental block or tip-of-the-tongue feeling that is relieved when they turn their minds to other activities. The answer is realized when solutions rise through the ladder of consciousness or sublimate from non-conscious to conscious in the form of sudden insight, or the classic 'a-ha' moment (Bennett, 2011). A recent dissertation using VHRD and this informal learning model as a conceptual frame found that online adjunct instructors, who are less likely than full-time faculty to be provided with ongoing professional development due to their temporary positions, relied on informal learning to prepare to teach online (Plachuta, 2016). In this study, the participants experienced sudden insight into their teaching practices when they were involved with activities that took their minds off online teaching, such as driving or mowing the lawn, when they were technically not on the job. In some cases, a problem solution was visualized, which supported the theory that the highly visual nature of web technology can promote implicit learning. Extending this idea, learning that involves the five senses can be integrated into OLS online courses and may be brought to mind years later to solve new problems.

Learning in one domain of life, such as a virtual environment, can trigger learning in another domain. Whether in virtual classroom discussion boards or in workplace knowledge systems, individuals share experience and application of new concepts when they engage in discussion and reflection. Online OLS programs can be designed to include experiential and informal learning that not only enhances program outcomes but prepares leaders for working with and leading through technology. The next section discusses leadership, experiential learning and virtual teams.

LEADERSHIP, EXPERIENTIAL LEARNING AND VIRTUAL TEAMS

Doctoral OLS programs fuse leadership in practice with leadership as a discipline within a number of conceptual areas. An underexplored area is how best to prepare leaders for virtual leadership, both general leadership and, more significantly, guiding virtual teams. Leaders practice communication, reflection, organizing and team processes in a virtual learning environment, which may put them at an advantage for leading virtual teams and groups in practice. This section of the chapter explores some of the emerging trends with a focus on the scholar-practitioner perspective. It first addresses virtual teams with an emphasis on trust development research and the notion of swift trust, then innovative experiences, and finally credible research as a capstone of experiential learning in online doctoral OLS programs.

Virtual Experiences and Trust Development

Today's leaders utilize various technology platforms, mobile and web-based, for work and everyday interactions. Many professionals work in groups or teams, whether as ad hoc arrangements or ongoing structures, and trust in virtual teams has been identified as critical for team functioning (Bennett and Bierema, 2010; Germain and McGuire, 2014). Seminal scholars have shown trust is a key factor for enabling teamwork and group performance effectiveness (Hackman and Morris, 1975; Hackman and Oldham, 1980), and this finding is reaffirmed in the research on global virtual teams (Gibson et al., 2014; Gibson and Cohen, 2003; Hoch and Kozlowski, 2014; Jarvenpaa et al., 1998; Lipnack and Stamps, 1999; Pinjani and Palvia, 2013; Townsend et al., 1998). Highlighted in recent research on virtual teams is the evolving nature of leadership and the importance of swift trust, which is a skill that can be transplanted from team to team so that new virtual teams can be up and running quickly (Germain and McGuire, 2014). Leadership of virtual teams is more distributed, collaborative and focused on relationships rather than solely on tasks (Gibson et al., 2014). Trust development may occur more quickly and earlier in virtual teams, particularly when there is a specific task focus.

In online doctoral OLS programs, a common education technique is to have students work in virtual teams. Because members must move to a task focus quickly to meet term deadlines and they are mutually responsible for the outcome, they have to negotiate team dynamics in short order. At Northeastern, using a formal team charter to establish goals, preferred communication modes and articulate expectations tends to reduce the problems that teams experience, including interpersonal conflict. Peer assessment allows teams more accountability to one another and reduces the need for faculty to mediate conflict. Barring rare circumstances, leaders should be expected to resolve conflict without appealing to someone else's authority.

The three primary theories of trust development are: (1) Media Richness Theory (Daft and Lengel, 1986; Zack, 1993), which is based on the premise that the higher the equivocality or ambiguity of the task, the stronger the need for face-to-face interaction, and the inverse, meaning the more unequivocal or clear the information or decision, the more virtual exchange is appropriate; (2) Social Presence Theory (Short et al., 1976), which highlights the distinctions between the feeling of personal interaction and the number and types of communication channels; and (3) Social Information Processing (Walther, 1996), which argues it may take longer to integrate a team through interaction. These perspectives remain important when exploring their relevance in today's context.

More tenuous and equivocal information may require organic conversation, requiring synchronous communication such as in a video conference, rather than through frustrating and hard-to-follow email exchanges. OLS students select and use appropriate synchronous tools embedded in an LMS, or external tools that allow for face and voice exchange, or potentially other formats needed for a disability, such as captioning and text readers. Northeastern's program encourages tools beyond those offered in the LMS, which could make assessment of team process more difficult, but should not affect assessments based on team products. Research has shown that trust in traditional courses is not significantly different from online (Beranek and French, 2011), and others have shown that having a face-to-face kick-off class can enable trust in a primarily online class (McDonald, 2012). At Northeastern, summer residency is a key ingredient for trust building and student motivation because it provides face-to-face and personal contact with peers and faculty.

Whether in virtual teams or a virtual learning community, OLS can promote healthy interaction skills important for VHRD, and instructors can model conflict resolution processes. One of the most important conflict resolution approaches is to ensure that team members communicate directly with one another rather than look to an authority to solve personal conflicts and thus practice leadership skills. In VHRD, community building is one of the identified outcomes of the media-rich and culturally relevant environment of VHRD, and effectively dealing with conflict is just as important in a virtually mediated environment as it is face-to-face. While physically co-located teams are sometimes believed to be more efficient, the nature of a virtual team requires members to be more intentional in their engagement with each other, which in turn can enhance feedback and knowledge sharing, and result in more robust experiential learning for the whole team.

Leveraging Insights to Design Innovative Experiences for Leaders

Experiential education has fully embraced the value of learning through experience as an effective pathway for personal and professional development. The blending of formal education with work experience has long been the formula used for career advancement, but it is now a way for academic institutions to bridge the professional experiences of leaders with their classroom experiences in a manner that is flexible and self-paced. Simultaneous work and learning has a tremendous advantage for two reasons. First, students can apply knowledge gained in class more immediately, and use their own problems of practice to drive learning and even offer solutions back to their home organizations. This creates a dialectic between environments. Second, online programs allow greater participation of practitioners from myriad organizations, which extends a student's exposure to how leadership is enacted in other environments. They can learn vicariously when, for example, they engage in application discussions typical of online assignments. These informal and experiential moments promote learning agility and innovation through exposure to new ideas explored through discussion (Bennett and McWhorter, 2017a). LMS platforms enable vicarious or second-hand learning (Goldman et al.

2014) or informal learning characteristic of VHRD, when students learn from other students.

The question becomes what, if any, are the trade-offs on the original ideas of experiential learning (Dewey, 1938; Kolb, 1984; Lindeman, 1926) and what are the mechanisms to engage in higher order learning through which adults reflect on their experiences and on their learning (Argyris, 1989; Mezirow, 1990; Miettinen, 2000; Revans, 1980; Schön, 1984)? In some cases this means questioning intuition and prior understandings derived from practice. Given that leadership development based on experiential learning is well accepted (Day, 2000; Dentico, 1999; Hirst et al., 2004; Kets de Vries and Korotov, 2007), the focus centers on how reflective practices are fostered in the virtual world to enable leaders to advance their awareness, insight and personal development.

Experiential learning projects and service learning (Bringle and Hatcher, 1996; 2000; Bringle et al., 2012; Butin, 2006; Jones and Abes, 2004) have been the dominant approaches to date to provide students with real-life experiences to enhance their learning. There is no need to confine online doctoral education to just what is in an LMS; students can easily engage in fieldwork and bring what they learned to the class. Healthcare, specifically medical education, has been a leader in the use of online learning platforms and simulations, and it represents a higher education-to-workforce continuum where students move increasingly from the classroom to the clinic with a system of advanced learners mentoring junior learners (Bennett et al., 2012). It is also increasingly interdisciplinary. Leaders in these environments are taught to practice risky procedures in safe formats, such as physical patient simulators or avatars in online programs similar to video games, before proceeding with live people. Scaffolding of skills at each stage must take into account how the experience of the simulation differs from reality; the feel of pulling a needle and thread through simulated tissue will never be exactly like suturing a person.

Simulation and gaming have a significant ability to foster technical and team skills in a safe but engaging environment (Bennett, 2011; Reeves and Read, 2009). Leadership scenarios foster important skills, such as decision-making in an evolving crisis or practicing the delivery of performance feedback, and they involve creative thinking practices that are important for innovation. At Northeastern, field projects are built not only to explore and critique concepts from literature, but also to enhance doctoral skills. For example, in an organizational culture course, students work in teams to build an interview guide based on theoretical concepts from literature, engage in interviews to field test ideas, and analyze the data to deepen understanding of culture. They sometimes find theory lacking. They also practice data collection, which will be reinforced and expanded in research courses. These experiences, though virtually mediated, bring the learning from virtual to the real world and back again when teams share results in online presentations. They develop organizational inquiry skills over time with multiple conceptual frameworks. The next section examines the final outcome of an OLS doctoral program: credible research.

Credible Research and Useful Theory: Transformation of Thinking

Lewin (1945) once said that there is nothing more practical than a useful theory. The OLS doctoral program is grounded on the premise that real-life experiences by scholar-practitioners engaged in field studies using credible research strategies and applying useful theory will not only provide new insights to workplace puzzles but also transform their perspectives. One of the most important outcomes is transformation of thinking, not only through coursework, but through the experience of the research process itself. Much of what follows here is something not often discussed in the literature and so this chapter provides perspective from practice as faculty of an online doctoral OLS program. Leaders who enter a doctoral program are coming to develop deeper insight, though they do not necessarily know how this will occur. Mentoring by faculty is a critical part of the transformation process, including challenging assumptions and testing logic. This involves raising subjectivities, sometimes to uncomfortable levels, and making conceptual logic explicit even if an idea starts with intuition or a gut feeling about what is important in practice. The nature of scholarship is to make logic explicit through written documentation, thus defensible and shareable, even though it can be a complex and sometimes painful part of the process. Further, scholarship must be fully embraced to form the scholar-practitioner identity (Ruona and Gilley, 2009; Short et al., 2009; Short and Shindall, 2009) of developing leaders who want to enhance patterns of thinking and analysis, and achieve rigor of evidence for decision-making.

There are some things about research that cannot be fully learned until they are experienced. The research process of the dissertation is highly experiential because ideas in the literature and assumptions about practice are tested in a real-life environment. This means it is a critical form of experiential learning. At Northeastern, students start with a problem of practice rather than gap-spotting a problem found in literature, emphasizing the local and particular. For a discussion on gap-spotting versus consensus-challenging research see Alvesson and Sandberg (2013). Their perspective not only values practitioner knowledge but actually increases the value of deep conceptual understanding, without privileging one as more important than the other. This approach emphasizes that leaders should produce research that is meaningful and useful to their organizations or to the field of practice. Furthering a single line of inquiry is secondary.

Through online coursework and then through faculty mentoring during the doctoral thesis, students explore their practitioner knowledge, illuminating the textures and edges of their problems of practice, and try on different theoretical lenses to find what may have explanatory power. It is a powerful blend of knowledge from practice, literature and theory that formulates the research problem and establishes important research questions. OLS students engage in a thoughtfully crafted applied research project in the organizational setting, artfully moving through an iterative data collection and analysis process, and then integrate perspectives gathered from the field with scholarship to formulate new, useful knowledge. They not only address implications for general research and practice, but they discuss how they have transformed through the experience of research and how they plan to change their own practice as a result of what was learned in the study. In this manner, they are encouraged to be active change agents rather than producing a study that gathers dust on a shelf. Some students find themselves making changes to practice while the research is in progress, an example of which can be found in Plachuta (2016), who created new online teaching resources and communication channels for faculty, as reported in the concluding chapter of the doctoral thesis.

Powerful learning through research can be achieved using online modalities. Where faculty and students once huddled around a conference table to pore over transcripts and data sets, they now exchange them through technology. Highlighting text and using the comment features in word processing software and cloud-based file sharing programs, such as Dropbox.com, enable faculty to provide highly specific feedback. Research discussions and defenses can be done just as easily through teleconferencing software as in person. One thing discovered early on in the program at Northeastern was that it was difficult to use teleconferencing software in a hybrid fashion with some members of the committee in a room together and some online. This was primarily due to echoes and background noises when microphones were not muted. Moving defenses fully into teleconferencing software was found to be more successful, creating a uniform experience and reducing the cost of travel. As with any doctoral program, students must develop an appreciation for the iterative nature of doctoral research and the process of incorporating feedback from multiple sources.

The process takes consensus-building and complexity management skills to produce a strong final product, which are also important leadership skills. While some may think that scholar-practitioner research is 'PhD-lite', involving the local organizational context can increase the complexity and sophistication of a study. Indeed, context statements are important for providing richness of detail that supports why the particular research questions are important to answer. The intention is often not to generalize, though others can learn from the new knowledge the study produces. Some Northeastern students conduct more general studies and others are practice-based where the questions are designed for only one organization or population. Following rigorous and meticulous research processes will have lifelong consequences for developing leaders, though little research has been done on how OLS alumni approach new problems with transformed thinking after they have left the program, which is an important area of investigation for higher education and for VHRD. Anecdotal evidence indicates that former students have transferred skills to justify new programs and projects, and Northeastern is considering innovations to the capstone project, such as further enhancing student change agency. The next section addresses implications and concludes the chapter.

IMPLICATIONS AND CHAPTER CONCLUSION

Virtually mediated online OLS programs have the capacity to transform leaders as well as transforming practice in organizations. As VHRD postulates, this occurs both through formal learning and informal learning. Online programs can reinforce a leader's ability to manage and administer organizational processes through technology because the leader must learn how to do this within the program itself. Students learn to navigate and interpret what is in the technology. Further, exposure to online learning processes helps students view themselves not only as leaders of groups of people, but leaders of learning and innovation.

Clearly there are advantages and disadvantages to online learning. This chapter has addressed some of the advantages, although a major drawback is that there are some things that simply cannot be done with current technologies. Online coursework must be planned in advance to avoid technical glitches and student frustrations when materials are difficult to find or written instructions are not clear. Asynchronicity allows working adults accessible learning opportunities but, at the same time, introduces delays in communication and may reduce the feeling of social connection. Like many online programs, Northeastern has primarily chosen the asynchronous model to accommodate students who have varying schedules and live in different time zones. Students in this program are not required to be online simultaneously; however, polysynchronous learning can be achieved when students choose which modes are best for teamwork.

Program design must be intentional, scaffolding skills and concepts from the beginning of the course to the end, and then scaffolding across multiple courses to support the ultimate outcomes of the program. A major outcome is not only the doctoral thesis, but the transformation of thinking it represents. While learning technologies are becoming increasingly sophisticated and better able to mirror social processes, there are still many new technologies and techniques that revolutionize learning online. These include simulation, gaming and avatar-based learning in three-dimensional virtual worlds. However, faculty need to have the time to learn new technologies and develop curriculum, which can be at odds with program administration that looks to online platforms to realize efficiencies and cost savings, and run courses year-round or in an accelerated format. Though faculty have multiple roles in an online class, including facilitator, lecturer, instructional designer and content expert, a critical faculty role is to develop intellectual relationship with OLS students.

A focus on informal and experiential learning promoted by VHRD emphasizes that online learning is not separate from experience but rather forms a part of a leader's experience; that is, online learning *is* experiential. The question then becomes: how are experiences through virtually mediated technologies different from face-to-face experiences, whether at work or in a degree program? Faculty and students alike are leaders in OLS programs. Brown et al. (2007) suggest nine leadership dimensions for those who lead virtually: charisma, individual consideration, intellectual stimulation, courage, dependability, flexibility, integrity, judgment, and respect for others (pp. 14–15). This chapter advocates self-direction as an important part of virtual leadership and online learning. These dimensions can be used to evaluate new technologies and pedagogies. Ultimately, both education and the workplace have gone through a sea change that has made technology a part of even the most traditional settings. Skills in virtuality are necessary for leaders to engage in OLS doctoral programs and to foster the virtual environment that develops people, and organizations they lead, through virtual HRD. Leaders need ongoing development even beyond the doctorate to adapt to new technologies and solve problems of the future, which means that doctoral programs should prepare them for lifelong learning and agile innovation.

REFERENCES

Alvesson, M. and J. Sandberg (2013). *Constructing Research Questions: Doing Interesting Research*. London: Sage.
Anderson, T. and J. Dron (2011). Three generations of distance education pedagogy.

The International Review of Research in Open and Distributed Learning, **12**(3), 80–97.

Argyris, C. (1989). Strategy implementation: An experience in learning. *Organizational Dynamics*, **18**(2), 5–15.

Bashir, T., T.M. Ali, M. Asrar and S. Babar (2015). Performance and progress of OIC countries towards building technology development capacity. *Current Science*, **109**(5), 878–88.

Bennett, E.E. (2009). Virtual HRD: The intersection of knowledge management, culture, and intranets. *Advances in Developing Human Resources*, **11**(3), 362–74.

Bennett, E.E. (2010). The coming paradigm shift: Synthesis and future directions for virtual HRD. *Advances in Developing Human Resources*, **12**(6), 728–41.

Bennett, E.E. (2011). Informal adult learning in simulated and virtual environments. In Information Resources Management Association (ed.), *Gaming and Simulations: Concepts, Methodologies, Tools and Applications* (pp. 1914–32). Hershey, PA: IGI Global.

Bennett, E.E. (2012). A four-part model of informal learning: Extending Schugurensky's Conceptual Model. *Proceedings of the Adult Education Research Conference*. Saratoga Springs, NY: AERC.

Bennett, E.E. (2014). How an intranet provides opportunities for learning organizational culture: Implications for virtual HRD. *Advances in Developing Human Resources*, **16**(3), 296–319.

Bennett, E.E. and L.L. Bierema (2010). The ecology of virtual human resource development. *Advances in Developing Human Resources*, **12**(6), 632–47.

Bennett, E.E. and R.R. McWhorter (2014). Virtual human resource development. In N.E. Chalofsky, T.F. Rocco and M.L. Morris (eds), *The Handbook of Human Resource Development: The Discipline and the Profession* (pp. 567–89). Hoboken, NJ: Wiley.

Bennett, E.E. and R.R. McWhorter (2017a). IHRD and virtual HRD. In T. Garavan, A. McCarthy and R. Carbery (eds), *Handbook of International Human Resource Development: Context, Processes and People* (pp. 268–94). Cheltenham, UK and Northampton, MA, USA: Edward Elgar Publishing.

Bennett, E.E. and R.R. McWhorter (2017b). Organizational learning, community, and virtual HRD: Advancing the discussion. *New Horizons in Adult Education and Human Resource Development*, **29**(3), 19–27.

Bennett, E.E., R.D. Blanchard and G.L. Fernandez (2012). Knowledge sharing in academic medical centers: Exploring the nexus of higher education and workforce development. In V.C.X. Wang (ed.), *Encyclopedia of E-Leadership, Training, and Counseling* (pp. 212–32). Hershey, PA: IGI Global.

Beranek, M.M. and M. French (2011). Team trust in online education: Assessing and comparing team-member trust in online teams versus face-to-face teams. *International Journal of E-Learning & Distance Education*, **25**(3).

Boje, D.M. and C. Rhodes (2005). The virtual leadership construct: The mass mediatization and simulation of transformational leadership. *Leadership*, **1**(4), 407–28.

Boje, D.M., A. Pullen, C. Rhodes and G. Rosile (2013). The virtual leader. In A. Bryman, D. Collinson, K. Grint, B. Jackson and M. Uhl-Bien (eds), *Sage Handbook of Leadership* (pp. 518–30). Thousand Oaks, CA: Sage.

Bringle, R.G. and J.A. Hatcher (1996). Implementing service learning in higher education. *The Journal of Higher Education*, **67**(2), 221–39.

Bringle, R.G. and J.A. Hatcher (2000). Institutionalization of service learning in higher education. *The Journal of Higher Education*, **71**(3), 273–90.

Bringle, R.G., J.A. Hatcher and S.G. Jones (eds) (2012). *International Service Learning: Conceptual Frameworks and Research*. Sterling, VA: Stylus Publishing.

Brown, M.K., B. Huettner and C. James-Tanny (2007). *Managing Virtual Teams: Getting the Most from Wikis, Blogs, and other Collaborative Tools*. Plano, TX: Wordware Publishing.

Burkhardt, J.B. and E.E. Bennett (2015). Shaping the future of a globalized world: A qualitative study of how undergraduate international students' everyday cross-cultural experiences were impacted by university diversity initiatives. *European Journal of Training and Development*, **39**(3), 162–81.

Butin, D.W. (2006). The limits of service-learning in higher education. *The Review of Higher Education*, **29**(4), 473–98.

Cho, E., Y. Cho and G.N. McLean (2009). HRDs role in knowledge management. *Advances in Developing Human Resources*, **11**(3), 263–72.

Daft, R.L. and R.H. Lengel (1986). Organizational information requirements, media richness and structural design. *Management Science*, **32**(5), 554–71.

Dalgarno, B. (2014). Polysynchronous learning: A model for student interaction and engagement. In B. Hegarty, J. McDonald and S-K. Loke (eds), *Rhetoric and Reality: Critical Perspectives on Educational Technology* (pp. 673–77). Proceedings of the ASCILITE 2014, Dunedin.

Day, D.V. (2000). Leadership development: A review in context. *The Leadership Quarterly*, **11**(4), 581–613.

Dentico, J.P. (1999). Leadsimm: Collaborative leadership development for the knowledge society. *Developments in Business Simulation and Experiential Learning*, **26**.

Dewey, J. (1938). *Experiential Education*. New York, NY: Collier.

Fain, P. and R. Seltzer (2017). *Purdue's Bold Move*, 28 April. Inside HigherEd. Accessed 3 July 2017 at https://www.insidehighered.com/news/2017/04/28/purdue-acquires-kaplan-university-create-new-public-online-university-under-purdue.

Friedman, J. (ed.) (2016). Study: Enrollment in online learning up, except at for-profits. *U.S. News & World Report*, 6 February. Accessed 2 July 2017 at https://www.usnews.com/education/online-education/articles/2016-02-09/study-enrollment-in-online-learning-up-except-at-for-profits.

Germain, M. and D. McGuire (2014). The role of swift trust in virtual teams. *Advances in Developing Human Resources*, **16**(3), 356–70.

Gibson, C.B. and S.G. Cohen (eds) (2003). *Virtual Teams that Work: Creating Conditions for Virtual Team Effectiveness*. San Francisco, CA: Jossey-Bass.

Gibson, C.B., L. Huang, B.L. Kirkman and D.L. Shapiro (2014). Where global and virtual meet: The value of examining the intersection of these elements in twenty-first-century teams. *Annual Review of Organizational Psychology and Organizational Behavior*, **1**(1), 217–44.

Goldman, E.F., M.M. Wesner, M.M. Plack, N.N. Manikoth and Y. Haywood (2014). Secondhand learning from graduates of leadership development programs. *Journal of Workplace Learning*, **26**(8), 511–28.

Graham, C.M. (2010). Communications technology, emotional intelligence, and impact on performance: A conceptual exploration of connections. *Advances in Developing Human Resources*, **11**(6), 773–83.

Hackman, J.R. and C.G. Morris (1975). Group tasks, group interaction process, and group performance effectiveness: A review and proposed integration. *Advances in Experimental Social Psychology*, **8**, 45–99.

Hackman, J.R. and G.R. Oldham (1980). *Work Redesign*. Reading, MA: Addison-Wesley.

Hirst, G., L. Mann, P. Bain, A. Pirola-Merlo and A. Richver (2004). Learning to lead: The development and testing of a model of leadership learning. *The Leadership Quarterly*, **15**(3), 311–27.

Hoch, J.E. and S.W. Kozlowski (2014). Leading virtual teams: Hierarchical leadership, structural supports, and shared team leadership. *Journal of Applied Psychology*, **99**(3), 390.

Horn, M.B. and H. Staker (2015). *Blended: Using Disruptive Innovation to Improve Schools*. San Francisco, CA: Jossey-Bass.

Jarvenpaa, S.L., K. Knoll and D.E. Leidner (1998). Is anybody out there? Antecedents of trust in global virtual teams. *Journal of Management Information Systems*, **14**(4), 29–64.

Jones, S.R. and E.S. Abes (2004). Enduring influences of service-learning on college students' identity development. *Journal of College Student Development*, **45**(2), 149–66.

Kets de Vries, M.F.K. and K. Korotov (2007). Creating transformational executive education programs. *Academy of Management Learning & Education*, **6**(3), 375–87.

Kolb, D. (1984). *Experiential Learning: Experience as the Source of Learning and Development*. Englewood Cliffs, NJ: Prentice Hall.

Langer, A.M. (2010). *Information Technology and Organizational Learning: Managing Behavioral Change Through Technology and Education* (2nd edn). Boca Raton, FL: CRC Press.

Lewin, K. (1945). The research centre for group dynamics at Massachusetts Institute of Technology. *Sociometrics*, **8**, 128–35.

Lindeman, E.C. (1926). *The Meaning of Adult Education*. New York, NY: New Republic.

Lipnack, J. and J. Stamps (1999). Virtual teams: The new way to work. *Strategy & Leadership*, **27**(1), 14–19.

Marsick, V.J. and K. Watkins (1990). *Informal and Incidental Learning in the Workplace*. London, UK and New York, NY, USA: Routledge.

McDonald, P.L. (2012). Adult learners and blended learning: A phenomeno-graphic study of variation in adult learners' experiences in blended learning in higher education. Unpublished dissertation: George Washington University, Washington, DC.

McLagan, P.A. (1989). Systems model 2000: Matching systems theory to future HRD issues. In D.B. Gradous (ed.), *Systems Theory Applied to Human Resource Development* (pp. 61–90). Alexandria, VA: ASTD.

Mezirow, J. (1990). *Fostering Critical Reflection in Adulthood: A Guide to Transformative and Emancipatory Learning*. San Francisco, CA: Jossey-Bass.

Miettinen, R. (2000). The concept of experiential learning and John Dewey's theory of reflective thought and action. *International Journal of Lifelong Education*, **19**(1), 54–72.

Pinjani, P. and P. Palvia (2013). Trust and knowledge sharing in diverse global virtual teams. *Information & Management*, **50**(4), 144–53.

Plachuta, A. (2016). A qualitative study of community college online adjunct faculty experiences with informal learning and virtual human resource development. Unpublished dissertation: Northeastern University, Boston, MA.

Polanyi, M. (1966). *The Tacit Dimension*. Garden City, NY: Anchor Books.

Poulin, R. and T. Straut (2016). WCET distance education enrollment report 2016. Available at WICHE Cooperative for Educational Technologies website: http://wcet.wiche.edu/initiatives/research/WCET-Distance-Education-Enrollment-Report-2016.

Quirk, M. (2006). *Intuition and Metacognition in Medical Education: Keys to Developing Expertise*. New York, NY: Springer.

Raelin, J. (2016). It's not about the leaders: It's about the practice of leadership. *Organizational Dynamics*, **45**, 124–31.

Reeves, B. and J.L. Read (2009). *Total Engagement: Using Games and Virtual Worlds to Change the Way People Work and Businesses Compete*. Boston, MA: Harvard Business Press.

Revans, R.W. (1980). *Action Learning: New Techniques for Management*. London: Blond and Briggs.

Ruona, W. and J. Gilley (2009). Practitioners in applied professions: A model applied to human resource development. *Advances in Developing Human Resources*, **11**(4), 438.

Schein, E.H. (2010). *Organizational Culture and Leadership* (4th edn). San Francisco, CA: Jossey-Bass.

Schön, D.A. (1984). *The Reflective Practitioner: How Professionals Think in Action*. New York, NY: Basic Books.

Schugurensky, D. (2000). The forms of informal learning: Towards a conceptualization of the field. NALL Working Paper No. 19-2000. Accessed 11 May 2017 at http://www.nall.ca/res/19formsofinformal.htm.

Schwandt, D.B. and D.B. Szabla (2007). Systems and leadership: Coevolution or mutual evolution towards complexity? In J. Hazy, J. Goldstein and B. Lichtenstein (eds), *Complex Systems Leadership Theory: New Perspectives from Complexity Science on Social and Organizational Effectiveness* (pp. 35–60). Mansfield, MA: ISCE Publishing.

Short, D.C. and T.J. Shindall (2009). Defining HRD scholar-practitioners. *Advances in Developing Human Resources*, **11**(4), 472–85.

Short, D.C., J. Keefer and S.S. Stone (2009). The link between research and practice: Experiences of HRD and other professions. *Advances in Developing Human Resources*, **11**(4), 420–37.

Short, J., E. Williams and B. Christie (1976). *The Social Psychology of Telecommunications*. London: Wiley.

Swanson, R.A. and D.E. Arnold (1996). The purpose of human resource development is to improve organizational performance. *New Directions for Adult and Continuing Education*, **72**, 13–19.

Thomas, K.J. (2014). Workplace technology and the creation of boundaries: The role of VHRD in a 24/7 work environment. *Advances in Developing Human Resources*, **16**(3), 281–95.

Townsend, A.M., S.M. DeMarie and A.R. Hendrickson (1998). Virtual teams: Technology and the workplace of the future. *The Academy of Management Executive*, **12**(3), 17–29.

Walther, J.B. (1996). Computer-mediated communication: Impersonal, interpersonal, and hyper-personal interaction. *Communication Research*, **23**(1), 3–43.

Zack, M.H. (1993). Interactivity and communication mode choice in ongoing management groups. *Information Systems Research*, **4**(3), 207–39.

PART III

Delivery: across disciplines, courses and borders

7. Online doctoral programs: a call for caring educators

Cynthia J. Brown and Delene Volkert

> If we are open to creativity and change, ongoing technological advances coupled with a firm intent to care will continuously open new and exciting possibilities for caring across distance, time and culture. (Sitzman and Watson, 2017, p. 56)

As doctoral programs evolve into online settings, how can educators best support students? The online format may be a course or program that has a hybrid structure with some aspects online and some face to face, or courses and programs that are completely online. With faculty role modeling positive leadership traits, students will learn to lead in the online educational environment, advancing in their chosen field. In this chapter, as two nursing faculty we share our thoughts regarding caring in the online educational setting. Nurses in doctoral programs must learn leadership skills and may be practicing in a variety of settings. Research conducted by nurses covers a multitude of topics that range from education (Hickey et al., 2017), clinical practice (Butler et al., 2015), informatics (Cubas et al., 2017), administration (Melnyk et al. 2016), to policy issues (Bae, 2016).

The chapter begins with an overview and definition of caring, introducing a philosophy on caring (Mayeroff, 1971) and a caring theorist from the field of nursing (Watson, 1999). Caring will then be described in the online educational doctoral setting, highlighting caring communication: (1) between students on the course; (2) between faculty and students; and (3) between faculty, particularly those co-teaching a course. Case studies and the experience of the authors is intertwined throughout the chapter to provide the reader with examples of caring communication in the online, doctoral, educational setting.

Caring is defined by the *American Heritage® Dictionary of the English Language* as 'Feeling and exhibiting concern and empathy for others' ('Caring', 2017). Sitzman (2010) describes caring as 'one person mindfully and appropriately attending to the spoken and unspoken needs of another'

(p. 171). Mayeroff (1971) defines caring as being composed of eight essential ingredients; 'knowing, alternating rhythms, patience, honesty, trust, humility, hope and courage' (p. vii–viii). These ingredients lend themselves to a deeper experience of caring.

Mayeroff's (1971) philosophy suggests caring includes not forcing a direction on the other, but rather allowing the other to guide what is needed. This concept is so important for doctoral education; allowing independence and respect of others, while guiding the student throughout the process. Taking the time to develop a collegial relationship with the student can allow the instructor to recognize what is needed at different times throughout the doctoral program. 'Alternating rhythms' includes looking at parts of the dissertation in relation to the whole, to make sure every section flows together. Also, the rhythms of providing feedback to the student, developing a timeline that works for both faculty and student, and encouraging the student to develop a rhythm for submission of writing are further examples. This is especially important after the course work has ended and the student does not have the structure of courses, but is on an independent schedule for their dissertation. 'Patience' from faculty allows the student to work at their own pace and in their own style and is balanced by 'honesty' to allow the faculty to see objectively how they are assisting the student and helping the student to move forward. 'Trust' permits the doctoral student to engage in the process of doctoral education and allows the student to grow. 'Humility' is a reciprocal relationship, where the faculty and students learn from each other. The possibilities of the student progressing in the doctoral process may bring the concept of 'hope' both to the faculty and student. 'Courage' is shown by faculty and doctoral students in being open to the unknown aspects of the doctoral research journey, allowing the student and faculty to grow in the process.

Watson's Caring Theory (Watson, 1999) and Caritas Processes ('Caring Science Theory', n.d.) began as a guide for caring in the world, recognizing the interconnectedness of all life and has now evolved into 'cybercaring' (Sitzman and Watson, 2017, p. 8). An intention to create a caring environment, both online and in the face-to-face classroom includes communication, engagement, presence, promptness, and assisting the student as needed (Sitzman and Watson, 2017, pp. 62–3). This chapter will focus on caring communication in the doctoral education setting where we as educators aim to support the growth and education of nurse leaders.

STUDENT–STUDENT COMMUNICATION

Caring Groups and Collaboration

Caring student groups may be used to create an online support system throughout the semester and encourage engagement, communication, and self-care practice (Brown and Wilson, 2016). Caring groups are small groups of 4–5 students, assigned either in the online or face-to-face setting. In our university, techniques are used such as asking the students to complete a personal self-care assessment, create goals for the semester and engage with their peers in the discussion area. Students are introduced to the caring groups in the orientation period. They are assigned to groups each semester and asked throughout to engage in discussion with their caring group to provide support for each other. Faculty can ask questions such as: 'Please set a goal for self-care and reflect on how you can best complete this goal during your doctoral education'; 'What helps you to deal with stress in challenging times?'; and 'How are you doing with the self-care goal that you set at the beginning of the semester?' 'Would you like to make any changes to your plan?' The questions are posted on the course news, in the discussion area, and in an email with the weekly announcements.

Interacting with students in their cohort helps build connection and presence, even for students enrolled in online programs. This interaction helps students come to know this important collegial group of peers. Students in any type of program, particularly distance programs, can seek support from student peers (Litalien and Guay, 2015) or participate in student-led support groups (Hadjioannou et al., 2007; Pancheri et al., 2013). These supportive groups can become part of formal processes, such as dissertation or capstone writing groups, or journal clubs (Walker et al., 2008), and in the field of nursing even promote collaboration between students in PhD and DNP programs (Buchholz et al., 2015; Murphy et al., 2015). These collaborations can occur at any point in student coursework, although instituting these collaborative relationships early in the program may lead to continued collaboration throughout students' doctoral study and into their careers after graduation. In practice fields such as nursing, these collaborations have the potential to be vitally important in the future. As Bellini et al. (2012) stated, academia can become separate from clinical practice. These collaborative partnerships initiated during educational programs may help bridge the gap between education and practice.

Use of Social Media

Supportive relationships with doctoral cohort peers can be enhanced by exchanging email and telephone numbers at face-to-face or virtual orientations. Students in any program can interact through varieties of social media, such as Facebook, Twitter and Instagram. Hrastinski and Stenbom (2013) suggested online student-to-student coaching, where a new student can be mentored or coached by a more experienced student. With creativity, any of these interventions can be implemented into any program delivery type, whether live, hybrid or online.

One way for students to connect with other students, particularly in online programs, is through the use of social media and digital platforms. An example is presented here from our experience with a doctoral cohort in an online PhD program. The seven members of the cohort lived in four different states. Immediately after the program's single required face-to-face meeting, one cohort member set up a private Facebook page. The students in the cohort used this page to communicate with each other during their doctoral studies and even after finishing their programs. Students shared thoughts about coursework and dissertation ideas. The page was used to coordinate meetings at conferences that many of the students attended. Finally, and probably most importantly, the page was used to share inspirational messages and provide support for each other. Over half of the cohort has successfully completed their dissertations and remain in touch with this group through the Facebook page. This supportive group served the dual purpose of helping to develop lifelong friendships.

Challenges

The student–student relationship can be difficult, as there can be a competitive component to the relationship. This competition can be as simple as attention from the instructor, to something as large as competition for grant funding. This type of dynamic means it is important for students to strive for caring and a professional demonstration of respect for their peers. This can manifest itself in a variety of ways. Haenen et al. (2003) define learning classrooms, whether live or virtual, as 'a shared problem space, inviting the students to participate in a process of negotiation and co-construction of knowledge' (p. 246). Building the same types of reciprocal learning relationships with each other that they will build with their faculty will add to the learning environment.

Doctoral students are often learning to teach at higher levels of academia and, as such, should begin practicing collaborative relationships amongst themselves as they begin their courses. Online discussions can be challenging, as the important component of non-verbal communication is removed from the setting. Students can only judge the meaning and intent of a written passage through the words alone. This means that students must strive to write more clearly and distinctly when interacting with peers in discussion boards and other online settings. Using honesty and trust, they can come to know each other as scholars and peers. Language should be professional and courteous and any misunderstandings should be addressed immediately.

Peer Review and Group Leadership

Peer reviewing and leadership in group projects is a natural place for students to begin building and developing their faculty–student interactive relationship skills. As peer reviewing and group leadership is conducted in settings with acknowledged peers, there can be misunderstandings if roles are not defined and agreed upon early in the task. This would indicate the need for open and honest communication, where the group leader outlines their expectations of their own role and the roles of each group member. This communication should occur before the project begins and can become a model for later faculty–faculty relationships and faculty–student interactions. It is important that the group leader extend the desire for a collaborative working group, while taking ownership of finalizing the finished product of the group work. Mutually agreed-upon timelines should be established in the first meeting, with responsibilities for each component of the task clearly outlined. Working in a shared setting, such as Google Docs, provides a space for collaborative work that is accessible to all group members.

It is important to remember, as Cramp and Lamond (2016) stated, that learning often has an emotional context. This may be even more evident in group projects, as the group members see themselves as equals. Clear and precise language is important in all written communication, as are frequent opportunities to either meet verbally by phone, or visually through video conferencing platforms such as Facetime, Skype, Google Hangouts or Zoom. These added personal settings allow for verbal and non-verbal communication to occur and provide real-time opportunities for questions to be asked and misunderstandings to be addressed. In peer-review settings, professional and courteous written comments are a must. Students should provide positive comments along with critiques for improvement. The peer-reviewer can offer suggestions for improvement or share resources that will help build greater understanding of concepts and topics. Ultimately, the most important component is for the peer-reviewer to provide all comments with respect and kindness.

FACULTY–STUDENT COMMUNICATION

Building authentic relationships with students is a valuable component of a successful faculty–student relationship. Hills and Watson (2011) state that relational pedagogy is required for caring in the curriculum, as it is important to transform relationships between faculty and students from those of submission and dominance. Using honesty, patience and humility, faculty must strive to create a sense of presence, understanding and acceptance so that learning can occur. Walker et al. (2008) discussed that for the formation of doctoral scholars, students must become a part of the intellectual community during their doctoral program. These types of reciprocal caring and trusting connections can help promote acceptance and support the building of collegial relationships. Faculty should be 'authentically present, instilling faith and hope ... and authentically listening to the other's story' (Sitzman and Watson, 2017, p. 25). Jackson et al. (2009) discussed that faculty-designed and faculty-led support can be beneficial to students in doctoral programs, as ultimately faculty must demonstrate a supervisory role in the relationship.

Feedback Techniques

Continuous feedback throughout the course

Particularly as faculty strive to develop a sense of presence in the online environment, frequent communication is important. The faculty member should strive to guide their students toward growth in their own understanding. Hills and Watson (2011) remind us that students are capable by stating, 'our responsibility as teachers is to create ambiguity, to challenge taken-for-granted assumptions, and to create an environment in which learners feel free to wrestle with ideas, challenge us and other learners, share half-baked ideas, and engage in critical dialogue about the issues at hand' (p. 63). So, rather than giving answers to student questions, use Socratic or challenging questioning to create dialogues to help students find their own answers. This allows students to build on their prior knowledge base and unique worldview. It is also important to bring in the perspectives of others. This can be done by including peers in the process. Not all the feedback and dialogue should be from or with the instructor, but it should also take place with peers. Peers will bring their own unique perspectives and experiences to the process.

It is the faculty role to help guide and direct thinking through feedback. This feedback should occur with each discussion or assignment, not just with one or two large assignments. It may be beneficial to scaffold this work. Rather than a large assignment or paper submitted all at once, faculty can scaffold the work to build to one final assignment submission. This provides numerous opportunities for students to both give and receive feedback along the way. Cramp and Lamond (2016) outlined that course design that allows students to use feedback to improve their work is one way to communicate caring in an online environment.

Giving the student feedback using the 'sandwich' method may be beneficial: beginning with written positive aspects of the assignment that the student has completed, inserting constructive feedback, and ending on a positive note. Some online platforms allow verbal comments that may add to the understanding. In thinking of 'alternating rhythms' related to grading for the doctoral student, it may be helpful to give feedback that is specific to the task at hand and how it relates to the bigger picture of doctoral studies. Being 'honest' regarding assignment objectives and how the student met the objectives is important for growth.

Organizing the online calendar

Providing dates for the entire course from the first day of class provides a 'roadmap' for students. Adult learners have multiple responsibilities in their lives. Organization from the beginning of the course allows them to plan their work, school and life schedules as needed. Faculty should strive to only make changes to the calendar when it is absolutely necessary and any changes made should come from listening to and responding to student concerns. If changes are necessary, transparency is key. The faculty should outline their reason for these changes and then make sure to notify students in multiple ways and at numerous times. Changes can be communicated through course announcements for the group as a whole and email, for individual contact. A revised or updated calendar with the new dates highlighted in a way that draws attention to the changes should also be posted in the course. It is important to remember that even in online classes, many students print material such as syllabi, course calendars and assignment instructions at the beginning of the course and then do not go back to review these documents later. If making adjustments to the course calendar changes or even removes any assignments, faculty should think about how this will influence all aspects of the course. If the removal of the assignment changes the weight of assignments, weights will need to be adjusted too. Due dates would need to be revised for any future assignments impacted by the change. Thinking about how change affects the course as a whole, and making adjustments along the way, provides a clear direction for the student.

Online meetings

Regularly scheduled times that the instructor is available and accessible, such as a Google Hangout, Skype, Facetime or Zoom meeting, which students are free to join as desired, helps build instructor presence and caring online. Faculty may want to vary the days and times for these meetings from week to week, to accommodate differing schedules. However the faculty decides to implement these meetings, the dates and times of meetings should be clearly communicated within the course. Sitzman and Watson (2017) suggest that it shows caring in an online environment when faculty are 'dependably present online' (p. 28).

As an example, we use a weekly newsfeed in an evidence-based practice/ statistics course. A recurring YouTube video we created and titled 'Brief but (p) Moment' was posted to describe difficult concepts and provide universal feedback regarding assignments. The title was adapted from the PBS NewsHour series called 'Brief but Spectacular' ('PBS NewsHour', n.d.). Using video was a way for students to see us, hear our voices and keep the momentum going in a 16-week course. Faculty are able to build caring relationships with students using videos. For some faculty, this may involve 'courage' to engage in video production.

Another way to have regularly scheduled meetings is to inform students at the beginning of the course that there will be a meeting opportunity at the beginning of each module and midway through a multi-week module. This allows the faculty to help clarify and guide the students, such as answering any questions, clarifying any misunderstandings, and providing the opportunities for students to share ideas. Sitzman and Watson (2017) stated that communicating with students 'quickly, clearly, and often' (p. 37) helps to develop trust in the online classroom.

Faculty members can have 'digital office hours' which are communicated on their syllabus, where faculty are dependably available by phone, email, or in virtual meeting spaces. Whether meetings are synchronous or asynchronous, faculty can make recordings of all course video meetings. This permits the student to watch the video multiple times if desired and allows for recall of instructions (Cramp and Lamond, 2016). Faculty can even pre-record and share audio or video messages with the class. Faculty members can set up meeting discussion boards, meeting Google Documents, and even meeting Wikis. The important issue is for the faculty to be creative and find methods that best fit their students. If students are divided into and working in groups, faculty can ask groups to share the responsibility for facilitating meetings for each course module. Then the student-led group can decide when content is delivered and how or even when to meet.

Weekly announcements

These are another important form of communication within the online setting. This allows the instructor to summarize, review or highlight key concepts this way. The faculty can also address common issues discovered in grading, and praise students for jobs well done. Video or audio is preferable, so students see or hear their instructor, which also helps the faculty build presence.

Without lecturing, the instructor can create instructional time in announcements. Before the online meeting or pre-recorded video, the instructor can ask students to post questions or request clarification about the muddiest point for the upcoming week. Then announcements can address these issues briefly, rather than just always having an announcement of a housekeeping variety, such as what is due and where to find or submit things. This creates a source of contact that is more meaningful for the student.

Listening to the student

'Listening' in the online environment is observing and noticing student clues. This 'way of knowing' may be 'implicit', without direct words from the student to the instructor, or 'explicit', a clear verbal message sent by the student (Mayeroff, 1971, p. 20). For example, in the online setting a student may use an 'Ask the Instructor' posting area or 'Q & A' discussion for students. An open discussion board can facilitate listening and may involve more than one student. One student may send an email about having difficulty reading and understanding the assignment guidelines (explicit). Conversely, a student may post to the 'Ask an Instructor' board allowing input from several students. This allows students to realize that they are not alone and others have the same questions. Having an instructor 'listen' through the discussion board can assist with student–faculty communication. A student that may be embarrassed to ask about the course guidelines (implicit) may benefit from an open communication discussion board. Sitzman (2015) found three themes in her qualitative survey of faculty related to caring in the online setting: 'sense, connect, and facilitate' (p. 25). In the study, sensing or implicit listening was reported by faculty using phrases such as 'pick up that they are worried' (p. 25), 'Feel the frustration in their words' and 'If I sense students are struggling. . .' (p. 26).

Flexibility

One aspect of andragogy is related to the self-concept of the learner. The adult learner is responsible for his or her own decision-making. It is important to involve adult learners with the timeline for assignments and provide flexibility as needed (Knowles et al., 2012).

As an example, the first author always begins her introduction to the course with the caveat that communication is particularly key in an online course. If more time is needed for assignments or there are conflicting dates with other courses, she asks that students let her know ahead of time so adjustments can be made. This involves 'patience' with the process.

In summary, even simple strategies can show thoughtfulness. Organizing the online calendar and providing flexibility whenever possible helps role model caring for future leaders. By providing clear and frequent feedback, communicating through weekly announcements, planning online meetings and 'listening' to the students in the online setting, the instructor can build presence and develop caring relationships.

FACULTY–FACULTY COMMUNICATION

Co-teaching can offer a varied and more robust experience, utilizing the strengths and experiences of two faculty members. An example of a positive co-teaching experience from an online EdD program follows. With class sizes of approximately 10 students each semester, a course that focuses on writing the methodology chapter is divided between two faculty members. One faculty member focuses on quantitative research and the other on qualitative research. This is the ideal scenario, and it does not always work out perfectly, as it depends on the methodology selected by the students. This course occurs in the summer semester, is one of the final courses taken by the students, and is an eight-week intensive course. This is the fifth year that the course has been taught in this manner in an online setting. Different faculty members have taught the course and added in their individual expertise. Students are guided in writing the methodology chapter with the assignments divided into three sections. The students share their writing in a discussion format three times over the semester, and two students are paired for peer review for each discussion. While co-taught classes provide students with the opportunity to work with faculty with different styles, it is important for faculty to demonstrate consistency when interacting with students through communications and grading.

In order for the course to be successful, faculty must agree in advance on course design, course workload, grading schedules, course participation by faculty, and grading techniques. Although co-teaching is a commitment of time and work involvement, it allows faculty to share their expertise. Opportunities for co-teaching can offer problem-solving between faculty, ideas sharing, and reflection on the course and program outcomes (Buss et al., 2013). Faculty can role model caring behaviors in their communication with each other and their teaching styles, allowing the students to see faculty teamwork in action. 'Humility' (Mayeroff, 1971) is a necessary attribute between faculty members to allow for learning from each other. This openness to lifelong learning is an important quality to role model to the student.

CONCLUSION

Leadership, communication skills and online teamwork can guide the student to prepare for future leadership roles in a technology-based world. Communication between students will include discussion etiquette, peer review styles, leadership in group projects, and being a member of a caring team. Caring for students from faculty will include feedback techniques, organizing the online calendar, flexibility, communication through videos, online meetings, weekly announcements, grading in a caring manner, and continuous feedback throughout the course. Faculty should listen and make changes as needed, providing a flexible environment that is often valued by an adult learner. Caring student groups may be used to promote an online support system throughout the semester and encourage self-care practices. Faculty who are co-teaching a course need to be in agreement regarding course assignments, grading schedules, grading techniques and course workload. A focus on caring can bring a unique aspect to the online doctoral educational setting that is beneficial to all.

REFERENCES

Bae, S.H. (2016). The Centers for Medicare & Medicaid services reimbursement policy and nursing-sensitive adverse patient outcomes. *Nursing Economic$*, **34**(4), 161–81.

Bellini, S., P. McCauley and R.M. Cusson (2012). The doctor of nursing practice graduate as faculty member. *Nursing Clinics of North America*, **47**(4), 547–56.

Brown, C.J. and C. Wilson (2016). One university making a difference in graduate education: Caring in the online learning environment. *Journal of Holistic Nursing*, **34**(4), 402–407.

Buchholz, S.W., C. Yingling, K. Jones and S. Tenfelde (2015). DNP and PhD collaboration: Bringing together practice and research expertise as predegree and postdegree scholars. *Nurse Educator*, **40**(4), 203–206.

Buss, R., D. Zambo, S. Painter and D. Moore (2013). Examining faculty member changes in an innovative educational doctorate program. *Innovative Higher Education*, **38**(1), 59–74.

Butler, A., G. Willetts and B. Copnell (2015). Nurses' perceptions of working with families in the paediatric intensive care unit. *British Association of Critical Care Nurses*, **22**(4), 195–202.

Caring (2017). *American Heritage® Dictionary of the English Language* (5th edn). Accessed at https://ahdictionary.com/word/search.html?q=caring.

Caring Science Theory (n.d.). Accessed at https://www.watsoncaringscience.org/jean-bio/caring-science-theory/.

Cramp, A. and C. Lamond (2016). Engagement and kindness in digitally mediated learning with teachers. *Teaching in Higher Education*, **21**(1), 1–12.

Cubas, M.R., L.E. Pleis, D.C. Gomes, E.C.R. da Costa, A.P. Peluci, M.A. Shmeil and C.M. Carvalho (2017). Mapping and definition of terms used by nurses in a hospital specialized in emergency and trauma care. *Revista de Enfermagem Referencia*, **IV**, 45–54.

Hadjioannou, X., N.R. Shelton, D. Fu and J. Dhanarattigannon (2007). The road to a doctoral degree: Co-travelers through a perilous passage. *College Student Journal*, **41**(1), 160–77.

Haenen, J., H. Schrijnemakes and J. Stufkens (2003). Sociocultural theory and the practice of teaching historical concepts. In B. Kozulin, V. Gindis, S. Ageyev and S. Miller (eds), *Vygotsky's Educational Theory in Cultural Context* (pp. 246–66). Cambridge: Cambridge University Press.

Hickey, K., J. Rossetti, N. Oldenburg, M. Abendroth, C. Uhlken, K. Musker, B. Peters and P. Paramore (2017). Moving nursing program portfolio assessment from midterm to end of program: Lessons learned. *Nurse Educator*, **42**(4), 172–5.

Hills, M. and J. Watson (2011). *Creating a Caring Science Curriculum: An Emancipatory Pedagogy for Nursing*. New York, NY: Spring Publishing.

Hrastinski, S. and S. Stenbom (2013). Student online coaching: Conceptualizing an emerging learning activity. *Internet and Higher Education*, **16**(1), 66–9.

Jackson, D., P. Darbyshire, L. Luck and K. Peters (2009). Intergenerational reflections on doctoral supervision in nursing. *Contemporary Nurse*, **32**(1–2), 83–91.

Knowles, M., E. Holton and R. Swanson (2012). *The Adult Learner: The Definitive Classic in Adult Education and Human Resource Development* (7th edn). New York, NY: Routledge.

Litalien, D. and F. Guay (2015). Dropout intentions in PhD studies: A comprehensive model based on interpersonal relationships and motivational resources. *Contemporary Educational Psychology*, **41**, 218–31.

Mayeroff, M. (1971). *On Caring*. New York, NY: HarperCollins.

Melnyk, B.M., L. Gallagher-Ford, B.K. Thomas, M. Troseth, K. Wyngarden and L. Szalacha (2016). A study of chief nurse executives indicates low prioritization of evidence-based practice and shortcomings in hospital performance metrics across the United States. *Worldviews on Evidence-Based Nursing*, **13**(1), 6–14.

Murphy, M.P., B.A. Staffileno and E. Carlson (2015). Collaboration among DNP and PhD prepared nurses: Opportunity to drive positive change. *Journal of Professional Nursing*, **31**(5), 388–94.

Pancheri, K., D.L. Fowler, C.M. Wiggs, R. Schultz, P. Lewis and R. Nurse (2013). Fostering completion of the doctor of philosophy degree through scholarly collegial support. *The Journal of Continuing Education in Nursing*, **44**(7), 309–12.

PBS NewsHour: Brief but Spectacular (n.d.). Accessed at https://www.pbs.org/newshour/brief/.

Sitzman, K. (2010). Student-preferred caring behaviors for online nursing education. *Nursing Education Perspectives*, **31**(3), 171–8.

Sitzman, K. (2015). Sense, connect, facilitate: Nurse educator experiences of caring online through Watson's lens. *International Journal for Human Caring*, **19**(3), 25–9.

Sitzman, K. and J. Watson (2017). *Watson's Caring in the Digital World: A Guide for Caring when Interacting, Teaching, and Learning in Cyberspace*. New York, NY: Springer.

Walker, G.E., C.M. Golde, L. Jones, A.C. Bueschel and R. Hutchings (2008). *The Formation of Scholars. Rethinking Doctoral Education for the Twenty-First Century*. San Francisco, CA: Jossey-Bass.

Watson, J. (1999). *Nursing: Human Science and Human Care: A Theory of Nursing*. Sudbury, MA: Jones and Bartlett.

8. Social media identity in doctoral leadership education: SMILE

Jackie Bruce and Sara Brierton

INTRODUCTION

Don't let your social media identity happen by accident; be intentional and have integrity. It can and should be curated. A SMILE can make it happen.

Social media is a major influence on, and reflection of, society. For many, what started as teenagers 'chatting' with friends using made-up acronyms and abbreviations is now a significant and powerful form of communication and connection for people of all ages. As early as the 1970s through the Bulletin Board System (BBS), people were communicating via electronic messages. That system was technically prohibitive and had only the most specialized users. The 1980s had more systems like BBS, but the audience was still very small (Sundheim, 2011). When the World Wide Web made access (relatively) easier, communication became more social, 'Site(s) like Compuserve and Prodigy were the first attempts to engage social media with more mainstream culture, but their early iterations were slow and expensive. As the Internet became more readily available, however, and service became faster, chat systems such as the AOL instant messenger began to take hold' (Sundheim, 2011, para. 5).

Academia in general has been slow to adopt social media, doubting its legitimacy and usefulness and decrying its informal nature, lack of grammar rules, and initial audience. Within the study of leadership, however, social media is a learning tool and acts as an almost real-time case study. There is no doubt that the far reach and continuous access to social media makes it a powerful tool for leadership education.

We see social media as an evolutionary construct. It changes as it is used and new uses are determined, and this creates change in the audience and environment. It is no coincidence that leadership can be viewed much the same way, as it influences change and is changed by its influencers. To that end, we believe it is crucial that social media users exercise greater control and intention over their social media use and identities. If social media is to have a positive impact on education and leadership it must meet the needs of its audience. If we, as leadership educators and scholars, intend to use it for leadership education and research we must be willing to acknowledge its influence on us and our students.

This is especially true in graduate leadership education programs. Ideally, doctoral leadership students direct their own learning by choosing the topics and focus of their research. For these students, the opportunities that social media affords can vastly improve their work, their research, their sense of belonging and their leadership. We feel, however, that social media should primarily be an instrument of connection. Its greatest strength is not its power of dissemination but its capacity for reciprocity.

This chapter looks at three general leadership arenas: the self, groups and teams, and organizations. Within those arenas we attempt to break down the key components of leadership and explore the development and role of a social media identity (SMI) in each case.

Our priority is to help students determine their needs. We believe the way to do that is to help formulate a Social Media Identity in Leadership Education via the SMILE questions. We find it appropriate that in the world of 'like', 'share' and 'retweet', a SMILE has a place. Enhancing and improving work, professional relationships and sense of self through social media is a goal for most doctoral leadership students and practicing leaders. Once students determine their SMI needs, we will focus on the 'how'. The following are crucial for burgeoning social media and leadership identities: how to talk with colleagues, professors and students; how to use skills to strengthen research and teaching; how to take those skills to new or returning work environments; and how to engage with the community and broader social sphere. Through social media, leadership students can provide themselves and others comfort, cohort, communication and connection. Doctoral educators and students are influenced by and are an influencer of social media and leadership studies. The key is to control those influences and maximize their benefits.

The intent is for faculty to use the SMILE as a teaching tool, distributing it to students to complete. Students should answer the SMILE questions at the beginning of their studies and whenever there are significant changes in the groups or organizations in which they have membership. The questions may also be helpful when there is a social media mishap or poor decision made. Contemplating these ideas can help identify what went wrong and offer a means of correction. All questions should be answered thoughtfully, but without attempt to manipulate the responses. Just like social media, students will get out of it what they put in. Honest answers beget honest guidance. Tables 8.1, 8.2 and 8.3 are the three levels

Table 8.1   SMILE assessment of self

Social Media Identity in Leadership Education: Assessment of Self

---

View yourself from within [be gentle, but honest with yourself]
What is my personal identity?
What is my personal message?
What leadership qualities do I see in myself?

View yourself from outside [be honest, but only register constructive thoughts]
What do others believe to be my identity?
What do others believe to be my message?
What leadership qualities do others see in me?
Do others see me as I see myself?
Can I reconcile the difference?
What is my Social Media Identity?
Am I creating a Social Media Identity that reflects learning and is improving?
   [It's not perfect, but is it genuine, honest, and growing?]
What can I do to feed that growth?

Table 8.2   SMILE assessment of groups and teams

Social Media Identity in Leadership Education: Assessment of My Groups & Teams

---

To what group identities do I belong?
What is the message of the groups to which I belong?
Are these messages incongruous?
[Now focus on just one or two groups]
Who is the leadership face of these groups?
What is the leadership aspect of these groups?
Is the group controlling its influence online and the reciprocal influence on the group?
Is there enough participation and commitment that we reflect the group, and the group reflects us?
Even if it is 'just a social group' do we have integrity?
Are we genuine, honest, and growing?
Does it exemplify learning and improving?
Not every statement made by a group reflects exactly the thoughts and attitudes of each member, however are group members comfortable with the group's Social Media Identity?

Table 8.3   SMILE assessment of organizations

Social Media Identity in Leadership Education: Assessment of Organizations
What is the identity of the organization in which I am a member? Who is (are) the leadership identities of this organization? Am I comfortable being represented by them? What is my role in the organization? What does my face-to-face and/or online behavior say about the organization? Am I okay with that message? Are the other members also okay with that message? Is the organization genuine, honest and growing? Does it exemplify learning and improving? Is there enough participation and commitment that we reflect the group, and the group reflects us? Even if it is 'just a social group' do we have integrity? Are we genuine, honest and growing? Not every statement made by a group reflects exactly the thoughts and attitudes of each member; however are group members comfortable with the group's Social Media Identity?

of questions for assessment of self, groups and teams, and organizations respectively.

Faculty can also use the SMILE questionnaires as a part of their own reflective practice as practitioners of leadership, but also (and perhaps more importantly) as a way to frame reflective conversations with their students about the development of their social media use and identity as a piece of their leadership journey. Folding social media into the paradigm of reflective leadership practice is essential as doctoral students are simultaneously crafting their leadership and social media identities. DeRue and Ashford (2010) propose 'that a leadership identity is co-constructed in organizations when individuals claim and grant leader and follower identities in their social interactions' (p. 627). In the case of students developing their own leader identities, the act of reflection, particularly using the SMILE instruments, allows for students to start claiming those leadership identities in ways that make sense for their own emergent development.

Komives et al. (2005) describe 'the process of developing a leadership identity [is] informed by the interaction of developing self through group influences that change[d] one's view of self with others and broadened the view of leadership in the context of the supports of the developmental influences' (p. 606). This is especially the case in social media where interactions and group influences are expanded in breadth and depth. Not only might students be connecting with peers and developing networks within their academic programs, which in and of itself might offer a very different group of people with whom a student might interact, but they are also accessing field experts, researchers and authors who lead their field. Also in the development of these new leadership identities, students will be exposed to and create opportunities for their own professional and personal development in the form of fellowships, grants, teaching or research opportunities, and potential publishing partners and opportunities. All of these serve to engage students in crafting these new identities.

The questionnaire can be used in several ways. Faculty can decide to use the questionnaire in a class as they scaffold SMIs into course content. With students new to the idea of social media as an aspect of their leadership journey, faculty might want them to work on the questions individually and then debrief them as a group. This gives an instructor some idea of where students are as individuals and can help more accurately guide the debrief and future conversations.

In courses where the idea of social media and leadership has already been planted, or when students are establishing social media groups, faculty could switch their technique and have the students answer the questions as a group. This can provide insight into the group's development process. As faculty debrief the group, more insight can be gained into role assignment and norms that might emerge as the group continues to develop. Faculty can use this insight in their own facilitation. Within the online learning context, this could also be used as a discussion board, blog or written assignment.

It could be helpful to do this in a variety of ways. Sitting in a classroom talking about online learning is a good approach. Online discussions (for example, blogs, wikis and forums) create opportunities to put ideas into practice. Faculty and students can model appropriate online conversations and actions. Learning by doing is as important when discussing appropriate online speech as it is in any active or physical skill acquisition – just think of it as digital Dewey.

Outside the classroom, faculty can use the questionnaire to help start conversations with students. As part of the mentoring process, reflective conversations about social media practice are a key component of the student's learning. This questionnaire should be used to jump start conversations, but is by no means a strictly held template. Faculty should feel free to use the questionnaire as a guide and ebb and flow with the students to meet their needs.

In addition to the use with students, faculty can use the questionnaire to help guide their reflective practice with leadership and social media. Again, the questionnaire is not something which must be strictly adhered to, but it is a starting point from which faculty may begin or continue their own reflection on the role social media play in their journey as both faculty member and leadership practitioner.

LEADERSHIP, SOCIAL MEDIA AND THE SELF

Leadership often starts with a study in personal leadership. Good personal leadership begins with asking tough questions: what are your opportunities; what are your challenges; what is your role; and what is your goal? Answering these questions is paramount for successful doctoral leadership studies students, and these questions guide and focus what educators can accomplish with social media. What positive impacts could each individual have and what influence can they exert via their SMI? What is obstructing those impacts? What mistakes have you made or might you make in the future that would deter those positive influences? We will discuss roles in greater depth in the groups and teams section, but it is important to ensure there is a fit between the individual and his or her SMI. People in leadership roles should always be asking what their goal is. Doctoral leadership education students need to have and explore goals beyond their dissertation or graduation. Very often doctoral programs begin with reflective exercises such as visioning or goal setting. For the student, knowing themselves as that student (person) helps them find an appropriate leader self-image. Understanding social media may help operationalize those roles.

Ultimately, this is about the student putting themselves into the world as a leader, exhibiting leadership that is beyond context, and then applying it to their context. There is a need for students to learn to progress from no context to each increasingly understood, focused and specific context, and then on to the next one. This progression is crucial for students, faculty, administrators, and the community at large. As so many students (and faculty) identify in one or more of these roles, we believe that social media can be a powerful vehicle to capitalize on the understanding of self.

A comprehensive walk through of Bennis's (1989) core tenets of personal leadership and developing self-knowledge help the doctoral leadership education student (or anyone) begin to really understand themselves and define their leadership identity. These tenets are:

- you are your own best teacher;
- accept responsibility; blame no one;
- you can learn anything you want to learn;
- true understanding comes from reflecting on your own experience (Bennis, 1989).

This understanding is paramount to establishing a student's SMI. Self-reflection allows a student to know their values and what choices reflect those values. Developing self-knowledge may be step one for personal leadership development and SMI development. By the time a graduate student is at the doctoral level they most likely have a fairly well-defined sense of self. That self, however, is probably being challenged with new and greater roles. The roles of researcher, teacher, cohort member and future leader are all vying for attention and maybe even for social media space. A doctoral leadership education student who is focused on building their SMI with purpose should trust Bennis's (1989) first lesson of personal leadership: you are your own best teacher. Taking it further, that student must understand that to be their own best teacher they need to be aware of what they are teaching to themselves and what they are learning. The first section of the SMILE questionnaire helps students focus on those ideas.

In tandem with being one's own best teacher is the idea that each individual can learn anything (Bennis, 1989). Graduate students who believe that they can learn anything are not preoccupied with the minutiae of any single technology; rather, they focus on process and goals and know that if a new piece of equipment or a new application gains popularity they can learn the steps and master it. Being able to learn anything also applies to leadership. Leadership styles, approaches, the hard work of personal leadership reflection, group and team development, and organization building are all skills that we are all continually learning, relearning and expanding. Students who trust they can learn anything have the confidence to expand their learning into new arenas and to greater heights; they are more likely to share their learning with peers, supervisors and clients. An attitude of learning can come across in the student's SMI. Curiosity and learner confidence, when noticeable in an SMI, convey a person, group or organization that is genuine, open and interested in growth. Leaders do not know everything, but they are willing to learn anything. An SMI that shows an active learner shows someone who can lead.

The reflexive nature of being one's own best teacher and trusting self-learning prowess demands reflection upon experience. The SMILE sparks that reflection, and the reflection informs the developing SMI of the engaged doctoral leadership students. Bennis (1989) reminds us that we must reflect on our experience to understand what we have done and what we choose to do in the future. In many ways the SMI is another type of reflection, a reflection of who the student was and who they are. Continuing to study and develop an SMI is an ongoing process requiring self-reflection upon experiences in face-to-face and cyber life regardless of whether students see these as separate or the same. The key is to tease apart the two perspectives and compare them to each other. For many students these worlds are so tightly interwoven that they do not see them as separate. This is a problem when purposefully developing the SMI. The two worlds are not the same; one has tone, inflection, body language, the possibility of immediate correction, and the sometimes fleeting nature of spoken words and demonstrable actions. The other has fewer and less established clues and indicators of nuance, and it is permanent (or at least virtually permanent). These differences are why an SMI must be intentionally cultivated; these differences are why a comparison between self-image and identity in one needs to be compared to image and identity in the other (McNally and Speak, 2012). Each student must reflect upon the reflection. Is there fidelity between the two? Does your SMI reflect who you are? Would others say it does?

An interesting exercise for faculty and advisors to use with doctoral leadership students relies on case studies of behaviors and how these behaviors are perceived in different environs. It develops the self-reflection muscle by letting students pretend they committed certain actions in a variety of scenarios. The case study can be as simple as two environments – social versus work. It can be as complex as face-to-face (social, organization, business), online (social, organization, business), or hybrid (social organization, business). A matrix like this allows nine or more scenarios and the contrast and comparisons between and among scenarios can tease out how small changes can make a big difference.

The last lesson in developing self-knowledge is to accept responsibility (Bennis, 1989). In the context of an SMI, responsibility really has two meanings. The first is recognizing mistakes that may have been made. These include things that were said or written that were incongruous to the desired SMI. For many academics (new or established) there are many options for 'open' exchanges and pathways to share research and ideas and ways to track and quantify those exchanges, like an author's h-index or an ORCID (Open Researcher and Contributor ID) (Delasalle, 2016). These avenues may be used to build or support an SMI. Responsibility also has a forward-looking interpretation. Everyone has the power and the responsibility to manage and curate an SMI that is self-reflective. All students have the responsibility to have an SMI that is intentional and has integrity and fidelity.

Personal leadership starts with asking the tough questions. The honest answers to those questions guide each student's journey through social media mastery. Having the strength to acknowledge those answers demonstrates their level of leadership acumen.

LEADERSHIP, SOCIAL MEDIA, AND GROUPS AND TEAMS

The connection between social media and group and team leadership seems straightforward. The social and connected nature of social media opens connections and increases activity between and among people in groups. Developing team leadership acumen via social media takes more intention and planning than just tweeting about what the group is doing. Well-directed social media deployment helps to set group tone, expectations and even behavior. Roles and norms are social building blocks for group behavior (Kinicki and Fugate, 2016). A role is a set of behaviors we expect from members of a group in a particular position; group roles are those for groups as a whole (Kinicki and Fugate, 2016). Just as in face-to-face interaction, there is an opportunity in groups and teams for users of social media to set the tone by their words, actions and attitudes.

For students of leadership education, social media can serve as a learning lab and a proving ground. Again, integrity and intentionality are key. Students must be consistent in online behavior; there must be group agreement as to what technologies will be used for what activities or processes. This includes simple decisions, such as all meetings being sent via a calendar app, topics and discussions being on a public forum, and new members all having an organizational profile. While the specific tasks and technologies are not important, the consensus and process of choosing them is. All elements need to move in the same direction, toward the same goal. Each plays a part in reinforcing the group identity and success.

Students are not alone in this process; faculty should be engaged partners. For example, faculty should, in part, be responsible for facilitating the discussions and eventual consensus on technology use. Inclusion of new members in a group is also a job to be started by faculty. With faculty setting the tone for tasks such as these, students come into a situation having some behavioral parameters and templates. Faculty members' roles here are essential to smooth group beginnings. For example, helping a group create norms by which all members will abide and creating opportunities where students might connect (could be icebreakers, could be more in-depth assignments, or setting up of sub-groups or affinity groups which could connect students with more specific interests) are both important pieces of a faculty role in these beginning stages. Staggers et al. (2008) provide further ideas for ways to facilitate teams in online environments.

If roles are what we expect from a group or team, the norms are the building blocks of those roles. Norms are attitudes, opinions and behaviors shared by two or more people that guide behavior (Kinicki and Fugate, 2016). Nowhere is the power of one person within a group to affect that group more apparent than in social media. We have seen countless times when one member of a group can say or do something that is conveyed via social media and it changes how the entire group is perceived (sometimes for the better, and sometimes to its detriment). In this age of prevalent and pervasive social media use, almost everyone's behavior and words are under the microscope. Again the separation between the group and the individual is at times almost indistinguishable. The pressure this puts on those moving into the workforce is great. This pressure may be at its apex for a doctoral student, a student who may have one foot firmly planted in their role as student and one stepping toward a higher profile professional role. How should that mantle of leadership get transferred from one foot to the other? Carefully. With intention and integrity.

An already established (curated or not) SMI does not disappear at each new stage of life. To that end it is never too early or too late to improve an SMI. Here the advantage may go to those who have been active online for a greater proportion of their life. They can 'get in on the ground floor' with professional and research identity aggregators. These online tools give users a platform to share their work. Interestingly these platforms add an air of legitimacy because they are collective and run by an independent (not the individual user's) group. The reality is that these platforms are only as legitimate or independent as the rules of use allow. These platforms are, however, an excellent way to broaden and deepen an SMI, adding points for triangulation and sometimes input and corroboration from others.

Additionally, these students are also navigating this transfer with others who may be at very different ages and stages with a myriad of experiences. A doctoral student (or any higher-ed student) is in a group, a cohort of other students that they did not choose, that may or may not have a shared past, and may not even have a shared future or goals (other than graduation). It is not unreasonable (and might even be wise) for graduate programs to have their cohort members take the group level of the SMILE and use it as a discussion point, a point of commonality, and a jumping off point for determining group roles and norms. Again in this space, faculty advisors' roles cannot be understated.

Intentionality is not only for students. Faculty should be intentionally engaged in the use of social media with their students. Understanding the individuals in a cohort, and by extension how to help the development of group norms, will make the use of social media significantly smoother with an active facilitator. Debriefing in this process is key. Helping students talk through their own role and the roles of others in the use of social media, and how that affects them personally and professionally, can provide vital insight. Students should reflect back to their personal leadership (focuses). How does their sense of self impact and reflect the group identity? How is it influenced by other group members? Communication among group members is essential to build and support the group. Members must agree to be accountable and responsive to one another.

The use of Tuckman and Jensen's stages of group development (1977) and Maples' (1988) extension of the same, can be a useful tool in the online environment. While social media was not a part of the group dynamics scene when the authors developed their stages, it is still a useful tool as students develop groups and group identity, and maximize group potential. Leadership students and faculty should be very familiar with the forming, storming, norming, performing and adjourning model, but may not have thought to apply it in this context.

Social media is about connection. This is essential as we think about group development. As groups are forming (Tuckman and Jensen, 1977), or as new members are joining existing groups, the tenants of group formation should be remembered. Students should be cognizant that as they come together for the first time, some people will be hesitant to be their authentic selves, instead waiting to see how things unfold. Allowing space for everyone to find their own place is key here. For faculty, creating a situation where everyone can become acclimatized is key. Forced participation in groups at this stage is not encouraged. A looser participation where everyone can come and go as they please might be warranted.

As the groups further coalesce, students may find themselves testing their limits and those of their fellow group members. The storming stage (Tuckman and Jensen, 1977) is a particularly key place for intentional faculty facilitation. Positive testing of group parameters is encouraged, but faculty must be on guard to watch for testing which becomes a deterrent to participation and group development. As testing subsides and roles become clear, students will emerge within their groups with new norms (Tuckman and Jensen, 1977). These roles should be developed for and by the group's members. The faculty advisor's job in this setting should be as clarifier, asking questions including: 'Is this a role behind which we can all throw support; what does this role practically provide for our group and why do/ should we follow; and how does this role further our group's purpose?' These clarifying questions can also be used throughout the group's development as a temperature check. No social media group is purposeless, and as the roles develop, the purpose of the group should be always in the forefront of members' minds. This means that as the group emerges from the setting of rules they should be focused on fulfilling their purpose. Faculty at this stage should continue to keep the group engaged toward their purpose.

Finally, as the group runs its course toward adjourning (Tuckman and Jensen, 1977), as all groups do, faculty should be engaged in the guiding of a group toward closure. In some cases this means the smooth transition of some members leaving the group as they conclude their time as students. In other cases, it means closing the group all together in order to create space for other, more appropriate groups, to take their place.

LEADERSHIP, SOCIAL MEDIA AND ORGANIZATIONS

As a doctoral leadership student moves from creating connection in small groups to creating community and connection in larger settings, understanding some foundational principles of leading in larger environs is key. Creativity and empowerment are powerful tools in a leader's toolkit. When these tools are applied to social media use, they can be leveraged to expand one's community and foster connections outside of an insular educational setting network.

Creativity or 'producing new and useful ideas concerning products, services, processes and procedures' (Kinicki and Fugate, 2016, p. 394) should be encouraged within leadership, education, organizations and social media for a variety of reasons. Creativity sparks new solutions to (old) problems, finds new avenues of revenue, and identifies new ways to meet the needs of constituents. One of the needs of our society is the feeling of human connection. The feeling of disconnectedness in an ever more connected society is very real. While the world is seemingly at our fingertips, the feelings of true connectedness may simultaneously feel very elusive. Feelings of isolation may be more likely for some segments of the population; one of these subsets is doctoral students (Ali and Kohun, 2007). Doctoral students often have to focus time and energy on a specific, long-term and independent set of tasks and responsibilities. By default there is less time available for established social connections and little time to make new ones. Ironically even doctoral students in online programs that rely on technology-mediated communication may not be getting enough meaningful communication within their program. Feelings of social isolation are often considered a root cause of attrition in doctoral programs (Ali and Kohun, 2007).

The creative use of social media to expand our connections in new ways is imperative. While doctoral students, and even faculty, may be comfortable in creating connectedness in small group settings, there is a wider world out there to which they can and should become connected. How to do that, however, is an interesting puzzle to solve. Doctoral leadership education advisors and faculty should first create space, literally and figuratively, for students to take calculated risks in their use of social media. We say calculated risks, because while social media may be 'old hat' for some students it could be very new for others.

Further, using social media to expand one's leadership connections and toolkit might be a new notion for many. Encouraging students to take calculated risks to develop their online social media personas is the first step. Some examples of important risks one might take include the searching out of new groups or expanded groups online. Finding the groups is first, joining the groups is second, and participating in the groups is third. Why is this considered a creative tool? By the very nature of searching out new forums, students are able to view leadership in larger contexts, to see content and problems through new lenses, and to connect with new people and expand their world. However, the role of encouragement should not be limited to faculty and advisors. Peer-to-peer support is a catalyst for further growth and development as students navigate these calculated risks.

A second and equally important step is to provide feedback for students in their leadership development/social media presence. It is not enough to simply advise students on what *not to do*; we must encourage them to know what *to do*. It is easy to have a litany of examples for all of the things that one should not do with social media, and one does not need to look far to see the long-reaching ramifications of poor social media choices. However, we must not rely simply on cautionary tales. We must provide guidance based on identified best practices and then allow the space for creativity to flow.

This guidance should take the form of consistent, constructive feedback, but should also include pointing out positive leadership role models in social media (of which there are many). Faculty should not be afraid to do some leg work in identifying positive social media role models from a multitude of leadership backgrounds (for example, education, business, government) to provide the roadmap for students. These role models can and should change regularly as modes of social media change and the needs of students (and society) also change. In other words, do not rely on the same individuals over and over; instead, we must engage in the search for positive role models regularly to always keep up to date with our students and their needs. Important to note, however, is that these roadmaps should be just that: a map. They are not a template, and students should be encouraged to make their presences uniquely their own. In those cases, faculty are encouraged to treat feedback on the use of social media the same way that they would any active, reflective practice. And as with encouraging calculated risks, students should also be encouraged to develop strong peer-to-peer relationships that would be an outlet for this type of feedback.

Doctoral students should also feel (be) empowered by faculty (and their larger educational programs and institutions) to harness the possibilities that full engagement in social media holds. How might we, as faculty, empower students to harness the power of social media as part of their leadership journey? One way to do this would be to encourage self-direction in social media use as pieces of course learning and assessment. Searching out networks, establishing a presence, and crafting those presences specifically related to their leadership journey are all small, incremental steps in developing this tool.

An additional way to help students feel empowered would be to share the reins to the educational program's social media presence. Students could effectively be mentored by faculty as they craft the social media presence for their educational programs. This notion of shared responsibility will create a sense of empowerment for students as they use the knowledge gained in one setting (managing the presence of their educational program) in another (managing their own presence). Ideally, the sense of empowerment will lead to a greater comfort with creativity and a cyclical process begins and perpetuates itself.

Faculty should feel free to explore multiples uses of SMI. While for some it will make more sense to include it in a specific lesson or activity within a larger program, others might find use in weaving it throughout a program to address one or more larger issues. And development and cultivation of SMI should not end with the academic year. Students who are between years or entering into a new professional identity can feel isolated. The SMI and subsequent networks built thereon can be a source of socio-emotional support as students transition between years or out into their newest professional positions.

CONCLUSION

Leadership educators and students need to cultivate fidelity between what and how we deliver content into the social media world and what and how we receive content. It will not be perfect, but it should be genuine and we should expect that level of integrity from what we say and what we read. Demonstrate a persona of openness, kindness and commitment to growth and learning. This is imperative for doctoral leadership education students who may already have an SMI as they mold it into the SMI of a professional, an academic, a citizen and a leader.

Reflective practice is key. If social media use should be intentional, then a foundational piece of that is reflection. How do we use social media? What are we receiving from our participation in social media? What are we contributing to the learning space that social media can be? How is our leadership growing and changing in positive (or negative) ways by what we contribute and what we receive? There is one caveat regarding reflection; because of the constant and almost limitless nature of social media, reflection could become relentless. It is best to establish boundaries on the dissemination, reception, participation and even reflection. Review, reflect, teach, learn, accept and move on.

Faculty members who are advising doctoral leadership education students should be inculcating social media into their advising structures. Even if faculty are not social media users or consumers, their role as conscientious advisors demands that they work with students as they continue to craft and refine their SMI. Class is only one piece of that advising and is a great starting point. Providing real world opportunities for SMI development in individual and group settings is beneficial. Additionally, engaging in discussions outside the classroom throughout a doctoral student's education is invaluable in helping that student craft (and recraft) their identities as needed. Faculty should be intentional about the questions that they ask in order to guide students' thinking towards positive development.

REFERENCES

Ali, A. and F. Kohun (2007). Dealing with social isolation to minimize doctoral attrition: A four stage framework. *International Journal of Doctoral Studies*, **2**, 33–49.

Bennis, W.G. (1989). *On Becoming a Leader.* New York, NY: Basic Books.

Delasalle, J. (2016). Talking to your researchers about the h-index. *Library Connect.* Accessed at https://libraryconnect.elsevier.com/articles/talking-your-researchers-about-h-index.

DeRue, D.S. and S.J. Ashford (2010). Who will lead and who will follow? A social process of leadership identity construction in organizations. *Academy of Management Review*, **35**(4), 627–47.

Kinicki, A. and M. Fugate (2016). *Organizational Behavior: A Practical Problem Solving Approach.* New York, NY: McGraw Hill/Irwin.

Komives, S.R., J.E. Owen, S.D. Longerbeam, F.C. Mainella and L. Osteen (2005). Developing a leadership identity: A grounded theory. *Journal of College Student Development*, **46**(6), 593–611.

Maples, M.F. (1988). Group development: Extending Tuckman's theory. *Journal for Specialists in Group Work*, **13**(1), 17–23.

McNally, D. and K.D. Speak (2012). *Be Your Own Brand: Achieve More of What You Want by Being More of Who You Are.* San Francisco, CA: Barrett-Koehler.

Staggers, J., S. Garcia and E. Nagelhout (2008). Teamwork through team building: Face-to-face to online. *Business Communication Quarterly*, **71**(4), 472–87.

Sundheim, K. (2011). Where they started, the beginning of Facebook and Twitter: A brief history of social media. *Business Insider.* Accessed at http://www.businessinsider.com/a-brief-history-of-social-media-2011-7.

Tuckman, B.W. and M.A.C. Jensen (1977). Stages of small-group development revisited. *Group & Organization Studies*, **2**(4), 419–27.

9. Beating anxiety and building community: best practices for teaching doctoral research methods and statistics online

Leslie Dinauer

In 2007 I was teaching a graduate-level research methods course online that included a quantitative data analysis component. When the time came to discuss the standard normal curve, I presented the usual graphics, including an image much like the one in Figure 9.1.

Unknown to me, this particular class included a student who had been completely blind since birth. She took classes online because technology allowed her to move 'undetected' through the program. She had never disclosed her disability to the university nor requested accommodations. She used a reliable service that recorded all of her textbooks to tape, and a sophisticated screen reader for other content that was made available in the online classroom. Statistics, however, caused her an anxiety she had not felt in her other courses. The normal curve, specifically, completely stymied this straight-A student enough to request a one-on-one appointment and to share her story. In a phone call of tremendous emotion and vulnerability, she let me know that the statistics content overwhelmed her in general, and she could not make sense of the narrative built around the 'area under the curve', specifically.

Our ensuing discussions were enlightening. The student shared general feelings of breathlessness she said she had never felt before. She also explained that she could conceptualize what the curve might look like, and infer how the blank space beneath such a representation was the ubiquitous 'area under the curve'. However, she could not parse the meaning of the words in the textbook or in the lecture enough to generate an understanding of the symmetry of the curve, how it was sliced up by standard deviations and t-values, or how the area represented a probability value. When she reflected on her thoughts and feelings she stated, 'This class is killing me'.

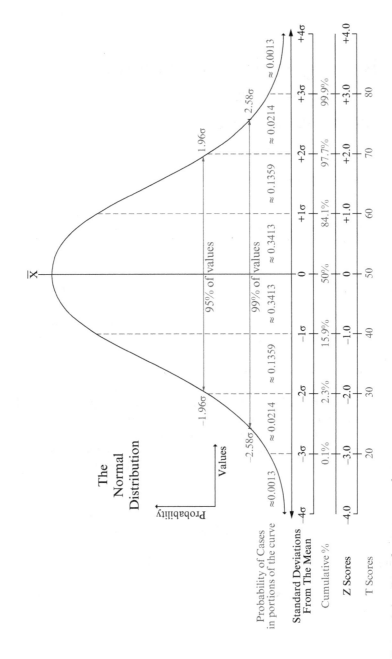

Figure 9.1   Distribution example

A resolution did not come easily. Godfrey and Loots (2015) had not yet shared their personal experiences as blind students – and then professors – of statistics, nor offered their useful guidance. As a relatively new professor, I had not yet dived into the literature on statistics anxiety. Nevertheless, through the magic of Google and several well-placed phone calls I discovered tactile drawing film on which a curve could be drawn which would subsequently be raised so the student could trace it with her fingers. We began a FedEx correspondence, sending raised curves back and forth, and spoke on the phone every week. Once she internalized the visual characteristics and spatial relationships of the curve, we had a common understanding to underpin our discussions; her grasp of statistical concepts snapped into place. Once she trusted me, we had an authentic relationship within which we could address the anxiety, and her self-efficacy also snapped into place.

Resolving this difficulty completely changed how I approached the teaching of statistics online. It made explicit for me the critical importance of both visualization and extremely detailed, careful narrative description in statistical teaching to *all* students. More broadly, however, the experience illuminated some of the dark corners of the online statistics classroom. I gained a better appreciation for the role of each student's individual orientation to the material, to the classroom – both affectively and cognitively – and to me.

This chapter will share some of the insight that emerged from that experience, beginning with a discussion of the need to build a statistics course deliberately within an online doctoral program as opposed to allowing instructors to simply reproduce the face-to-face coursework. Next, statistical anxiety is examined as a fundamental force to be defeated within the classroom, followed by the best practices that emerge from these understandings.

DEVELOPING A STATISTICS CLASS FIT FOR PURPOSE

Best practices within the online statistics classroom begin at the program level where such courses should be built intentionally. Most online doctoral programs in leadership require students to take at least one course in research methodology; the ability to find, use and interpret data critically is a highly desired graduate attribute. Residing as they do in the social sciences, these required methodology courses have been primarily quantitative and have adhered generally to a post-positivist epistemology (Combs and Onwuegbuzie, 2012; Garfield and Ben-Zvi,

2007; Hassad, 2010). Thus, most programs also include a mandatory course in statistics.

Beyond this orientation, however, there is often not much thought given to the strategic development of quantitative research methods and statistics courses. Most of the faculty in online doctoral leadership programs obtained PhDs, and many of them did so in traditional environments. Methodological doctrine – the 'quants' versus the 'quals' – tends to embed itself deep within PhD graduates who, in turn, go out into the academic world and reify their positions (Bernauer et al., 2013; Hassad, 2010). The methods and statistics classes that they develop as professors look very much like the ones they took as students, frequently including: descriptive statistics, probability, probability distributions, sampling distributions, hypothesis tests, analysis of variance, regression, time-series, chi-square, and maybe some non-parametric tests. It is not that those topics are not necessary or useful . . . under the right circumstances.

Doctoral-level research methods training, however, particularly in online programs, should be 'fit for purpose'. That is, the methods taught should be tied to concrete learner outcomes. Of course, programs in general should possess thoughtful curricula in which each course has clear utility to the practitioner-scholars who enroll. But this is especially true for research methods and statistics courses. Learners in these programs frequently cannot see the value of these courses; or, if they understand the general necessity of quantitative research methods in writing a dissertation, they often find specific course content useless and needlessly anxiety provoking: 'I will never, *ever* use a Poisson distribution in my dissertation or my life!' (for example, Bernauer et al., 2013; Llamas and Boza, 2011).

Since doctoral-level learner outcomes are usually related to dissertation work, aligning outcomes to methods training requires a program-level examination of the range of dissertation methodologies being executed, and an inventory of the content required to support students in making progress. It also requires program directors to examine their personal research philosophies and consider the extent to which those personal research worldviews influence student requirements in the program. They need to consider whether the approach to dissertation research should be methodologically driven (often quantitative) or question driven within the program (for example, Onwuegbuzie et al., 2011). Is statistics an end unto itself or a means to an end? One student in Bernauer et al.'s (2013) examination of a doctoral program in educational leadership shared, 'I have a feeling that students are now choosing methodologies first before research questions because methodology is front-loaded into the program. Methodology is perceived as "this is incredibly important" and then all of a sudden the students have to identify a dissertation topic after methodology has been the focus' (p. 184).

The clear articulation of a program's research philosophy, and the dissertations it will support, is an important one as it creates the parameters around acceptable dissertation research. Mixed methods (or mixed research) is a methodological approach that is increasing in prevalence and that offers scholar-practitioners research avenues that many find relevant to their work (Onwuegbuzie et al., 2011). Similarly, in Bernauer et al.'s (2013) study, where students have a broad choice in their dissertation methodology, they have turned away from purely quantitative research for several years. Supporting such approaches, however, may require a wholesale re-imagining and re-orienting of methodological training, particularly in terms of the statistical skills required by students. If the primary purpose of statistics courses in online doctoral programs in leadership is to give students the tools that they may need to conduct original research for their dissertations, then it is logical that a one-size-fits-all course may not fulfill that purpose.

EVERYONE IS ANXIOUS IN THE STATISTICS CLASSROOM

Thirty-five years ago, Kathleen Dillon at Western New England College coined the term 'statisticophobia' to describe the anxiety that she observed in the statistics courses that she taught (Dillon, 1982). Dillon asked her students in the first class 'to complete, anonymously and honestly the following two sentences on a piece of paper:

When I think of taking this course in Statistics, I feel _____.
When I look at this equation:

$$t = \frac{\bar{x} - \mu}{s / \sqrt{n}}$$

I feel _____.' (p. 117).

She reported that the responses were usually fairly consistent, including "'unsure," "nauseous," "panicky," "uneasy," "sick," [and] "worried"' (p. 117). To acknowledge and validate their feelings, she then gave a lecture on statistics anxiety and how to combat it.

Unfortunately, in the years since Dillon shared her observations and her classroom exercise, little has changed. Most programs have not successfully addressed the prevalence of statistics anxiety in their students. This can have a significant negative impact on student satisfaction, performance and retention. For this reason, understanding the components of statistics anxiety is critical to developing best practices in the online statistics classroom.

Statistics anxiety has been defined as 'feelings of anxiety encountered when ... doing statistical analyses; that is gathering, processing and interpreting data' (Cruise et al. 1985, p. 92). It is characterized by both affective and cognitive dimensions including stress, worry, disorganized thoughts, physical discomfort arising from personal attitudes about the worth of statistics, feelings of computational inadequacy, fear of asking for help, and fear of statistics teachers (Onwuegbuzie, 2000; Onwuegbuzie and Wilson, 2003). A complex phenomenon, statistics anxiety is probably related to mathematics anxiety, but it has shown to include additional dimensions (see a discussion of this in Cruise et al., 1985). In fact, Zerbolio (1999) argued that statistics is more related to *verbal* reasoning than to mathematical reasoning, and suggested that success in statistics is linked more strongly to logical reasoning skills than mathematical skills. So, there is something unique about the cognitive demands of a statistics course that causes a great deal of stress in students.

Both program directors and instructors should be concerned about anxiety in their methods and statistics classrooms because student outcomes are significantly affected; statistics anxiety has been shown to be negatively related to performance and student success (Onwuegbuzie and Wilson, 2003). Baloglu and Zelhart (2003) found a negative relationship between statistics anxiety and student achievement, as did Lalonde and Gardner (1993). Zanakis and Valenza (1997) have also demonstrated that the general underlying mathematics anxiety that is often co-morbid with statistics anxiety is a significant detriment to academic success.

To make matters worse, students taking statistics *online* are prone to even higher levels of anxiety, which exacerbates negative outcomes like poor persistence and retention (DeVaney, 2010; Dunn, 2014; Ni, 2013). This is a result of not only discomfort with the statistical content of a course, but also of the asynchronous learning environment in which they must wrestle with little or no access to instant feedback and the increased cognitive load of managing both the learning management software system as well as a statistical analysis program (Collins and Onwuegbuzie, 2007; Hsu et al., 2009). Indeed, Dinauer's (2012) study of doctoral students in a required online statistics course found that every student in the classroom indicated feelings of isolation and anxiety:

I had trouble with this last week on my own and now I am swallowing my pride and asking for help. Is anybody else stuck?

Am I the only one who still gets sweaty palms when looking at statistics?

My statistical knowledge is pretty much null and void. This class is going to be very difficult for me. Does anyone want to form a study group?

I'm having a tough time. . . Any suggestions or help you can provide would be great. I'm out on a limb here. (Dinauer, 2012, p. 105)

These findings were consistent with Collins and Onwuegbuzie's (2007) finding that, 'Many students report higher levels of anxiety in statistics courses than in any other course in their degree programs' (p. 118).

Instructors' behaviors can frequently exacerbate learner anxiety in the online statistics classroom (McGrath et al., 2015). Many online research methods faculty do not have access to (or do not know how to use) technology that allows them to compile graphs or derive formulas dynamically, which in the face-to-face classroom allows students to gain a sense of process, and understand a 'reason why'. In the absence of such explanations, students are forced to follow derivations on the printed page of their textbooks, with no opportunity to ask questions at any step along the way. However, many students do not possess the reading ability to adequately process even those text-based explanations (Collins and Onwuegbuzie, 2007). The notion that instructor interactions are critical to online student success is supported by Sebastianelli and Tamimi (2011), whose findings suggest that online classroom features involving professor–student interaction are the most useful of the virtual classroom. They also argue that conference discussion forums, such as student-to-student communication, are of limited value in learning highly quantitative content.

PRIMARY PRODUCERS OF ANXIETY IN THE ONLINE STATISTICS CLASSROOM

Students learning statistics online face four distinct challenges that magnify the difficulty of the content: unreadable textbooks; the lack of immediate, synchronous feedback; difficulty navigating the Learning Management System (LMS); and trouble learning the statistical data analysis software. Indeed, with respect to the LMS and data analysis software, specifically, Wick et al. (2017) found online statistics students identified technology as a significant hindrance to their learning.

Textbooks

A cottage industry of statistics self-help books has grown up around the pervasive understanding that statistics textbooks are difficult to read. With titles like *Statistics for Dummies* (Rumsey, 2003), *Statistics for People Who (Think They) Hate Statistics* (Salkind, 2007), and *This is the Statistics Handbook Your Professor Doesn't Want You to See* (Deviant, 2014), these books promise to clarify the mathematical jargon found in traditional texts. The perceived difficulty of the textbooks is not imagined. Collins and Onwuegbuzie (2007), for example, demonstrated how reading ability among African American graduate students could diminish their ability to read the texts and, consequently, generate high levels of anxiety. Aside from the general complexity of the content of statistics textbooks, it is also the case that the language and logic around common statistical concepts are difficult for students to comprehend, particularly off the printed page. Kaplan et al. (2009) found lexical ambiguity around students' understanding even of terms that instructors would find fairly straightforward, like *average* and *association*. Such lexical confusion contributes to students' feelings of frustration and anxiety. These conditions support assertions like that of Herrick and Gold (1994), who stated that, 'Choosing an effective statistics textbook can . . . be a difficult task for instructors because the instructors are unlikely to feel "math anxiety," whereas their students may not have had a mathematics course in many years, or otherwise may not feel comfortable with mathematical thinking' (p. 1). This is especially true with professional doctoral students who enroll in online or hybrid doctorates and who are returning after years out of school.

The Challenge of Delayed Feedback

In a face-to-face classroom, students can raise their hands to ask questions, and have them answered, at the instant they arise. They can talk with their classmates before, during and after class to process the material with which they were just engaged. In the online classroom, students cannot ask for immediate clarification of information or material; they frequently must wait 24 hours or longer for an email to be answered or for a discussion post to receive a reply. Dinauer (2012) found this lack of immediate feedback in the online classroom was certainly a disadvantage; on a number of occasions small misunderstandings quickly grew into a source of great stress:

> I'm so confused. I thought we wanted alpha to be .75 or higher, not .05 or less. If I know the average, why do I need to know the mean?

I would like to understand what is the difference between Interquartile range and Interquartile range of data?

Question – is the researcher creating the dummy variable or do they show up in the data somehow? I am not sure I understand this concept at all.

Why is the regression linear? (Dinauer, 2012, p. 106)

Many similar questions arose simply due to either a poor or highly literal reading of the text or lecture material. The effect of waiting in uncertainty seems to increase students' anxiety levels and create a cognitive load that makes the statistics feel that much more difficult. According to Dunn (2014), 'students report that the asynchronous nature of online interactions increases their frustration and sense of isolation' (p. 35). This is consistent with Wick et al.'s (2017) finding that 'For remote students, any technical issues with software were compounded by the fact that no onsite assistance was available to immediately help resolve them' (p. 143) and 'Though question-and-answer sessions were a weekly event, online students were also likely to be concerned with the lack of immediate feedback sent via email by the course instructor. This, at times, caused a delay in completing assignments or moving on in the material because of unanswered questions' (p. 143). Overall, the time lapse of the asynchronous environment is a huge anxiety-producing component that instructors should address and can possibly be reduced through the use of technologies that allow faster and easier access to the instructor.

The Challenge of Mastering the Learning Management System

Students often have difficulty with not only the statistical content of the online course but also its delivery method (Hsu et al., 2009). Depending on where the statistics course falls within the curriculum, and the degree to which various features have been used in previous courses, students frequently encounter difficulty in navigating their workspace: 'Where can I find the syllabus?' 'Where can I find the homework?' 'Where do I post the homework when it's completed?' And, more specifically, 'How can I type equations into the discussion area?' 'How can I make Greek letters in my discussion posts?' Although these tasks are usually fairly easy to do, they increase students' cognitive load when interacting with statistical content. They can increase frustration as well as interfere with learning. Students in Dinauer's (2012) study of doctoral students in an online statistics classroom articulated some of these frustrations:

I had trouble with my password, so that is why I am just now getting started with the course.

> I have been looking around in the classroom and did not see any informa-
> tion on the homework assignments. Can you please tell me where I can find
> them?
> I see that Homework 1 is due this weekend, and I am still unable to find it.
> Has anyone found it? Where is it located? (p. 107)

In a face-to-face classroom, there is no corresponding challenge to learning
the LMS that contributes to the overall sense of anxiety.

The Challenge of Mastering the Statistical Software

Contrary to the assumptions that many people make about them, students
in online doctoral programs frequently are not adept at working with technology in general. Learners are drawn to online programs because they fit
into the complex lives of working adults, not because they like computers
(Henriksen et al., 2014). So opening up the syllabus of a required methods
or statistics class and finding a brief paragraph stating something like
'Students should purchase a 6 month license and download SPSS Statistics
Standard GradPack24 from http://estore.onthehub.com' can be intimidat-
ing and, depending on how the subsequent installation and computation
goes, often quite frustrating.

Compounding such frustration is the fact that students in the online
classroom are quick to interpret the normal learning curve for statistical
software as personal failure, and view that learning curve as evidence of
their own inability to master the content. This, in turn, compounds the
anxiety that they feel in the statistics classroom. Dinauer's (2012) observations supported this notion:

> I'm unable to open the third document that starts with 'public perceptions'. Is
> anyone else having difficulty? If you've already downloaded it to your computer,
> can you please send it to my personal e-mail. I hate this.
> Hello XXX, Did you install SPSS in your computer? You should be able to
> open the file if you had SPSS.
> I tried just to delete that value, but I ended up getting rid of the whole column
> and I can't get it back so I'll never make it.
> With me, it's usually 'user error' so I will try again.
> Thank you Apple, Java and IBM for another job well done. . ... NOT!!! I can't
> make this work!!! I will never catch up!!! (p. 108)

In a face-to-face classroom, of course, there can be similar challenges
with learning a statistical software package. Very often, however, in a
traditional bricks-and-mortar setting students have the opportunity to
visit a computer lab with their instructor and work through statistical
processes together. Or, instructors can use projectors in the classroom to

share a screen, and show students what each point-and-click looks like; they can walk around a classroom to assist students on their laptops. Many online classrooms lack the infrastructure to support a similar learning experience, so the software that is intended to make statistics 'easier' ends up exacerbating its difficulty (Mills and Xu, 2005).

Therefore, the choice of data analysis software is important. Data analysis packages like SPSS can be powerful, but come with steep learning curves and a steep price (Tabachnick and Fidell, 1991). R, which is software for statistical computing and graphics, is free and open-source but it also has a steep learning curve due to the disparate nature of its command packages. Microsoft Excel can be a solution to the learning curve as most doctoral students have had at least some exposure to Excel in the workplace. However, it is not designed as statistical data analysis software and has been shown to have flaws in numerical accuracy, estimation and generating distributions (Mélard, 2014). Additionally, it does not perform more sophisticated statistical analyses often encountered in doctoral dissertation research. So, much like constructing a course that is fit for purpose, programs need to choose statistical software with purpose, considering the specific relevant combination of ease of use, institutional support and long-term student needs (Hulsizer and Woolf, 2009). Then, the rationale for the software choice should be communicated with students. Table 9.1 provides a brief comparison of the most popular data analysis software tools used in online doctoral programs in leadership.

TOP FIVE RECOMMENDATIONS AND BEST PRACTICES FOR TEACHING STATISTICS IN ONLINE DOCTORAL LEADERSHIP PROGRAMS

When the unique challenges of teaching research methods and statistics online to practitioner-scholars in a doctoral leadership program are considered, a set of best practices emerges that should improve the overall learning experience.

1. Develop a Course that is Fit for Purpose

As discussed earlier, the students who tend to enroll in online doctoral programs want to see how each course in their program contributes to their overall degree goals, and will be most successful in data analysis courses that are directly relevant to their dissertation research. Onwuegbuzie et al. (2011) have recommended a purposively designed curriculum that

Table 9.1   Advantages and challenges to consider when choosing statistical calculation software for use in an online doctoral program in leadership

Software	Advantages	Challenges
Microsoft Excel	• Most students already possess Excel on their personal computers; no cost • Most students are familiar with how it works, and are comfortable with it • Most students will see and use Excel in their organizations	• Many statistical computations are clunky or absent • Output is sometimes incomplete with respect to desired tests • Does not manage missing values well • Can be inaccurate
Minitab	• Relatively easy to use • Offers more complete computational options and output than Excel	• Expensive for students to purchase individually • Students will never see it outside of the classroom environment
R	• Free and open-source • Offers more complete computational options and output than Excel • Can handle very large datasets • Visualization capability is excellent • Positioned to be the dominant data analysis software overall in the future (Muenchen, n.d.)	• Relatively steep learning curve in writing scripts and programming • Does not run on Chromebook without using a remote Linux or cloud server
SPSS	• Offers more complete computational options and output than Excel • Variable and value labeling relatively easy • Currently the dominant package in the social sciences, although use is trending downward (Muenchen, n.d.)	• Expensive for students to purchase individually • Moderate-to-steep learning curve

integrates both quantitative and qualitative elements, in alignment with the goals of many contemporary doctoral students. Bernauer et al. (2013) also have addressed the recommendation of fit for purpose when they suggested:

having the individual student's methodological choice influence their personal curriculum [. . .], exposing students to a diversity of epistemologies [. . .], taking a scientifically-based approach to the research process and focusing methodological training on action research projects in order to promote self-reflection in relation to methodological assumptions and choices (p. 176).

Moreover, when research methods course content is well aligned with students' dissertation work, doctoral students in an online program can find themselves at an advantage. The nature of online courses allows not only textbooks and articles to be persistent resources for students, but also entire lectures and classroom discussions. Indeed, students can revisit entire courses. Designing online statistics courses with the foresight that students will return to the content at dissertation time can be a 'win–win' for instructors and students: it helps ensure that course content is focused and relevant when it is first delivered, and also creates a useful methodological resource for students a year or two later, which can alleviate the need for advisors to 'reteach' specific concepts or procedures that may have been forgotten.

2.   Determine Student Preparation for the Course and Address It

Doctoral students come to online leadership programs from diverse master's-level backgrounds and a wide variety of life experiences. Some students may have had significant prior coursework in quantitative research methods and statistics; others may have had none. A number of those with prior coursework may have taken those classes many years ago, having retained little. Both program management and statistics faculty should be aware of the degree of student preparation for required methods courses. And although it is usually not realistic to separate more- and less-prepared students and offer ability-differentiated sections of statistics courses, there are strategies to support the range of students in the program. For example, individual pre-enrollment advising and expectation setting can assist students with identifying supportive resources and putting them into place. Chiesi and Primi (2010) have shown that explicit support and direct interventions aimed at improving cognitive functions (for example, offering lessons in basic mathematical knowledge) as well as non-cognitive factors (for example, exploring and unpacking student attitudes about statistics) can positively affect student performance.

Also, an extra-curricular statistics boot camp can provide a catch-up opportunity for students with no or stale experience with statistics, as well as a normative starting place. It can introduce or review fundamental material like descriptive statistics, probability and distributions without the assessment pressures of the formal classroom, which relieves anxiety and promotes questions. A boot camp is also a good, low stakes environment in which to introduce the data analysis software used in the program, and to provide students with the opportunity to install and learn to operate the software before they need to use the software to complete assignments and meet deadlines. The key here is to set the conditions for student success before the course begins.

3.   Address Attitude and Anxiety Explicitly

Students online tend to suffer alone, at home, in silence; they imagine they are the only learners in the class feeling stricken with anxiety. Therefore, as has been the suggestion for many years (at least as far back as Dillon, 1982) statistics instructors need to acknowledge learners' fears at the beginning of the course and explicitly validate their anxiety. Talking openly about anxiety normalizes it, and illuminates its commonness. Combs and Onwuegbuzie (2012) suggest also discussing the apparent causal link between attitude toward statistics (correlated with anxiety) and statistics achievement (p. 370), to further help students create a cognitive defense against anxiety.

4.   Disentangle Statistical Content, Data Analysis Software, and Learning Management System Challenges

Technical difficulties are one of the most frequent complaints – and sources of anxiety – of students in online statistics courses (Mills and Xu, 2005). Although students naturally view their instructors as the target for their questions about statistical content, they similarly feel that their instructors are not the 'proper' resource for their technical questions since the statistics domain seems so distinct from the software and LMS domains. Instructors should explicitly reassure students that technical issues are normal and to be expected, and then clearly identify the help resources and points of contact for questions around the LMS and data analysis software (Mayne and Wu, 2011). Instructors are well-served to have a technology helper (or two!) in the classroom. This can be a teaching assistant or even a student volunteer. In fact, a student who has recently successfully completed the course is a good choice, as current students find such a volunteer both credible and sympathetic to their difficulties. Additionally, all online statistics classrooms should have a dedicated discussion thread and FAQs for 'Technical Issues'.

Doctoral programs with residencies should consider doing LMS training at the very first residency and statistical software training at a later residency (depending on where the statistics course falls in the curriculum), to capitalize on the benefits of synchronous communication in learning technology.

5.   Actively Cultivate and Promote Opportunities for Social Interaction

Mann (2005) has explained that students learning online may feel 'held back, blocked, inhibited, estranged or isolated from what it is they are learning, and the study practices and learning processes, both individual and social, which are part of their particular learning context' (p. 43). This is because students in the online statistics classroom are on their own. They do not come to class each week, making it more difficult to form connections with both the instructor and other students, and they often fail to ask for help when they need it, for fear of 'looking stupid'. Often, students who need help stop logging into the class and disappear for days or weeks at a time.

To compensate for the loss of the synchronous environment, online statistics courses should be carefully designed to promote frequent learner-to-learner and learner-to-instructor interactions; it is critically important to create a sense of community in the classroom (Dunn, 2014). To do this, Mayne and Wu (2011) suggested a range of effective social presence strategies including: *personal* (not group) welcome emails, personal emails inviting questions from each individual student, active instructor presence in the discussions, and a student-only discussion area that is 'off limits' to the instructor (p. 113). Group projects or problem sets executed via synchronous collaboration tools like Google Hangouts, WebEx and GoToMeeting also serve to keep students directly engaged with and accountable to each other.

CONCLUSION

Overall, teaching statistics to doctoral students online can be a challenge for both instructors and students. The Learning Management System (LMS) technologies required to deliver classes are not usually integrated with statistics computational technologies, and neither of these are considerations of the designers of collaboration technology. It can be difficult for even the most motivated instructors to make the rich learning experiences they can envision for their students accessible across the myriad home machines, operating systems and internet providers.

But there is reason to be hopeful. Technology is trending in the right direction. For example, SoftChalk cloud content creation software allows instructors to produce multimedia course content that can be uploaded (and updated) across multiple LMS platforms with one click. Screen capture capability is moving from the realm of downloaded software like Jing and Screencast-O-Matic, which are operating system dependent, to simple cloud-based browser add-ons like Loom. Moreover, when a screen capture video is combined with a browser-based speech recognition program like Speechnotes, instructors can create transcripts and adhere to the principles of universal design in creating classroom modules easily accessible to all students with just one click. Additionally, advances in the gamification of statistical content promise interactive course content in which students can learn statistics while immersed in a 'real' application, solving meaningful contemporary problems or perhaps while 'standing' next to William Sealy Gosset and observing the shape of the distribution of yeast cell samples.

New technologies have brought online pedagogy a long way from my mailing a raised normal curve to a single student. They are poised to continue to transform statistics education in the years to come.

REFERENCES

Baloglu, M. and P. Zelhart (2003). Statistical anxiety: A detailed review. *Psychology and Education*, **40**, 27–37.

Bernauer, J.A., G. Semich, J.C. Klentzin and E.G. Holdan (2013). Themes of tension surrounding research methodologies education in an accelerated cohort-based doctoral program. *International Journal of Doctoral Studies*, **8**, 173–93.

Chiesi, F. and C. Primi (2010). Cognitive and non-cognitive factors related to students' statistics achievement. *Statistics Education Research Journal*, **9**(1), 6–26.

Collins, K. and A. Onwuegbuzie (2007). I cannot read my statistics textbook: The relationship between reading ability and statistics anxiety. *The Journal of Negro Education*, **76**, 118–29.

Combs, J.P. and A.J. Onwuegbuzie (2012). Relationships among attitudes, coping strategies, and achievement in doctoral-level statistics courses: A mixed research study. *International Journal of Doctoral Studies*, **7**, 349–75.

Cruise, R.J., R.W. Cash and D.L. Bolton (1985). Development and validation of an instrument to measure statistics anxiety. In *Proceedings of the American Statistical Association* (pp. 92–6). Alexandria, VA: American Statistical Association.

DeVaney, T.A. (2010). Anxiety and attitude of graduate students in on-campus vs. online statistics courses. *Journal of Statistics Education*, **18**, 1–15.

Deviant, S. (2014). *This is the Statistics Handbook Your Professor Doesn't Want You to See! So Easy it's Practically Cheating* . . . (4th edn). Accessed at www.statisticshowto.com/practically-cheating-statistics-handbook.

Dillon, K.M. (1982). Statisticophobia. *Teaching of Psychology*, **9**(2), 117.

Dinauer, L. (2012). Students so close yet so far away: A case study and best practices for teaching research methods online. In *Proceedings of the 11th European Conference on Research Methods for Business and Management Studies*, 28–29 June, University of Bolton, pp. 102–109.

Dunn, K.E. (2014). Why wait? The influence of academic self-regulation, intrinsic motivation, and statistics anxiety on procrastination in online statistics. *Innovative Higher Education*, **39**, 33–44.

Garfield, J. and D. Ben-Zvi (2007). How students learn statistics revisited. *International Statistics Review*, **75**(3), 372–96.

Godfrey, A.J. and M.T. Loots (2015). Advice from blind teachers on how to teach statistics to blind students. *Journal of Statistics Education*, **23**(3), 1–28.

Hassad, R.A. (2010). C121: Toward improving the quality of doctoral education: A focus on statistics, research methods, and dissertation supervision. In C. Reading (ed.), *Data and Context in Statistics Education: Towards an Evidence-Based Society. Proceedings of the Eighth International Conference on Teaching Statistics (ICOTS8, July) Ljubljana, Slovenia*. Voorburg, the Netherlands: International Statistical Institute.

Henriksen, D., P. Mishra, C. Greenbow, W. Cain and C. Roseth (2014). A tale of two courses: Innovation in the hybrid/online doctoral program at Michigan State University. *Tech Trends*, **58**(4), 45–53.

Herrick, M.L. and K. Gold (1994). Establishing objective criteria for evaluating statistics texts. Paper presented at the Annual Meeting of the American Educational Research Association, New Orleans, LA, April.

Hsu, M., S. Wang and K. Chiu (2009). Computer attitude, statistics anxiety and self-efficacy on statistical software adoption behavior: An empirical study of online MBA learners. *Computers in Human Behavior*, **25**, 412–20.

Hulsizer, M.R. and L.M. Woolf (2009). *A Guide to Teaching Statistics: Innovations and Best Practices*. Malden, MA: Wiley-Blackwell.

Kaplan, J.J., D.G. Fisher and N.T. Rogness (2009). Lexical ambiguity in statistics: What do students know about the words association, average, confidence, random and spread? *Journal of Statistics Education*, **17**(3).

Lalonde, R. and R. Gardner (1993). Statistics as a second language? A model for predicting performance in psychology students. *Canadian Journal of Behavioral Science*, **25**, 108–25.

Llamas, J.M.C. and A. Boza (2011). Teaching research methods for doctoral students in education: Learning to enquire in the university. *International Journal of Social Research Methodology*, **14**(1), 77–90.

Mann, S. (2005). Alienation in the learning environment: A failure of community? *Studies in Higher Education*, **30**, 43–55.

Mayne, L. and Q. Wu (2011). Creating and measuring social presence in online graduate nursing courses. *Nursing Education Research*, **32**(2), 110–14.

McGrath, A.L., A. Ferns, L. Greiner, K. Wanamaker and S. Brown (2015). Reducing anxiety and increasing self-efficacy within an advanced graduate psychology statistics course. *The Canadian Journal for the Scholarship of Teaching and Learning*, **6**(1), Article 5.

Mélard, G. (2014). On the accuracy of statistical procedures in Microsoft Excel 2010. *Computational Statistics*, **29**(5), 1095–128.

Mills, J.D. and Y. Xu (2005). Statistics at a distance: Technological tools, learning, and design features for today's modern course. *Journal of Educational Technology Systems*, **34**(4), 427–46.

Muenchen, R.A. (n.d.). The popularity of data science software. *R4stats.com*. Accessed at http://r4stats.com/articles/popularity/.

Ni, A.Y. (2013). Comparing the effectiveness of classroom and online learning: Teaching research methods. *Journal of Public Affairs Education*, **19**(2), 199–215.

Onwuegbuzie, A. (2000). Statistics anxiety and the role of self-perceptions. *Journal of Educational Research*, **93**, 323–30.

Onwuegbuzie, A.J. and V.A. Wilson (2003). Statistics anxiety: Nature, etiology, antecedents, effects, and treatments – A comprehensive review of the literature. *Teaching in Higher Education*, **8**, 195–209.

Onwuegbuzie, A.J., R.K. Frels, N. Leech and Collins, K.M.T. (2011). A mixed research study of pedagogical approaches and student learning in doctoral-level mixed research courses. *International Journal of Multiple Research Approaches*, **5**(2), 169–99.

Rumsey, D. (2003). *Statistics for Dummies*. Hoboken, NJ: Wiley.

Salkind, N.J. (2007). *Statistics for People Who (Think They) Hate Statistics: The Excel Edition*. Thousand Oaks, CA: Sage.

Sebastianelli, R. and N. Tamimi (2011). Business statistics and management science online: Teaching strategies and assessment of student learning. *Journal of Education for Business*, **86**(6), 317–25.

Tabachnick, B.G. and L.S. Fidell (1991). Software for advanced ANOVA courses: A survey. *Behavior Research Methods, Instruments, & Computers*, **23**, 208–11.

Wick, J.A., H-W. Yeh and B.J. Gajewski (2017). A Bayesian analysis of synchronous distance learning versus matched traditional control in graduate biostatistics courses. *The American Statistician*, **71**(2), 137–44.

Zanakis, S. and E. Valenza (1997). Student anxiety and attitudes in business statistics. *Journal of Education for Business*, **73**(1), 10–16.

Zerbolio, D. (1999). A bag of tricks for teaching about sampling distributions. In M. Ware and C. Brewer (eds), *Handbook for Teaching Statistics and Research Methods*. 2nd edn (pp. 207–209). Mahwah, NJ: Lawrence Erlbaum Associates.

10. Teaching leadership research courses online at the doctoral level: why we do it and how it works

Jennifer Moss Breen and Jim Martin

There is no question the world needs good leaders. In today's complex economic, social and technological environment, leaders are needed who can create and deliver on pro-social goals using evidence, rather than opinion, to shape decisions. Many leaders are seeking a terminal degree that can help them acquire these critical thinking skills, as well as to advance their career (Pedersen, 2016). Similarly, employers are seeking individuals with critical thinking skills that can use research and knowledge building to give them a competitive edge. Many mid- to late-career professionals seek the doctoral degree to establish themselves in a second career or to be able to effectively 'give back' to society through teaching, service, consulting or research. The traditional Master's degree once afforded these opportunities; doctoral students are looking for new opportunities that the Master's degree may no longer provide.

Today's doctoral students tend to take one of two distinct paths. The first, the traditional, is to leave full-time work and work part-time as a graduate assistant while enrolled full-time within the university. Doctoral students pursuing this path are often seeking full-time scholarly work and a traditional academic career path upon graduation. The second path, the less traditional but increasingly in demand option, is the student who works full-time while pursuing their doctoral degree part-time. On this path, students must balance full-time careers with part-time doctoral coursework and research (Blessinger and Stockley, 2016).

The non-traditional path to a doctoral degree is thought to be in response to several factors, including the inability for students to leave full-time work and fund their schooling while pursuing their doctoral degree, limited availability of graduate assistantships, and the students' need for programs that are flexible both programmatically and in terms of providing for learning approaches that are accessible for working students. Additionally, many doctoral students are sponsored by their workplace as an employee development benefit and as a way to enhance the organiza-tion's human capital. A stronger, more theoretical rationale, however, emanates from the work of the Carnegie Foundation (Boyer, 1990), which challenged traditional university structure by compelling faculty not only to teach students, but also to learn from them through a shared learning community. The Boyer model encourages rich dialogue, context-based learning and instructor-facilitated courses that not only inform practice, but also draw from practice to inform research. Boyer contends that teachers can become much more than the 'sage on the stage' who directs knowledge toward the learner. Rather, teachers are facilitators who toler-ate ambiguity, acknowledge that they do not have all the answers, and ask students to bring their work-based context to the classroom.

The thought processes articulated by Boyer create enthusiasm in some faculty and terror in others. Boyer signals the need for universities and colleges to ask faculty to change, which is never easy. But, with the addi-tion of the Carnegie Foundation's work, universities and colleges could remember their call: to teach students whenever, however and wherever was best for the student. Thus, not only did universities consider adapting the traditional classroom with the new technologies becoming available in the early 1980s and 1990s, but online education became a viable option for delivering meaningful educational courses and entire programs online (Harasim, 2000).

With the emerging boom of online education, traditionalists became nervous, thinking that the value and outcomes of an online course or program could never equate with those of the traditional classroom. Early adopters included corporate universities and for-profit educational institu-tions that more easily acquired and embedded technology to quickly create online programs that were highly profitable. Students flocked to these programs because they could access education whenever, wherever, for the first time. Traditional universities lagged in the online learning market primarily because of their complex infrastructure, lack of resources, and internal disagreement about the value of online learning.

Today, the thinking around online education has shifted as educators and universities understand both the educational value, but also the fiscal value of offering courses to students across the globe (Berge and Donaldson, 2008). Now, learning can occur both synchronously and asynchronously with students across sectors, job roles and international boundaries, creating a rich learning environment that is not always avail-able in more traditional settings.

Still, online learning is not without its challenges. Attending to student engagement, teacher preparation and support, and program design is essen-tial (Bowers and Kumar, 2017; Heafner and Petty, 2016). Furthermore, while Boyer's model presents an ideal philosophical approach for online learners, such strategies must be balanced by the need to provide students with a rigorous academic experience. As doctoral educators, we have hurdled many of these barriers to learning, and through our lessons, we have adapted our policies and practices, curriculum and staffing. Like many other hybrid doctoral programs, our program is always a work in progress as we balance andragogy, academic rigor and practical administrative considerations.

This chapter shares practices, challenges and ideas concerning teaching leadership online at the doctoral level; specifically, we address the process of revising and implementing a series of reforms to an important element in the teaching of critical thinking skills: our online research courses. We also discuss how we ensure that students get the same experience across multiple sections of a course – and that full-time and adjunct faculty who teach our research courses are on the same page in terms of academic expectations. This chapter offers a broad overview of online teaching and provides practical, hands-on tips for those new to teaching in the online environment.

Our online doctoral program grew from a 2009 university initiative designed to enhance and encourage intra-professional and interdisciplinary programs at the university. The university created a task force of faculty experts that created the program's initial learning outcomes, crafted course syllabi and established the program in 2010. The first cohorts began the program in January of 2011; our program now has over 300 active students and over 150 graduates. Creighton views the success of this program as a function of its 100 percent online and short residency format, which allows the university to draw students from across the country and the globe.

THE BENEFITS OF AN ONLINE DOCTORAL-LEVEL LEADERSHIP COURSE

A unique challenge when teaching leadership and research courses at the doctoral level is embracing the varied levels of research, writing, applied leadership and technological experience that our students bring with them to the courses. Because our students are studying leadership, we emphasize leadership theory throughout the program as would be expected. A differentiation between online and in-class leadership and research courses, however, is that the online environment serves as an excellent leveling tool that can help instructors guide students and help them to meet their own individual learning needs. For example, students may be encouraged to interpret an assignment through the lens of their own organizational challenges. Faculty have more opportunities to provide concise, individual feedback to students on a weekly basis based upon student-written discussion board responses and papers. The online environment also balances class participation as both introverts and extroverts receive ample attention from the instructor, alleviating a common problem in the traditional classroom.

Throughout the doctoral online learning environment, we expect students to behave as leaders in both theory and practice, and we require weekly reflections (Ballantyne and Packer, 1995), or meta-cognition, that encourage the student to think about their own thinking concerning leadership and research. This is an important outcome of the online learning environment as students reflect both individually and with others, and it encourages a tolerance of ambiguity, problem solving, systems thinking, and understanding of multiple epistemological lenses. When comparing leadership programs at the doctoral level as opposed to the master's level, these doctoral-level skills stand out as those that support the creation of a leader who can work across disciplines effectively, apply leadership concepts in their context, embrace the differing stakeholders' perspectives, pace changes such that the system can adapt, and discern their own leadership strengths and weaknesses.

ADAPTING AN ONLINE DOCTORAL-LEVEL RESEARCH COURSE

Since the beginning of the EdD program, continuous improvement and refinement have been emphasized. During the early years, we revised courses at times, but eventually engaged in a larger remapping of our curriculum after a more comprehensive review. This effort was made in response to the trials our students faced when conducting dissertation research, writing, and quantitative and qualitative analysis. Teaching research design and methodology online is a challenge, though the online format provides many advantages. In the online environment, students have the luxury of time to review faculty videos, readings and assignments. They also have the benefit of a cohort of peers with varying degrees of expertise in research topics. The interdisciplinary nature of the program is another benefit of online as students can witness first-hand the differing research paradigms held by their peers.

The research curriculum remapping process was a step-by-step process that encompassed an entire summer and was initiated by deciding exactly which research skills our students needed to complete the dissertation successfully. We drew from a listing of research skills from a collection of research texts and prioritized the skills required for our students. Our query resulted in no less than 25 research skills including philosophical research perspectives, research design, quantitative and qualitative analysis methods, validity, reliability, research ethics, disseminating research findings, integrating research with social change activity, and professional writing. Once we identified what our students needed to know, we mapped research courses such that each of the topics could be introduced, reinforced and mastered. Notably, other doctoral programs, particular ones that focus on adult learners and an interdisciplinary approach, have engaged in similar exercises (Haywood et al., 2016; Ford et al., 2016).

Results of this remapping have been positive. We are beginning to see a dramatic improvement in the quality of dissertations and the timeliness of defending the dissertation, an important consideration for working doctoral students. Of course, graduate students often struggle with writing, initiating and leading their own analyses, a problem noted by many scholars working to reform graduate programs around the world (Lee and Dansby, 2012; Blessinger and Stockley, 2016). Furthermore, communication between students and dissertation committee members, and adherence to rigorous standards and expectations are important. Because adjunct faculty are often asked to chair or participate in dissertation committees, we invest time and effort to communicate with and support them. This accomplishes two purposes: first, it allows them to teach our students more effectively. Second, it creates a sense of community for the adjuncts and our core faculty, resulting in a better flow of ideas. We discuss this further in a later section detailing these efforts.

After completing the curriculum mapping process for our online research courses outlined in the previous section, the team then created new courses and extensively revised others. Here, we share the process of revising, building, teaching and managing one such course, an introductory graduate level research class. We discuss how the course was designed, the nature of the assignments and how they relate to student efforts to research leadership, the process used to build the online master version of the course, and how we coordinate teaching the course across multiple sections. Finally, we present a discussion of how improvements are made to the course from term to term.

After finishing the mapping process, we had a list of courses that required creation or revision and a list of research concepts that we wanted each course to introduce and reinforce. We have six focused research courses; these are presented below in the order students take them:

- Research Design and Professional Inquiry: an introductory, graduate-level research fundamentals course.

- A Literature Review and Ethics in Research Course: how to find, read, engage with, and use scholarly literature as well as sections on the ethical conduct of research.
- Research, Data Collection and Analysis: the general procedures used to conduct quantitative and qualitative research.
- Two research methods electives, each focused on qualitative or quantitative methods. These two courses are specifically focused on the practice of conducting research using either approach.
- A Proposal Construction Course: leads students through the process of developing a well-honed draft of the first three chapters of their dissertations.

As the first course in our research sequence, we viewed Research Design and Professional Inquiry as a leveling course intended to bring our students to a standardized level of knowledge. This was a challenge. Our program is interdisciplinary in nature; we have students from healthcare, business, federal, state and local government, the armed services, higher education, K-12 education, and other disparate fields. Given this variance, and considering that our students come from a variety of educational backgrounds, we could not assume that any of them had been exposed to social science research methods.

Research Concepts

The mapping process revealed the general tools and concepts that we want our students to possess as serious doctoral researchers. For our Research Design and Professional Inquiry course, we identified these general concepts:

- deductive and inductive reasoning;
- a sense of what theories are and how they are used in research;
- the skeptical nature of scientific inquiry;
- how to identify a practical topic;
- how to craft a research question;
- how to identify a population, a unit of analysis, and a sample;
- how to craft hypotheses;
- the nature of validity and bias;
- a sense of ethics in research;
- how to find and read research articles;
- the general steps in the scientific method within a social science context;
- a general sense of research designs and how they are used;
- a general sense of methodological choices.

Finding a Text Book

The next step involved finding an appropriate text. This was more challenging than one might think. We wanted a non-field-specific research concepts text book for a graduate student audience, written for an interdisciplinary audience. There are many fine research texts for specific fields. Yet, these texts, while useful to political scientists, psychologists or scholars of the business world, are less than accessible to a diverse student body. We ordered perhaps 15–20 different research methods text books for review. After a few weeks of parsing these books as a team, we identified Babbie's (2014) *The Basics of Social Research* as most useful to our students. We also identified scholarly articles that focused on a variety of research-oriented topics, reinforcing concepts outlined in the text.

The Creation of a Syllabus

In our program we use a template for the creation of revision of all syllabi. The template is one element to ensure that students have the same experience regardless of when they take a course or whom their instructor may be. The template is regularly updated to ensure that policy elements required by our program, our department and our university are present and accounted for. The template also incorporates our programs' learning outcomes, and, within the syllabus for a course, the learning outcome focus of the course. Starting from this template, we crafted a flow of readings, supplemental articles, and other required and recommended materials for the eight-week course.

It is important to recall that our program is online and that courses are eight weeks as opposed to a traditional 15- or 16-week semester. Because our students work full-time, we know that the time required to work on class assignments would be difficult for them to fit in as we expect students to spend about twenty hours each week working on coursework. Therefore, we adapted the traditional full semester by dividing it into two eight-week terms. By doing this, we require students to take only one course at a time, or two per semester, which allows them to focus fully on the content one course at a time (Smith, 2009).

Many students ask to take more than the required number of courses, and we strongly discourage this practice and reinforce to them the notion of embracing and pacing their learning. A common retort is that 'this is a marathon, not a sprint'. Many students have not experienced the higher order thinking required at doctoral level, and often push back as they want to complete the program more quickly. Time and time again we find that if we allow students to double up, they inevitably fall behind in one course or the other.

Assignments

Discussion and Writing Requirements. *(Instructor may modify these as the course proceeds.)*

Discussion Board Assignments
Discussion board exercises are featured in weeks 1, 3, 5, 6, and 7, of the course. These exercises will present opportunities for critical thinking and analysis during the course. Initial posts should use proper English, correct grammar, and employ scholarly evidence and critical thinking. **Initial posts are due on Thursday evenings of the course weeks in which they are due by 11:55 pm CT. Replies to at least two other students' initial posts are due no later Sunday, the last day of the course week in which they are due, by 11:55 pm CT. <u>Early replies (on Fridays or Saturdays) are strongly encouraged.</u>**

Figure 10.1   Expectations and timing for discussion board assignments

Because of the accelerated and focused pace of the eight-week course, clear instructions and discussions of expectations within each course are, in our experience, exceptionally important. Online students need to know what they are supposed to do and when they are expected to do it. This requires a more stringent approach to schedules. For example, we have a standardized expectation for assignment schedules during the flow of a course: lesson weeks start on Sundays and close on Sundays; discussion board posts, usually requiring students to craft a 3–5 paragraph response to a prompt, are due Thursdays by 11:55 pm, while interactive discussions (discussion board replies, for instance) are due no later than Sundays at 11:55 pm. We strongly encourage students to engage with interactive replies promptly, as engagement between students helps reduce the isolation that can occur in online settings (Bolliger and Inan, 2012; Vora and Kinney, 2014). We provide firm guidance on the nature and schedules for other sorts of assignments. Figure 10.1 presents a view of the language used to convey these within the syllabus for the course.

In the Research Design and Professional Inquiry course, we present three assignment types: discussion board posts and replies, short papers, and a more substantial Research Report due at the end of the course. Finally, we also present two views of the schedule: a detailed view and a summary view at the end of the syllabus as well. Figure 10.2 presents the detailed view of the first two weeks of the course.

This view of the first two weeks of the course provides students with the focused concepts for each week, the text book and articles presented as required reading (note that other supplemental materials can be added by instructors) and details on the type of assignment that is due and when the students must complete their work.

Note that specific details on exactly what students must do in the course assignments are not presented in the syllabus for Research Design and Professional Inquiry (or in most of our courses). Furthermore, we do not include rubrics either. Instead, these are contained within the online

ILD 812: SCHEDULE/ASSIGNMENTS (Note that other readings & resources are present in each module)			
Week	**Topics**	**Textbook Readings**	**Assignments: Discussion/Written Work**
Week 1	An introduction to social science research; paradigms and theories; reading and writing in the social sciences.	**Babbie 1-59; 447-471 Chapters 1, 2, 15**	**Discussion Board Exercise** *(Initial post due Thursday by 11:55 pm CT; replies due Sunday by 11:55 pm CT)*
Week 2	The ethics of research; research design & measurement principles.	**Babbie 60-158 Chapters 3, 4 and 5**	**Week 2 Short Written Assignment** *(Due Sunday by 11:55 pm CT)*

Figure 10.2   Detailed view of partial course schedule

master course shells (a feature of our approach discussed later). We want our syllabi to be short, to the point, and to present important strategic guidance on the course. We also want to encourage students to log into the course itself, thus encouraging them to engage with the real work of the course.

Another challenge associated with the accelerated, online learning environment is the necessity for both students and faculty to adhere to stringent timelines and due dates. For instance, because students write a lengthy discussion board post as well as a final paper, pressure is created for the instructor to provide feedback and the student to attend to that feedback, and do so within a week's timeframe. In the traditional class environment, students often submit a final paper after 16 weeks, allowing more time to develop their ideas, craft and edit their paper. In the online environment, however, we do not have this luxury. The learning is focused, quick and demanding. We continue to explore this problem and have considered the idea of 'chunking' the eight-week term into four separate modules that allow students and faculty to collaborate for a longer, two-week period as opposed to a one-week period.

Online courses are often a moving target that requires creative facilitation. Salmon (2004) discusses the concept of e-moderating, which resonates with our team as it encourages instructors to use video, web conferencing sessions (for example, WebEx), creative prompts, and real-time content to bring life to the class. Feedback can also be offered through phone meetings, video, or done individually and in group settings.

LEADERSHIP AND RESEARCH ASSIGNMENTS

Crafting assignments within an online interdisciplinary program presents interesting differences from approaches used to create learning exercises for an online field-specific or face-to-face course. Interaction with faculty members, as well as encouraging student-to-student interaction, is an important factor in building a sense of community and enhances student learning (Rovai, 2002; Baturay, 2011). Given that our students are seeking to apply what they learn to their own fields, assignments are designed, when possible, to allow students to bring their own leadership context and experience to bear. At the same time, assignments cannot be so student-oriented as to prevent instructors from being able to easily pick up the thread of the logic and application of the course materials and concepts to the topic at hand. These are also doctoral-level courses – mere recitation is not an option. We want our students to be critical consumers of the theories and research approaches required to study leadership, and this small group approach facilitates this (Ford et al., 2016; Mendenhall and Johnson, 2010).

Below is an example of a typical discussion board assignment that helps students focus on concepts and theories. This assignment encourages students to engage with the readings and resources, to critically consider them, and to apply these concepts within their own leadership-oriented field. It is also important to note that the instructions on content and the timing of the post and the required replies are presented here as well, reiterating the instructions presented in the syllabus – this is a common theme within our approach that we will return to later. Figure 10.3 presents an example of this sort of strategy in action.

The second type of assignment in the Research Design and Professional Inquiry course is the Short Written Assignment. These short papers are intended to push students to get into the weeds with the variety of research concepts and tools the course provides. They address topics of greater depth and breadth than possible within a discussion board context, setting a higher bar for students in terms of showing that they know how scholars use these tools. Figure 10.4 presents a view of one of these assignments.

This assignment encourages students to express their knowledge of concepts and materials that they engaged with that week, but also requires them to apply them to their own leadership experience.

Finally, the Research Design and Professional Inquiry course requires students to write a larger Research Report due at the end of the course. In this case, the assignment presents a variety of scenarios that students may choose to address within their papers. Figure 10.5 presents an abbreviated

Assignment #1: Discussion Board Exercise

After a careful consideration of the readings for the week, answer the question posed on the discussion board in an initial post of 2-3 paragraphs. This initial post is due **by Thursday by 11:55 pm CT.** As soon as it is feasible, complete **meaningful replies to two of your fellow students' initial posts.** Your replies are due <u>by Sunday at 11:55pm CT</u>, but **early replies are expected.** Your instructor may also comment on your initial post – keep an eye out for these comments as they are sure to be useful to your growth as a researcher.

Question: *Consider one of the theories discussed **in our readings** and identify it. How does it work? If people tend to act the way that the theory predicts, what might they do? Apply it to your own field of interest – consider how it might help you explain a problem or phenomenon important to you.*

Figure 10.3   A discussion board assignment

Using the Library site, **find a scholarly, peer reviewed, empirical research article (either qualitative or quantitative)** that deals with an aspect of leadership that interests you. In your paper, **briefly summarize the topic and findings of this article (1-2 paragraphs _maximum_).**

After reading this article, **create a single, simple research question** for a research study that would either address some aspect of this study that you believe wasn't fully addressed OR would build upon the results of the study. From this research question, **generate a single hypothesis that identifies a cause and effect relationship.**

Finally, discuss **both the concepts (conceptualization) and operationalization of the dependent and independent variables** inherent in your hypothesis.

*This paper should present a title page, abstract, body of <u>no more than 3 pages</u>, and a list of references (in accordance with APA requirements) and should cite any resource you use.**

This paper is due by Sunday at 11:55 pm CT.

Figure 10.4   Short written assignment

view of this assignment; be assured that the full assignment presents details on the format, stylistic requirements and deadlines. This final assignment is cumulative in nature. It requires the students to use and apply the concepts and tools they have learned about social science research throughout the course within a leadership context.

In sum, these assignments incorporate the concepts of social science research, encourage the application of these tools rather than the recitation of definitions, and approach the subjects from an applied leadership perspective. Additionally, the discussion board assignments encourage engagement between students. Finally, detailed directions on the format and deadlines are reiterated for each assignment, which is especially valuable to working professional students who do not have instant face-to-face access to their instructor when they may be completing assignments in other countries or late at night.

Week 8 Research Report
Choose ONE of the following puzzles as the subject of your paper:

Puzzle #1: *You are the provost of a medium sized liberal arts college. Your analysts have noticed that veterans attending your college tend to graduate at lower rates than the general population of college students. Moreover, this problem appears to be a relatively new phenomenon – graduation rates for veterans used to be considerably higher.*
OR...
Puzzle #2: *You are the mayor of a small city. Your legal team has noted that lawsuits by city employees (for a variety of issues) have increased dramatically during the past few years, placing a financial burden on the city budget, generating bad publicity and endangering morale among employees.*

Assignment Content Requirements:

- A title page with an interesting title that reflects the puzzle you've selected
- A properly formatted abstract with the content one typically sees in an abstract (given the nature of the assignment).
- Briefly, in a page or less, introduce the nature of the problem and some logical explanations for potential influences (causes). A few cites to back these contentions up would be nice, but aren't strictly necessary – if they are logical, I'll be satisfied. Do not overshare on the problem.
- After that section, share a single, properly formatted research question.
- Share your unit of analysis.
- Share your population and a realistic sample.
- Share three (3) distinct hypotheses – each with a cause and an effect. Provide a brief discussion of the logic behind these hypotheses.
- Describe the dependent variable AND how you might measure it.

Figure 10.5   Research report assignment

BUILDING THE COURSE MASTER

Once the syllabus and lessons for the course were completed and approved after a review by our Curriculum Review committee, the course itself could be built. This took place within the context of Blueline™, our university-specific Learning Management System (LMS). Our university uses Canvas™, a typical LMS with features familiar to any online instructor. Before sharing details on how this course was built, a discussion of systems and organizational approaches to course management is in order.

Our program has around forty courses (including electives). Courses are digitally stored in Course Masters, the repository for the fundamental elements of the course from term to term. Specific individuals are given the responsibility for the management of courses; we refer to these instructors (all of whom are faculty with our program) as

Course Directors. Course directors are responsible for building and implementing changes to course masters and are responsible for working with faculty members who may teach a course in any term. They provide guidance, instruction and assistance to these faculty who are frequently adjunct faculty residing in a variety of locales. While course directors may teach a section of a course they direct, it is often the case that they may not. In the case of the Research Design and Professional Inquiry Course, the course director is almost always an instructor when the course is offered – but given the fact that it is a required course, there are almost always two or three additional sections, each taught by another faculty member. Communication between the course director and the instructors (and between the instructors) is encouraged, a point we will return to later. A sense of these relationships is captured in Figure 10.6.

To return to the original point of this discussion, the course director is tasked with building the course master for the Research Design and Professional Inquiry course within our LMS. The basic architecture for our courses includes a variety of modules. The first is a Getting Started module; the others are modules for each specific weekly lesson. There

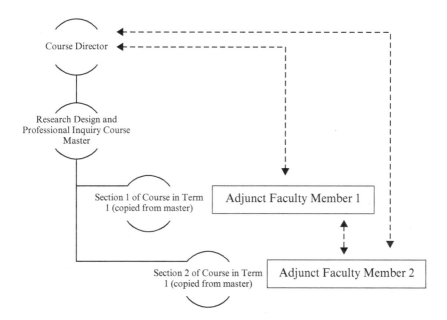

Figure 10.6   Course masters, course sections, course directors and course instructors

Figure 10.7   The Getting Started module in the Research Design course

are also links to resources and navigational tools for students common to online courses. The Getting Started module is worth exploring further. Figure 10.7 presents a view of the sections of that module.

The folders in this module are straightforward. The Rubrics folder is worth a detailed look. This provides general rubrics for the three assignment types in the course. While these are simply Microsoft Word documents, they form the basis for interactive rubrics within the course used to evaluate and grade assignments – the results of which are visible to students. Table 10.1 and Figure 10.8 present a view of one such rubric, its weighting scheme, as well as the interactive tool that is used to grade that assignment. The concepts in the rubric and the weighting scheme evaluate the students' ability to follow the instructions, use the course materials, employ critical thinking, and finally, grammar and adherence to, in our case, the style rules of APA.

These rubrics (detailed in Table 10.1 and Figure 10.8) are a pedagogical and technological advance in our program. These tools, while tedious to construct due to the variations in both assignment types as well as in their point values, provide a time saving and clear grading tool for faculty members (Wyss et al., 2014). These also provide students with a solid sense of how they will be evaluated, as well as feedback. In our program, these have proven popular among students and faculty and have benefits in assessment (Wyss et al., 2014) and ultimately for improvement and accreditation (Aggarwal and Lynn, 2012). We have also shared them with other programs at our university. Those interested in creating such rubrics might visit the excellent Canvas Community site (https://community.canvaslms.com/docs/DOC-10460) for more information.

Next, we include a Course Materials module, pictured in Figure 10.9. Note the 'writing guides' section; here, students can review a standardized

Table 10.1 Written paper rubric (used for short papers and the research report)

Description

A: Excellent to very good performance. Follows assignment instructions effectively. Provides useful supporting evidence that fits with the project and applies course materials successfully. Generates productive, insightful interpretations of the project at hand. Grammar is superlative and citations are presented effectively. Follows APA conventions.

B: Good to Average performance. Responds thoughtfully to assignment requirements. Demonstrates critical analytical inquiry into evidence and applies course materials but may miss some elements or opportunities. Grammar and citations executed properly but may display minor inconsistencies. Follows APA conventions but may present minor inconsistencies.

C: Below average performance. Demonstrates minimal or inconsistent responsiveness to assignment requirements. Summarizes evidence and presents course content but does not analyze or apply meaning. Grammar and citations may be haphazard. Inconsistent use of APA conventions.

F: Poor performance. Does not follow assignment requirements. Demonstrates poor ordering or organization of ideas, inaccurate application of evidence and course materials. Grammar is poor, citations may be inconsistent or lacking. Does not follow APA conventions.

Criteria	Ratings					Pts
Structure and Format 10% of Grade	Excellent 10.0 pts	Very Good 9.4 pts	Average 8.8 pts	Poor 7.7 pts	Not Present 0.0 pts	10.0 pts
Synthesis and Application of Evidence 25% of Grade	Excellent 25.0 pts	Very Good 23.5 pts	Average 22.0 pts	Poor 19.25 pts	Not Present 0.0 pts	25.0 pts
Synthesis and Application of Course Materials 25% of Grade	Excellent 25.0 pts	Very Good 23.5 pts	Average 22.0 pts	Poor 19.25 pts	Not Present 0.0 pts	25.0 pts
Critical Thinking and Analysis 25% of Grade	Excellent 25.0 pts	Very Good 23.5 pts	Average 22.0 pts	Poor 19.25 pts	Not Present 0.0 pts	25.0 pts
Grammar and APA Skills 15% of Grade	Excellent 15.0 pts	Very Good 14.1 pts	Average 13.2 pts	Poor 11.55 pts	Not Present 0.0 pts	15.0 pts
					Total Points: 100.0	

Figure 10.8 Interactive grading rubrics with concepts and weighting scheme

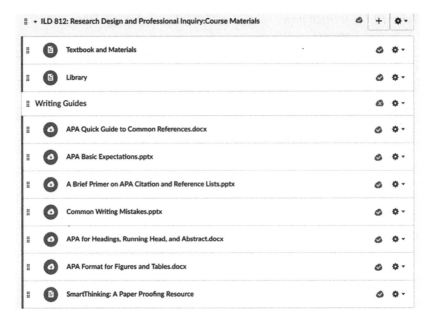

Figure 10.9   Course Materials module

set of writing assistance resources. Students in our program, like many others, occasionally struggle with writing or have not worked on their academic writing since they left graduate school many years ago. These guides help them overcome these struggles.

Next, we created weekly modules within a course that provide the actual content and assignments that students must engage with. These elements are featured in Figures 10.10 and 10.11. Figure 10.10 presents the Week 1 module: these modules typically contain a brief lecture on the topics covered in a week, a discussion of what assignments must be attended to and when they are due, a list of Readings and Resources, and finally, the actual assignment itself.

We provide a detailed view of one element of the weekly module in Figure 10.11. Within it, the required readings in the text book are listed, and a variety of useful supplementary videos and PowerPoints are also offered. We encourage faculty to use these, but also encourage them to add their own resources that bring out their individual personality and field knowledge.

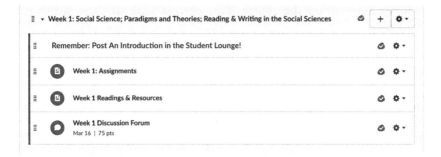

Figure 10.10   An assignment module

Week 1 Readings & Resources

Week 1 Readings and Materials

Required Readings

- Babbie Text Book: pages 1 - 59; 447-471

Power Points (Required)

- Induction & Deduction 2016_10_22.pptx
- Theory-A Gentle Discussion.pptx
- The Ladder of Abstraction - A Useful Tool.pptx
- A Quick Look at the Structure of Research Articles.pptx

Research Course Flow Chart for the EdD Program (Optional but Informative)

- EdD Research Course Flow Chart PDF.pdf

Figure 10.11   The readings and resources folder

BUILDING THE COURSE: A TIMELINE

The creation of the eight weekly modules and related components within the course master shell were built in the LMS. Consistency and steady work was key; this is not an activity that can be done in short bursts; it requires focused attention to ensure accuracy. A few ancillary activities included the creation of weekly announcements designed to prompt students on general tasks and concepts for particular weeks, the classification of assignment types, and double-checking links and the flow of navigation within the course. This process took us three weeks to complete.

TEACHING THE COURSE ACROSS SECTIONS

Once the course master for Research Design and Professional Inquiry was built, instructors were assigned, course sections were created for each instructor, and the students were enrolled in these respective sections. We deploy sections to instructors about three weeks before a course starts; students do not gain access to the course section until three days before the course formally begins. This allows course directors to ensure that the copying process is performed correctly and gives instructors time to review and customize the course to their own teaching approach. These three weeks are also used to coordinate the teaching approaches of the instructors, a responsibility of the course director.

Course Directors and Instructors

During the weeks before the course starts, course directors work with the faculty members teaching the course to ensure that they have access and are aware of the structure and materials in the course. They also share changes that have occurred since the previous iteration of the course. During the course, course directors serve as a resource, providing guidance on technical issues and with student issues that may arise. After the course concludes, faculty are also encouraged to share their thoughts about the course with course directors. This tactical-level approach to communications among instructors and course directors represents a strategic approach employed by our program that deserves a brief note.

Teaching Strategies in the Course

In our program, faculty members, whether full or part-time, are encouraged to engage with our students. This entails participation in discussion board activities and the provision of extensive private feedback on papers and graded assignments. To be sure, we do not wish to homogenize the approaches of our faculty members. However, we do expect that faculty will engage with and provide feedback to students commensurate with graduate courses. In the case of the Research Design and Professional Inquiry course, this is especially important. Many of our students are unfamiliar with research principles and need guidance. Faculty members also facilitate this using video messages (a tool available in Canvas) or sometimes through webinars and teleconferences with students. We encourage and familiarize our faculty members with these strategies and the tools used to provide them through a faculty development process.

Adjunct and Full-Time Faculty Review and Development

In many programs, adjunct faculty members are largely excluded from gaining a full sense of what is going on (Schreyer, 2012; Webb and Wong, 2013). As an online graduate program, we find that adjuncts who feel connected to full-time faculty are more engaged and can help students more than otherwise. We facilitate this in two ways: through a monthly newsletter that keeps faculty up to date on policy issues and upcoming events and through quarterly webinars in which a variety of teaching approaches, research issues and policy guidance are provided. Part-time faculty are also encouraged to share feedback during these webinars. We have found these communications are highly valued by our part-time faculty members during our yearly faculty evaluations. Furthermore, all faculty, including adjunct faculty, participate in a yearly review process with our director. These meetings are not merely critiques – rather they serve to provide faculty members with a sense of what they are doing well, as well as feedback on potential shortcomings. Furthermore, the director also shares opportunities for professional development. In many ways, this represents an approach that puts the leadership theory we teach into practice through the way the faculty are managed.

CONTINUOUS IMPROVEMENTS TO THE COURSE

From term to term, we acquire feedback from faculty and student evaluations on all of our courses, including the Research Design and Professional Inquiry course. This feedback, when considered by research faculty members and the course director, is used to make evolutionary changes to courses. For instance, we recently added a library of methods articles to serve as a supplementary resource for students and faculty members and have modified the schedule of assignments. This process ensures that our courses provide the best opportunity to students to learn and use the social science methods tools.

CONCLUSION

In this chapter, we have shared details on the tactical and strategic considerations we have developed to run a large, online graduate program in leadership. We have also discussed the mapping process we used to revise, create and deploy a series of research courses, then provided specific details on how we leveraged these strategies and the technology of our LMS within one particular course, the Research Design and Professional Inquiry class.

Additionally, we shared a variety of ways that our program manages courses and ensures that faculty members are informed and engaged within our program. These strategies are useful to consider for any program, but are particularly valuable for online programs that feature multiple sections of courses and that use a significant number of adjunct faculty members. While we know that there is always room for improvement, we hope that by sharing our experiences, we can encourage others to step into the world of online learning with graduate students. By sharing our experience, other programs may share in the pride and joy we have in our program.

REFERENCES

Aggarwal, A.K. and S.A. Lynn (2012). Using continuous improvement to enhance an online course. *Decision Science Journal of Innovative Education*, **10**(1), 25–48.

Babbie, E. (2014). *The Basics of Social Research*. Boston, MA: Cengage Learning.

Ballantyne, R. and J. Packer (1995). The role of student journals in facilitating reflection at doctoral level. *Studies in Continuing Education*, **17**(1–2), 29–45.

Baturay, M.H. (2011). Relationships among sense of classroom community, perceived cognitive learning and satisfaction of students at an e-learning course. *Interactive Learning Environments*, **19**(5), 563–75.

Berge, Z.L. and C. Donaldson (2008). Cost-benefit of online learning. In W.J. Bramble and S. Panda (eds), *Economics of Distance and Online Learning: Theory, Practice and Research* (pp. 179–94). New York, NY, USA and Abingdon, UK: Routledge.

Blessinger, P. and D. Stockley (eds) (2016). *Emerging Directions in Doctoral Education*. Bingley: Emerald.

Bolliger, D. and F. Inan (2012). Development and validation of the online student connectedness survey. *International Review of Research in Open and Distance Education*, **13**, 41–65.

Bowers, J. and P. Kumar (2017). *Students' Perceptions of Teaching and Social Presence: A Comparative Analysis of Face-to-Face and Online Learning Environments in Blended Learning: Concepts, Methodologies, Tools, and Applications*. Hershey, PA: IGI Global.

Boyer, E.L. (1990). *Scholarship Reconsidered: Priorities of the Professoriate*. Lawrenceville, NJ: Princeton University Press.

Ford, K., E. Yu-Polush and N.J. Brooks (2016). Living theory in action: Preparing a new generation of educational researchers. In P. Blessinger and D. Stockley (eds), *Emerging Directions in Doctoral Education* (pp. 111–28). Bingley: Emerald.

Harasim, L. (2000). Shift happens: Online education as a new paradigm in learning. *The Internet and Higher Education*, **3**(1), 41–61.

Haywood, K., K. Allen and F. Myers (2016). Client-based dissertation in practice. In P. Blessinger and D. Stockley (eds), *Emerging Directions in Doctoral Education* (pp. 171–88). Bingley: Emerald.

Heafner, T. and T. Petty (2016). Measuring candidate learning outcomes associated with program delivery models: Comparisons of online and face-to-face (F2F) using edTPA. In *Proceedings of the Society for Information Technology & Teacher Education International Conference* (pp. 1071–8). Savannah, GA.

Lee, A. and S. Dansby (eds) (2012). *Reshaping Doctoral Education: International Approach and Pedagogies.* New York, NY: Routledge.

Mendenhall, A. and T.E. Johnson (2010). Fostering the development of critical thinking skills, and reading comprehension of undergraduates using a Web 2.0 tool coupled with a learning system. *Interactive Learning Environments*, **18**(3), 263–76.

Pedersen, H.S. (2016). Are PhDs winners or losers? Wage premiums for doctoral degrees in private sector employment. *Higher Education*, **71**(2), 269–87.

Rovai, A.P. 2002. Sense of community, perceived cognitive learning, and persistence in asynchronous learning networks. *The Internet and Higher Education*, **5**(4), 319–32.

Salmon, G. (2004). *E-moderating: The Key to Teaching and Learning Online.* Abingdon: Psychology Press.

Schreyer, J. (2012). Inviting the 'outsiders' in: Local efforts to improve adjunct working conditions. *Journal of Basic Writing*, **31**, 83–102.

Smith, R.M. (2009). *Conquering the Content: A Step-by-step Guide to Online Course Design.* San Francisco, CA: Wiley & Sons.

Vora, R. and M. Kinney (2014). Connectedness, sense of community, and academic satisfaction in a novel community campus medical education model. *Academic Medicine*, **89**, 182–7.

Webb, A. and T. Wong (2013). Professional development for adjunct teaching faculty in a research-intensive university: Engagement in scholarly approaches to teaching and learning. *International Journal of Teaching and Learning in Higher Education*, **25**, 231–8.

Wyss, V., D. Freedman and C. Siebert (2014). The development of a discussion rubric for online courses: Standardizing expectations of graduate students in online scholarly discussions. *Tech Trends*, **58**(2), 99–107.

11. A technology-based glocal perspective for teaching in doctoral educational leadership programs

Emmanuel Jean-Francois

INTRODUCTION

The evolution of globalism through globalization, as well as other factors such as rapid technological changes, demographic shifts, migration, new forms of communication and interactions, and environmental and social challenges have served as drivers fostering the demand for new skills and competencies expected from university graduates by employers and other stakeholders. These social changes implicitly impose a greater sense of responsibility on post-secondary education institutions with respect to the teaching and learning of their students, especially those who will be called upon for leadership positions in organizations.

This new sense of responsibility inspires higher learning institutions, scholars, practitioners and other stakeholders to explore creative and innovative ways for teaching and learning at the local, global and trans-national levels. Consequently, the purpose of this chapter is to articulate a technology-based glocal perspective for teaching doctoral educational leadership programs. This chapter is informed by the transnational and glocal education frameworks (Jean-Francois, 2015; 2016) and includes key insights for practitioners to contribute to glocal teaching and learning in leadership education through technology.

GLOBAL REALITY AND ITS LIMITATIONS

The world is global when being considered as a whole. However, some global issues and the need for global solutions to address them are relevant only in a global context. Therefore, it is not surprising that some people living in one part of the globe may feel completely removed or detached from some issues that may be of critical interest to other people living on the other side of the globe. One may argue that this is because the members who feel detached from a global issue are uninformed or not educated enough regarding such issue. However, the supposedly 'uninformed' or 'uneducated' people may make the same argument from their own standpoint and point to the arrogance of others who believe in their sense of righteousness to determine what is a global issue and what is not. In other words, while there is an undeniable global reality of the world, it does not always create consensus to capture the needs, concerns and understanding of all people living across various corners of the planet earth. Yes, everybody on earth shares a common planetary citizenry. However, different citizens on the planet live, understand and embrace such citizenship differently, based on various cultural and national contexts, which envelop multiple sub-contexts such as racial, ethnic, religious, economic, political, geographical, regional, historical, biological and other factors.

When accounting for cultural or national contexts or sub-contexts, it is much easier to understand why the global reality tends to exist in the eyes of the beholder regardless of the fact that issues such as climate change, international migration and international trade are global in nature. The complexity is that even if the aforementioned issues are global they do not necessarily capture the needs and interests of particular people with the same level of awareness, concern or intensity simply because of cultural or national contexts. Therefore, it should not be surprising that some global frameworks can be intentionally well-constructed to improve the overall welfare of the globe, but rejected at the cultural or national level, or at sub-cultural or sub-national levels. The challenge is that the term 'global' aims to eliminate national borders and make itself the center of attention. In so doing, while global offers alternative solutions for global issues, the one-size-fits-all pretention that the global implies represents by itself a problem that adds up to other global issues.

This complexity of the global as a phenomenon is very important for proponents of global approaches or frameworks to understand. Such complexity of the global has built-in limitations that provide justification for glocal frameworks, which account for local realities as distinct, but also as part of the global (Jean-Francois, 2015; Robertson, 2006). In fact, glocal realities exist in various corners around the world. Some glocal realities are transnational, because they have relevance and implications across and beyond cultural or national contexts.

TRANSNATIONAL REALITIES

Contrary to the global, the transnational exists across and beyond national contexts without aiming to eliminate the national. Therefore, there is greater potential for the transnational to be receptive in cultural or national contexts or sub-contexts where the global might have been rejected. Before going further, the term 'transnational' refers to 'educational scholarship and practices between, across, and beyond the boundaries of two or more nations or countries' (Jean-Francois, 2016, p. 12).

There are some issues related to teaching and learning strategies and technologies that are concerns for policy makers, administrators, communities, employers and instructors within, across and beyond national borders or cultural contexts. On the surface, the perceptions of such issues may be different, but at their core, they carry the same concerns and desires to identify or find ways to overcome these challenges. Such issues are transnational.

INTERNATIONAL INSTRUCTIONAL TECHNOLOGY STANDARDS

In 2001, the Technology Standards for School Administrators Collaborative (TSSA), the American Association of School Administrators (AASA), and the National School Boards Association (NSBA) had produced six National Education Technology Standards for Administrators (NETS-A), to 'promote the idea that specific skills, knowledge, and practice were required for administrators to be ready to support the appropriate use of technology in a school' (Schrum et al., 2011, p. 242). The 2001 NETS-A standards were the following:

- *Leadership and Vision* (educational leaders inspire a shared vision for comprehensive integration of technology and foster an environment and culture conducive to the realization of that vision);
- *Learning and Teaching* (educational leaders ensure that curricular design, instructional strategies, and learning environments integrate appropriate technologies to maximize learning and teaching);
- *Productivity and Professional Practice* (educational leaders apply technology to enhance their professional practice and to increase their own productivity and that of others);
- *Support, Management and Operations* (educational leaders ensure the integration of technology to support productive systems for learning and administration);

- *Assessment and Evaluation* (educational leaders use technology to plan and implement comprehensive systems of effective assessment and evaluation);
- *Social, Legal and Ethical Issues* (educational leaders understand the social, legal and ethical issues related to technology and model responsible decision making related to these issues).

The standards were revised in 2009 (ISTE, 2009), and are now known as the ISTE Standards for Administrators (ISTE Standards-A), to evaluate technology leadership in schools (ISTE, 2014). The ISTE Standards-A were stated as follows (ISTE, 2014):

- *Visionary Leadership* (administrators inspire and lead development and implementation of a shared vision for comprehensive integration of technology to promote excellence and support transformation throughout the organization);
- *Digital Age Learning Culture* (administrators create, promote and sustain a dynamic, digital age learning culture that provides a rigorous, relevant and engaging education for all students);
- *Excellence in Professional Practice* (administrators promote an environment of professional learning and innovation that empowers ·educators to enhance student learning through the infusion of contemporary technologies and digital resources);
- *Systemic Improvement* (administrators provide digital age leadership and management to continuously improve the organization through the effective use of information and technology resources);
- *Digital Citizenship* (administrators model and facilitate understanding of social, ethical and legal issues and responsibilities related to an evolving digital culture).

There are other technology leadership models that are inspired by the ISTE standards (Arafeh, 2015; Davies, 2010) to assist educational administrators in technology leadership functions and responsibilities.

SOCIAL CONTEXT OF GLOCAL IDENTITY

A technology-based glocal perspective for teaching doctoral educational leadership is inspired by the desire to train leaders who are locally oriented and globally minded. In other words, it is to foster doctoral educational leadership programs that produce technology literate leaders with glocal identity. 'Glocal identity is one's identification to global citizenship (i.e., citizen of the world) in relation to the abilities to perform, behave, and understand with effectiveness and efficiency in a culture-specific context other than one's own native culture' (Jean-Francois, 2015, p. 149).

Glocal identity and technology are interrelated because humans live in a global world interconnected through information and communication technology and in local communities that are culturally diverse. The social construction of glocal identity occurs through factors such as global competence (awareness and possession of knowledge about global issues, as well as the abilities to use approaches and frameworks that are designed for worldwide application, regardless of cultural particularities), cross-cultural interactions (interactions with people from diverse cultural backgrounds), living abroad (living in a foreign country), the stranger experience (experiencing being a minority and helpless in a foreign social and cultural environment), and second language acquisition (going through the process of learning a second language) (Jean-Francois, 2015).

Academic leaders and faculty of doctoral educational leadership programs have a responsibility to help future leaders develop a glocal identity, because they will be called upon to manage multicultural and diverse teams, serve ethnically diverse students, and interact with communities that are also ethnically and culturally diverse.

It can be challenging for certain students to travel abroad for various individual, family, occupational or financial reasons. However, study away and technology can help create international-like learning settings that partially compensate for the potential lack of opportunities to travel abroad. Study away consists of providing students with an experiential learning experience like studying abroad but without having to travel overseas. A technology-based glocal perspective for teaching doctoral educational leadership programs aims to provide insights to help academic leaders and leadership education faculty design curriculum and instructional approaches that further such an endeavor.

TEACHING DOCTORAL EDUCATIONAL LEADERSHIP THROUGH TECHNOLOGY

Almost every aspect of daily living, including teaching and learning, and the administration of educational institutions is influenced by technology. From mobile technologies, hand-held devices and smartphones to social media, hardware, software and technology platforms, opportunities to use technology for leadership education are countless. At the doctoral level, priorities should be addressed for learning management systems and decision management applications or web-based software for instructional leadership, as well as administrative, logistic and human resource management purposes (Blackboard, CalDiem, Canvas, Coursesites, Moodle, Myicourse, Open EdX LMS, Schoology, and other similar applications or software).

Additionally, doctoral leadership education can help students (future educational leaders) become more familiar with applications, such as Trello, Taskworld and Slack, which allow teams to collaborate and work on projects in ways that are efficient and user friendly. Further, applications like Jing allow students to capture PowerPoint and record video instantly on their computers and share it with others, while Zoom helps organize video conferences and record meeting minutes that can be shared immediately.

However, technology should not be used just for the sake of using it and the claim to be innovative. Teaching doctoral educational leadership through technology requires first an understanding of the purpose of technology, the aims for which it will be used, and the expected outcomes. According to the US Department of Education (2017),

> Technology ushers in fundamental structural changes that can be integral to achieving significant improvements in productivity. Used to support both teaching and learning, technology infuses classrooms with digital learning tools, such as computers and hand-held devices; expands course offerings, experiences, and learning materials; supports learning 24 hours a day, 7 days a week; builds 21st century skills; increases student engagement and motivation; and accelerates learning. Technology also has the power to transform teaching by ushering in a new model of connected teaching. (US Department of Education, 2017, para. 1)

Therefore, teaching doctoral educational leadership through technology should have the ultimate purpose of improving teaching and learning in an educational institution. Academic leaders and faculty should ask key questions, such as: (a) how can I use technology in leadership education to provide transformative teaching and learning experiences to students? (b) What are the learning outcomes that particular technology devices, support and resources can better help to achieve? (c) How can particular technology devices, support and resources help remediate students who would have failed otherwise? (d) How can particular technology devices, support and resources be used to foster greater, more meaningful and impactful student engagement? (e) How can particular technology devices, support and resources be used to assess the achievement of learning outcomes or in making instructional leadership decisions? (f) How can particular technology devices, support and resources be used to nurture the glocal-mindedness of future educational leaders?

INTERNATIONALIZING THE DOCTORAL EDUCATIONAL LEADERSHIP CURRICULUM

Technology can help to internationalize the curriculum and lesson plans by creating a global classroom that enables students to interact with the rest of the world without going overseas. Simply put, a global classroom is a course that is intentionally designed to be an international and intercultural environment that uses opportunities and resources offered by Information and Communication Technologies (ICT) to provide participating students with meaningful, relevant and creative mutual learning interactions with qualified individuals from various other countries.

Many school districts focus primarily on educating children with the sole focus on the local community without an awareness of living in a globally interconnected world that forces future graduates to compete in a global marketplace, even when working at the local level. In many cases, the lack of global awareness of local educational leaders is one of the biggest obstacles to the infusion of global perspectives into the curriculum and lesson plans of local schools. Local educational leaders make decisions on curriculum, choice of textbooks and allocation of resources. Therefore, their glocal awareness or lack thereof is consequential in whether glocal perspectives are taken into consideration or incorporated in curriculum and instructional practices of local schools.

Internationalizing the doctoral educational leadership curriculum can help fill such a gap where it exists. For example, academic leaders and faculty of doctoral educational leadership programs can revise their curriculum to add learning outcomes related to glocal awareness, knowledge, skills and understanding (Jean-Francois, 2015). Similarly, students in a leadership education course can work, with the support of technology, on joint instructional leadership strategic plans with other doctoral educational leadership students from another country. Students can use technology to work with their counterparts in other countries in order to identify transnational trends (Jean-Francois, 2016) in educational leadership, as well as in teaching and learning.

Despite time differences, there is a variety of support and resources such as Google Docs and Dropbox (to share documents), Skype, Line, WhatsApp, Oovoo and Viber (for face-to-face communications), free teleconference numbers, and opportunities to interact with international guest speakers or guest speakers with international backgrounds via Skype or Google Hangouts, to name just a few examples that make such activities very realistic and feasible. Teekens (2006) asserted that cellphones, email and video conferences have taken away the barriers between countries. Obviously, there can be challenges related to time differences or lack of

ICT access in some developing countries. However, the main challenge to creating a global classroom is not necessarily the availability of ICT support and resources; it is mainly the desire to meticulously plan well in advance and implement with discipline and open-mindedness the interactions of one's students with stakeholders from other countries around the world. The creation of a global classroom requires revising the curriculum of a program with the support of academic leadership, revising course syllabi, and informing students about the relevance of glocal doctoral educational leadership.

The support of academic leadership is necessary for planning and attaining basic resources such as space and internet access that may emerge as helpful. The revision of course syllabi is required so that particular courses reflect new learning outcomes, objectives, content, activities and assessments related to glocal doctoral educational leadership. The collaboration of the doctoral educational leadership students is important. Collaboration enables students to be fully engaged and use the global classroom as an opportunity to influence change and policy at the local and national, or even global level.

TECHNOLOGY-BASED DOCTORAL LEADERSHIP EDUCATION AND ADULT LEARNING

Technology-based doctoral leadership education should be envisioned in support of effective pedagogy. In other words, faculty must have the pedagogy right first before envisioning the use of technology. Effective pedagogy in doctoral leadership education must be inspired by the foundational principles of andragogy, because students in these classes are most likely to be adults, and more specifically, non-traditional adult students who have to juggle multiple roles at the same time. Knowles (1980; 1984), considered as one of the pioneers of andragogy (facilitation of adult learning), stated six main characteristics of adult learners: they are self-directed or autonomous (adult learners make their own learning decisions with the support of their mentors); they utilize knowledge and life experiences (help learners connect past experiences with current instructional activities); they are goal-oriented (help adult learners link activities with specific learning outcomes); they are relevancy-oriented (adult learners are more motivated to engage in activities that directly contribute to help them achieve their learning objectives); they are practice-oriented (educators should identify activities to help adult learners link theories with real life situations); and they thrive in collaborative environments (adult learners thrive in learning environments that acknowledge their contributions).

To be effective, the choice of technology to teach adults must account for such andragogical principles. For example, adult learners should be treated with respect, as adults with self-knowledge and the ability to make the best decisions for themselves, including some flexibility in the ICT used in learning and its products. Instructors of adult learners should acknowledge upfront the potential for a technology gap, and the suggestion of readily available support and resources to help fill such a gap. Technology can be used to transform doctoral educational leadership students into engaged and creative learners, facilitate collaboration during and in between class sessions, foster experiential technology leadership practice, and foster individual learning and growth.

Technology integration into the curriculum is the direct responsibility of the teacher, given the role of teaching in daily curriculum implementation through instructions. However, research shows that the implementation of technology integration in curriculum and lesson plans cannot happen without the technology leadership of the school administrators, such as principals (Anderson and Dexter, 2005; West, 2003). According to Grady (2011), the principal's role as a technology leader includes: establishing the vision and goals for technology; carrying the technology banner; modeling the use of technology; providing support for the use of technology in school; engaging in lifelong learning; providing technology-related professional development opportunities to teachers; allocating resources for the use of technology as a support for teaching and learning; advocating for technology integration in teaching and learning; staying abreast regarding national technology standards and promotion of the attainment of the standards in the school; and communicating to school stakeholders about the utilization and importance of technology integration for enhancing learning outcomes and better academic performance. Many doctoral leadership education students are principals or fill similar leadership positions and need to be prepared to be technology leaders.

TEACHING DIGITAL EDUCATION LEADERS

While teacher education programs prepare teachers to use technology in their classrooms, Schrum et al. (2011) found in a study that the majority of principals felt that they had no specific instructional technology course in their licensure preparation program. Flanagan and Jacobsen (2003) asserted that principals should be prepared as technology leaders, because principals who are prepared in technology leadership are most likely to inspire the effective integration of technology into teaching and learning in their schools (Brockmeier et al., 2005). Rivard (2010) explained that

'Without basic technology competency, it stands to reason that most school leaders lack the ability to understand the various policy and planning issues related to the successful implementation of technology' (p. 10). Garcia and Abrego (2014) had also reported that 'too many principals do not have the adequate skills, dispositions, training or developmental experiences in integrating technology into the curriculum' (p. 13).

This is a problem to be addressed by academic leaders and faculty in doctoral educational leadership programs to ensure that future educational leaders can play their roles as digital leaders. As McLeod et al. (2011) suggested, the intersection between technology and school leadership preparation is one of the most significant for doctoral educational leadership programs. Creighton (2003) considered the principal as a technology leader who should use technology for instructional leadership purposes. The Wallace Foundation (2013) indicated, 'the principal remains the central source of leadership influence' (p. 6). Similarly, Afshari et al. (2009) argued that the principal as a technology leader should understand the technologies and how such technologies can help perform educational administrative tasks. The bottom line is that successful technology integration in schools cannot happen without the influence of educational leaders (Byrom and Bingham, 2001; Greaves et al., 2012).

Technology-based teaching in doctoral-level educational leadership studies does not mean injecting one technology course into a program of studies. Instead, it means integrating technology leadership application throughout the curriculum. In other words, learning outcomes related to technology leadership must be integrated into the program design. Students in doctoral educational leadership programs should have opportunities to explore how to use technology for planning, administration, instructional leadership, teaching and learning, enhancing student academic performance, assessment and evaluation, and continuous quality improvement. To acquire a glocal perspective, an educational leader must be equipped to plan and implement changes that create a digital culture in a school, and use such an opportunity to empower teachers to incorporate glocal perspectives into their lesson plans. The purpose must not just be to create a digital culture for its own sake, but a digital culture that nurtures students' 21st-century skills, such as content knowledge in 21st-century themes (English, reading or language arts, world languages, arts, mathematics, economics, science, geography, history, government and civics, global awareness, financial, economic, business and entrepreneurial literacy, civic literacy, health literacy and environmental literacy); learning and innovation skills (creativity and innovation, critical thinking and problem solving, and communication and collaboration); information, media and technology skills (information literacy, media literacy, ICT literacy); and life and career skills (flexibility and adaptability, initiative and self-direction, social and cross-cultural skills, productivity and accountability, leadership and responsibility), as suggested by Partnership for 21st Century Learning (P21st Century Learning, 2016).

INSTRUCTIONAL STRATEGIES FOR TEACHING EDUCATIONAL LEADERSHIP THROUGH TECHNOLOGY INTEGRATION IN DOCTORAL PROGRAMS

Technology-based teaching in educational leadership can take advantage of online learning, using games, simulations and virtual worlds to facilitate the education of K-12 students who must master 21st-century skills. It can use mobile technologies, hand-held devices and smartphones in combination with social media for enhancing pedagogy, fostering stakeholder engagement (for example, students, teachers, staff and parents), and creating learning-friendly environments. Faculty of doctoral educational leadership programs can help their doctoral students become aware of technology support and resources that they can suggest to teachers in their schools. Some of the strategies include, but are not limited to: revision of lesson plans to use technology as a support to provide international/intercultural experiences to students; using a digital camera in the classroom; using mobile technologies, hand-held devices and smartphones; using social media platforms to interact with students' parents; using digital storytelling in the classroom; using Google tools in the classroom; using free websites as learning and teaching tools; and using Web 2.0 tools for projects and more. Some examples of technology-based assignments or activities that can be used to engage students in a Doctoral Leadership Education program include:

- *Student-led live Google Hangouts meeting:* students can be asked to plan and lead a simulated teacher conference through a live Google Hangouts session.
- *Technology-supported presentations:* an assignment can be designed requiring students to use specific technology, with the purpose of helping the students become more comfortable with the utilization of such technology.
- *Inventory of technology support and resources:* students can work in groups to develop an inventory of technology support and resources, and identify how they can use it in a school to facilitate better teaching and learning experiences.

- *Digital story telling:* students can use recording devices to produce digital storytelling regarding their own perspectives on technology integration in schools.
- *LMS-based data collection and analysis:* students can be required to use a particular Learning Management System (LMS) to collect existing data, and analyze such data to make decisions to enhance teaching and learning in a school.
- *Reflective paper:* students can be asked to write a reflective paper on their perspectives regarding technology integration and glocal perspectives in curriculum and lesson plans.
- *Technology integration needs assessment:* students can work in groups to conduct a needs assessment regarding availability and utilization of technology for teaching and learning in a given school or school district.
- *Technology integration asset mapping:* students can work in groups to conduct an asset mapping or appreciative inquiry exercise regarding availability and utilization of technology for teaching and learning in a given school or school district.
- *Strategic plan for technology integration:* students can work in groups to develop a strategic plan for technology integration in a given school or school district.
- *Literature review on technology integration:* students can write a literature review synthesizing and critically analyzing existing studies on technology integration, educational leadership and glocal perspectives in school curriculum.
- *Instructional technology specialist interviews:* students can be asked to interview several instructional technology specialists and write an interview report.
- *Technology how-to-presentation:* each student in a course can be asked to select a particular technology support or resource and prepare a how-to presentation for classmates, including how such a resource or support can be used to enhance teaching and learning.
- *Glocal trends in education and technology paper:* students can work with counterparts in other countries to develop a report on glocal trends in education and technology.

The aforementioned activities or assignments constitute just a random and selective list as an illustration of instructional strategies that can be used in a leadership education program. When used to support curriculum goals and the teaching and learning process, technology can help facilitate greater student participation in class, enhance student engagement, strengthen peer interactions, and make it easier to collect feedback for formative assessment, continuing quality improvement, as well as summative assessment related to course learning outcomes.

OUTCOME-BASED ASSESSMENT USING TECHNOLOGY

The use of technology does not necessarily translate into enhanced educational or academic outcomes. However, proper use of technology can help enhance student academic achievement. For example, computer-based integrated learning systems (CILS) exist in most school districts in the US and can be integrated into the overall curriculum of doctoral leadership education programs to help future educational leaders become more familiar with how to make them more useful for student learning. CILS include courseware and management software run on network hardware. They include drill and practice in various school subjects (for example, language arts, mathematics, social studies, science, writing, foreign languages, computer skills) and thus help manage the curriculum, and track and report on student progress based on learning outcomes. CILS can help educational leaders advise teachers on how to focus on individual student academic performance and make data-driven decisions to improve student learning. Darling-Hammond et al. (2014) argued that technology can help schools improve student achievement and close the achievement gap.

Doctoral educational leadership programs, curriculum and instruction should adopt the use of particular technology devices, support or resources based on robust assessment and evaluation, and evidence-based frameworks related to the enhancement of teaching and learning. For example, data can be collected from cognitive data (for example, test scores), human behavioral data, and technology data (for example, smart glasses, wearable cameras and biosensors), in order to make instructional leadership decisions to provide personalized teaching and learning experiences to students. This requires, however, clear ethical commitments from those who would control the data.

CONCLUSION

Faculty teaching doctoral educational leadership programs and courses should envision educating glocal leaders through an intentional use of the opportunities offered by new information and communication technologies. As already explained, a glocal leader is one who is globally minded and locally grounded. This is important not only to respond to the ever-increasing demands of our interdependent world, but also to adapt to transnational trends requiring the revision and adaptation of traditionally-based curricula to meet the challenges of more complex environments that are yet to come.

This chapter has provided a technology-based glocal perspective that would facilitate the task of faculty teaching doctoral educational leadership. Further, this chapter explains that instructional technology leaders can help create an atmosphere that makes technology an enabler for learning as opposed to a disruptor. For example, social media, mobile technology devices, games, simulations and virtual worlds may enable faculty of doctoral educational leadership programs to simulate cross-cultural experiences when opportunities to travel abroad are not available. Instead of letting technology devices be perceived as a distraction, effective technology integration can provide instructional leadership to nurture collaborative learning. Doctoral educational leadership programs should prepare graduates who learn and reflect on how to make technology a tool for effective collaboration, and how to mentor their teaching staff to use technology as a support for transformative learning experiences.

REFERENCES

Afshari, M., K.A. Bakar, W.S. Luan, B.A. Samah and F.S. Fooi (2009). Technology and school leadership. *Technology, Pedagogy and Education*, **18**(2), 235–48.

Anderson, R.E. and S. Dexter (2005). School technology leadership: An empirical investigation of prevalence and effect. *Educational Administration Quarterly*, **41**(1), 49–82.

Arafeh, S. (2015). Educational technology leadership for education leaders: An integrated technology leadership model. In N.M. Haynes, S. Arafeh and C. McDaniels (eds), *Doctoral Educational Leadership: Perspectives on Preparation and Practice* (pp. 253–69). Lanham, MD: University Press of America.

Brockmeier, L.L., J.M. Sermon and W.C. Hope (2005). Principals' relationship with computer technology. *National Association of Secondary School Bulletin*, **89**(643), 45–63.

Byrom, E. and M. Bingham (2001). *Factors Influencing the Effective Use of Technology for Teaching and Learning: Lessons Learned from the SEIR-TEC Intensive Site Schools* (2nd edn). Greensboro, NC: University of North Carolina at Greensboro.

Creighton, T. (2003). *The Principal as Technology Leader*. Thousand Oaks, CA: Corwin.

Darling-Hammond, L., M.B. Zielezinski and S. Goldman (2014). *Using Technology to Support At-risk Students' Learning*. Accessed at https://edpolicy.stanford.edu/publications/pubs/1241.

Davies, P.M. (2010). On school educational technology leadership. *Management in Education*, **24**(2), 55–61.

Flanagan, L. and M. Jacobsen (2003). Technology leadership for the twenty-first century principal. *Journal of Educational Administration*, **41**(2), 124–42.

Garcia, A. and C. Abrego (2014). Vital skills of the elementary principal as a technology leader. *Journal of Organizational Learning and Leadership*, **12**(1), 12–25.

Grady, M.L. (2011). *Leading the Technology-powered School.* Thousand Oaks, CA: Corwin.

Greaves, T.W., J. Hayes, L. Wilson, M. Gielniak and E.L. Peterson (2012). *Revolutionizing Education Through Technology: The Project RED Roadmap for Transformation.* Eugene, OR: International Society for Technology in Education.

International Society for Technology in Education (ISTE) (2009). *NETS for Administrators* 2009. Accessed at http://www.iste.org/docs/pdfs/nets-a-standards. pdf? sfvrsn=2.

International Society for Technology in Education (ISTE) (2014). *ISTE Standards for Administrators.* Accessed at http://www.iste.org/standards.

Jean-Francois, E. (2015). *Building Global Education with a Local Perspective: An Introduction to Glocal Higher Education.* New York, NY: Palgrave Macmillan.

Jean-Francois, E. (2016). *Perspectives on Transnational Higher Education.* Boston, MA: Sense Publishers.

Knowles, M.S. (1980). *The Modern Practice of Adult Education: From Pedagogy to Andragogy.* Chicago, IL: Follett.

Knowles, M.S. (1984). *Andragogy in Action.* San Francisco, CA: Jossey-Bass.

McLeod, S., J.M. Bathon and J.W. Richardson (2011). Studies of technology tool usage are not enough: A response to the articles in this special issue. *Journal of Research on Leadership Education*, **6**(5), 288–97.

P21st Century Learning (2016). Framework for 21st century learning. Accessed at http://www.p21.org/our-work/p21-framework.

Rivard, L.R. (2010). Enhancing education through technology: Principal leadership for technology integration in schools. (Unpublished doctoral dissertation). Wayne State University, Detroit, MI.

Robertson, R. (2006). Glocalization. In R. Robertson and J.A. Scholte (eds), *Encyclopaedia of Globalization* (vol. 2) (pp. 545–8). New York, NY: Routledge.

Schrum, L., L. Galizio and P. Ledesma (2011). Doctoral Educational Leadership and technology integration: An investigation into preparation, experiences, and roles. *Journal of School Leadership*, **21**(2), 241–61.

Teekens, H. (ed.) (2006). *Internationalisation at Home: A Global Perspective.* The Hague: NUFFIC.

US Department of Education (2017). Use of technology in teaching and learning. Accessed at https://www.ed.gov/oii-news/use-technology-teaching-and-learning.

Wallace Foundation (2013). *The School Principal as a Leader: Guiding Schools to Better Teaching and Learning.* Accessed at http://www.wallacefoundation.org/ knowledge-center/Documents/The-School-Principal-as-Leader-Guiding-Schoo lsto-Better-Teaching-and-Learning-2nd-Ed.pdf.

West, B. (2003). Building the bridge to effective use of technology. In A.D. Wheatley (ed.), *How to Ensure Ed/Tech is not Oversold and Underused* (pp. 53–72). Lanham, MD: Scarecrow.

12. Integrating doctoral research and teaching with technology: a case from a Finnish business school

Peter Zettinig and Katja Einola

BACKGROUND

Both the academic field of international business (IB) and business school education seem to be at a crossroads. IB studies have recently been criticized for failing to move with the times in studying the vibrant field of IB and the complex process of globalization. Instead, the field is seen as fixated on traditional topics such as the internationalization of the firm, dramatically reducing its relevance (Delios, 2017). Arum and Roksa (2011) found in their study of over 2300 US undergraduates that students in business studies performed *worse* in their first few years of university than they had done in high school when it comes to cognitive abilities, raising some questions about what and how business students are taught. Some of the most prestigious business schools are being placed under scrutiny for 'moral failures' (McDonald, 2017) or lacking relevance due to alienation from the world of practice (Bennis and O'Toole, 2005). Meanwhile, the number of business PhD students has grown just as the number of increasingly research-driven academic jobs available for them has been shrinking ('The disposable academic', 2010), and the market for these jobs has been globalizing. Governments are cutting university budgets, and education is becoming a field where universities fight for the best students and donations, and sometimes existence, and PhD students compete against each other for scarce jobs.

In such an environment, how do educators build a practically relevant doctoral training program to prepare a future generation of educators and researchers capable of conducting meaningful social research (Alvesson et al., 2017) and finding their place in the volatile job market? In this chapter we discuss how we turned our master's level international strategy course into a shared laboratory for combining the completion of doctoral research, practicing teaching, course design and coordination, and acquiring practical management and leadership skills, using technology-mediated communication.

EDUCATIONAL SYSTEM IN FINLAND AND OUR SCHOOL

In Finland, education is generally seen as a public good, based on principles such as high quality learning outcomes and equal opportunity. Historically, the cost of the education system is widely understood as an investment in the future development of the society, and as an important economic factor that increases the potential knowledge resource base from which innovations are developed and future opportunities derived. For PhD students (as for most BSc and MSc students), this means that university education is tuition free, and admission is highly selective, in particular when it comes to programs and universities with the best reputations. Overall, this system has worked well for this geographically distant and scarcely populated North European country with moderate natural resources to draw from. The Finnish educational system has an important role in generating many desirable outcomes for society.

This is illustrated by international comparisons where Finland has been described as 'the most peaceful and sustainable country in the world' (Messner and Haken, 2016), 'the best higher education and training system in the world' (The Global Competitiveness Report, n.d.), 'the healthiest ecosystem in the world' (Hsu et al., 2016), and 'the most innovative country in the world' (Hallett, 2016; cited in 'Welcome to study in Finland', 2017, para. 5).

Students selected for doctoral programs often receive research project funding through different doctoral positions at the university, scholarships provided by foundations, by joining state-funded research projects or collaborative research projects with industry. Although globalization and tightening government budgets are making the field of education somewhat more competitive, in line with other Nordic countries, universities in Finland emphasize collaboration among schools over competition. This creates interesting settings for doctoral studies. For instance, Finnish universities cooperate in doctoral research education by offering joint courses in core areas such as philosophy and methodology, as well as main disciplinary areas such as finance, marketing and IB, drawing on a wider resource base. The same is happening across the Nordic countries. For instance in IB, doctoral candidates can select courses at partner universities and there is a regional collaborative program to study the field.

In Finland, students at all levels of education are expected to acquire a broad knowledge base and interdisciplinary studies are encouraged. Doctoral graduates are in general well-appreciated for their philosophical breadth, mastery of several methodological approaches, and diversity in methods of enquiry. They possess strong capabilities in terms of information literacy, coordination capabilities and autonomy, and ethical, social and professional understanding of their own potential impact on society (Zettinig and Vincze, 2008).

Another important feature of the doctoral education system is the broader institutional context that characterizes itself as *a national innovation ecosystem*. Among other institutions, the Finnish Academy takes the primary role to fund basic research projects, while Business Finland (Finnish State's Funding Agency for Technology and Innovation) focuses on collaborative research between industry and research institutions. These efforts are considered to produce highly relevant outcomes for the society and the economy. Thus, many doctoral candidates align their individual research projects with programs that both contribute to the advancement of disciplinary knowledge and are measured in terms of impact on stakeholders.

Both authors of this chapter are part of the IB faculty at the Department of Marketing and IB in a multi-disciplinary university in southwestern Finland. Being located in the former capital and having the longest university tradition in the country, starting in 1640, the university is the second largest in terms of student enrollment in Finland with about 20 000 students. In IB, our core research community consists of around twenty active doctoral candidates and eight academics. Despite the rather small size of our team, the nature and topics of our research are highly diverse and some are multidisciplinary in nature. We do not limit our research interests to narrowly defined phenomena or conceptual bases.

To get accepted, prospective doctoral candidates provide a detailed research plan that indicates good command of an important and (to us) relevant research topic, with both theoretical and practical implications. Although preliminary research plans must demonstrate a connection to our research community's interests and expertise, our approach is more to enable than to limit, as we appreciate pluralism in terms of theoretical, methodological and philosophical choices. Doctoral students on our staff typically also participate in teaching and administrative tasks.

Since our team is rather small, our resources are quite limited as well. We have also been facing budget cuts and organizational changes, most notably a merger of our business school with a much larger university, and ongoing changes to our curriculum and organizational structure. Our staff, just like many of our colleagues in other business schools, are increasingly stretched between teaching, supervising, conducting research, and performing other organizational duties. Combining teaching and conducting research together with outside stakeholders and creating experimental settings for both pedagogy and research is one way to work around constraints.

For us, technology is more of an enabler through which learning and collaboration takes place rather than an end in itself – in our case a realistic ambition is Finland being a pioneer in digital technology with a rich infrastructure and technology-savvy citizens. It is our understanding that a PhD candidate keen on a career in teaching and researching this field, must be a competent user of digital platforms and have a deep personal understanding of what it means to live and work in a world where technology can help build bridges across distances, as much of our personal and working lives are spent in virtual space offering limited opportunities for face-to-face interaction.

AN INTERNATIONAL COURSE ON BUSINESS STRATEGY AS A LEARNING LABORATORY FOR VIRTUAL COLLABORATION: INSIGHTS AND SYNERGIES

Communication technology is what enables IB and is key to most modern work life in general. Professionals spend their workdays engaged in chat groups, messaging services, document sharing systems, writing and reading emails, on the phone, in synchronous online or video conference meetings, and other collaboration platforms that the day-to-day practice of IB relies on. Like virtual communication in general, teamwork with geographically dispersed and socio-culturally different others is a matter of everyday practice to most professionals engaged in IB (Zander et al., 2015). To better understand how global virtual teams (GVTs) work and what drives their success is a research topic we thought was interesting enough to start building competence around, especially as prior research had not been able to conclude whether such aspects as virtual means of communication or cultural differences were liabilities or assets to team outcomes – they seemed to be both, depending on the study and research setting (for example, Brett et al., 2006; Chiravuri et al., 2011; Gibson and Gibbs, 2006; Gilson et al., 2015; Hertel et al., 2005; Jarvenpaa and Leidner, 1998; Mockaitis et al., 2009; 2012; Peñarroja et al., 2013; Townsend et al., 1998; Zander et al., 2013).

When initially starting to evaluate different research strategies and possible methodological approaches for studying GVTs in our emerging research group, we received significant interest from several large multinational firms willing to participate in this type of research. However, due to the high ambitions for our empirical goals (in-depth, process focused, and longitudinal in nature) to better understand what drives these teams from within, these companies responded with some reluctance, proposing more traditional research methods such as surveys and interviews.

Therefore, we decided to create our own setting, a social experiment. This allowed detailed observation of how a large number of virtual teams evolve over time and how these teams create and change their processes, build routines, make sense of their team environment, co-construct leadership–followership relations, and learn over time as a collectivity. It also enabled students to learn about virtual teamwork in practice.

The Phenomenon of GVTs in our Research

Over the past 15 years GVTs have moved to the center of interest in IB research as they provide organizational solutions to implement multinational corporations' worldwide strategies, and provide viable means for other types of international organizations to leverage their international resource base (Zander et al., 2013; Zettinig and Vincze, 2011).

These teams are interesting because they have the potential to integrate globally dispersed capabilities and resources, while through their members' localized understanding and presence, they have access to intimate knowledge of local needs and demands. They are in a prime position to gain from cultural diversity, with respect to values, beliefs, attitudes, perspective and experiences (Zander et al., 2012). At the same time, they are challenging social organizations in that they need to overcome difficulties such as lack of colocation, work in different settings, time zones, cultural and contextual frames, and members' differing proficiencies in a common trade language (Mockaitis et al., 2012).

In sum, virtual teams can be hugely successful, while at the same time, due to their complex nature, they often fail and are known to be difficult to lead, organize and manage. These teams in their virtual realms are largely dependent on technological means, virtual communication channels and shared digital work platforms, which is an added complication in comparison to traditional ways of managing and leading teamwork.

In our efforts to conduct meaningful research on GVTs uncovering new insights, we collected a rich set of research materials. We evaluated teams' case outputs (presented as 7-minute presentation videos directed towards the 'client'), collected six reflective individual essays from each participant, conducted focus groups and individual interviews based on structured questionnaires, carried out informal discussions with the participants and among course facilitators, and collected electronic materials from various sources.

Our doctoral candidates focus their research on a number of different aspects critical to the success of these teams, broadly striving to understand how and why certain phenomena emerge and evolve in GVTs. The unfolding of sensemaking at individual and team levels over time, how the team learns, and how trust can be established in GVTs, are the types of questions we aimed to answer. As an example, the second author of this chapter completed a doctoral dissertation on the *becoming* of well-performing teams, with socially constructed metaphors as one of the outcomes of the study, questioning the whole concept of a 'well-performing team' (Einola, 2017).

Broadly speaking, our aim is to leverage our unique setting and rich data, and challenge and diversify extant literature on GVTs, which typically offers simplified static models incapable of capturing the dynamic and varied nature of the phenomenon. The mainstream research on GVTs is largely based on input–process–output positivist thinking, testing one variable against another one (for example, Jonsen et al., 2012), with very little process or interpretative research available on the topic so far.

Our Course on IB Strategy as a Platform to Study GVTs

To form genuine GVTs and to create a shared learning environment for our students, we approached our colleagues who we knew were running similar courses at three other universities in the surrounding countries. These courses were mainly geared to students in professional MBAs and Master of Science programs, and many students already had significant professional experience making possible this type of set-up requiring considerable student autonomy.

We developed the course with the idea of simulating work in an international strategic consultancy, where team members are typically geographically dispersed and working on fast-paced and demanding projects. Approximately 120 students were placed in teams using virtual communication tools of their choice (mainly Skype, WhatsApp, SMS, email, Dropbox, OneDrive and Facebook) to overcome geographic spread (Zander et al., 2012). These teams, typically composed of five individuals of at least three different nationalities, solved consecutive case problems as a collaborative effort. During the course, students were given six consulting cases, which were partly previously published business school cases and partly real industry projects developed with partner firms from a Business Finland financed project. Our research setting can be described as a 'safari park' or a 'reality show', as the setting has similarities with a social experiment where researchers are able to closely observe teams being born and evolving over time while executing their tasks (see Einola, 2017 for details).

Since problems were defined and solved as a collective effort, the actual solution of a case was not limited to the individuals' subjective perceptions and mere factual knowledge of a limited kind, but required concerted problem-solving efforts, intense collaboration, joint decision-making, and aligned task execution in a high-speed stressful environment where students, in order to succeed, had to form as well-functioning teams and be able to solve conflicts that are unavoidable in this type of setting.

This approach to learning IB strategy is close to the *strategy-as-practice* stream of research (Vaara and Whittington, 2012), which considers strategy as an activity, something people *do*, rather than something that is as a property of organization. To date, over 500 students split over four cohorts have taken this course, and in total four PhD students have been involved (2014–17).

In parallel to master's students learning to work and solve strategic problems over virtual means, our international team of course facilitators also worked closely together in a parallel GVT to ensure alignment of goals and schedules, to grade the cases and other student work, to communicate with students and to solve any sudden problems that required attention. The PhD students participated fully in course planning, administration, teaching, grading, student communication, course development, and handled most of the coordination activities between the different universities. Before the course start, a shared document repository and structure was created in Dropbox for the teacher team, and a Facebook group was created to communicate with the course participants. However, over time, we found that the most reliable way to circulate important information was email, as some students from China and Russia, for instance, did not have Facebook accounts. Each team had to adjust its communication strategy to the multicultural background of its participants.

It was fascinating to see how student teams created radically different communication platform mixes to adjust to the needs of the team members. While some teams relied mainly on Skype and did most of their work in an almost face-to-face type of team via video conferencing, some other teams worked almost solely in Microsoft's OneDrive. Although more time consuming, for some teams this was the best means of communication, in particular when some members had problems with spoken English or the team had trouble finding time slots for simultaneous work sessions. The type of communication mix did not seem to be instrumental to the teams' success; it was more critical for the team to find platforms that optimized the inclusion of all its members.

To help align the different curricula of our schools and our teaching activities, we held an initial face-to-face meeting with our international colleagues and wrote a *Teacher's Handbook* for the course which we then adjusted along the way, and from cohort to cohort. We acknowledged from the start that we would not be able to control for 'everything' and agreed to try to fix any problems as soon as they emerged in the spirit of trial and error learning (Hull, 1930; Sosna et al., 2010).

Our core facilitator team quickly established a WhatsApp group we used as a hotline for any urgent problems that required our attention, either with the students or the rest of the teacher team located in different countries. At times we also used Skype – or simply met at the university café ad hoc to discuss ongoing matters. Our regular work hours stretched significantly, and while one of us was attending to student communication in late evenings, another one was up early in the morning. This approach worked quite well, although our workload for this course exceeded what we were used to by about 50 percent. Since we were also collecting research data and developing an international course format for virtual work, this was not much of an issue as overall synergies were significant.

When it comes to regular and planned communication, the facilitator team mainly used emails for better record-keeping and reach, but at times we had real problems, unrelated to the virtual communication mode which needed careful attention. For instance, students on one site were not receiving instructions from teachers that were sent to them. To avoid bypassing these facilitators or much less blame them, we instructed our local students to make sure their remote colleagues had all the information needed to solve the task, a tactic that also helped improve team cohesion. Another quite frequent problem was when one of the course participants was not very active or out of reach altogether. These situations caused tension in the concerned teams that were hard to deal with as we had very little control over students in other universities. However, they also offered our facilitator team an opportunity to experience work in a live GVT and we noticed that the problems faced were often similar to those the students were experiencing (slow response from some team members, unclear goals, sudden changes, stress, overwhelming and unevenly distributed workload, and so on).

Synergies

While this elaborate research setting is useful for doctoral research and learning, it also has to produce synergies with other key activities in our department in order to justify the high resource inputs needed to run such experiments. The synergy comes when aligning different objectives from different core activities. For instance, the research setting also enabled the creation of a meaningful educational setting for our master's degree students to help them understand strategy-as-practice, rather than seeing strategy as a merely static act of conceptual problem-solving as it is often portrayed in textbooks. Here, it is more important to be able to apply theoretical and book knowledge than to memorize it, and more important to be able to establish and work in a virtual team using technology-mediated communication than to read about what makes them successful.

The setting also helps students to develop self-awareness and reflective capabilities about the possibilities and limitations of work in these types of teams and of the technologies used. It also helps them develop their own personal approaches to collaboration and work in GVTs, and to gain an understanding of their relative strengths and weaknesses in these types of settings.

Importantly, our course is also a means to develop international cooperative relations with colleagues and universities abroad, as both students and faculty greatly benefit from being exposed to international management tasks and virtual team environments. The experimental setting turns our doctoral education into a practical apprenticeship of a sort, where not only research and cognitive skills are enhanced, but also where teaching skills and capabilities to develop and run master's degree courses are honed. Ideally, and with initial insights to build on, this type of course is also an opportunity to develop windows for further research projects and collaboration with industry players and practitioners. Outcomes of innovative experiments in a controlled setting like ours can help better understand very tangible real-life strategic challenges with virtual teamwork as the focus of interest.

DOCTORAL MENTORING AND LEARNING

Doctoral studies can be seen from many viewpoints. In order to offer a rich understanding, two perspectives are presented: the first one represents the point of view of a doctoral supervisor (Peter) responsible for facilitating and advancing doctoral candidates' learning to become an academic, and the second one reflects thoughts of a recent graduate (Katja), who looks back at her own journey of becoming a PhD.

Peter's Story

Originally from Austria, I have been part of our school's faculty for about 15 years, with a four-year position as senior lecturer in New Zealand in between, as well as with experience as an entrepreneur and consultant. Quite different from the Anglo-Saxon tradition I experienced in New Zealand, the research community built around our doctoral program here is very collegial, with very low hierarchical distance. It is a community of curious people. We like to engage with real-life problems of our wider stakeholder networks to contribute to our conceptual and more general understanding of the world. These values strongly shape our identity as an organization characterized by a strong desire to adhere to a variety of ideas, approaches, philosophies and ways of doing things. We favor creative but also critical thinking, as we understand that organizational continuity and progress need to balance stability as well as enable change; we also believe that making ethical thinking and debate a central part of all of our activities leads to more sustainable and desirable futures.

These clear stances on who we are and what we do as an organization attract likeminded doctoral candidates. Some of the new recruits return after having graduated from our programs, usually after a professional career, because they value further learning and have a desire to be part of changing the world in some aspects. This leads to a good basis for a collaborative atmosphere and many joint projects, where academics and doctoral candidates team up and bring their individual capabilities to accomplish higher learning goals.

At our university, as may be likely in many other universities as well, the personnel cuts and the added workload that comes from change projects, accreditation processes and requirements to publish create tension as many feel teaching and students receive less attention than they should. I could spend less time in teaching and coaching and take fewer PhD students to supervise, but for me this is the part of my work that is most rewarding. In a way, what I do is neither work nor a hobby, but rather a mission. It is personally meaningful to try to have an impact on the real world by helping students, no matter their level, to find their own ways in their careers and what they want to do in life, and learn new things myself in the process.

What we do here in our strategy course is to create what first could be seen as unnecessary work for ourselves as interacting between four sites and 120 students and giving individual feedback on over a thousand assignments is a daunting task. However, when we use this same material as data for research and see how students struggle but manage to pull through as they learn, it all starts to make much more sense. It is fascinating to learn about team dynamics and discuss issues within our teacher team as well as with the students, while facilitating a practically inspired course we all consider a valuable learning experience.

I like to think of our way of working as setting up an initial frame for minimal structure, and then co-creating and refining the rest together (the course, teamwork and research). As we go we facilitate our individual learning experiences together, 'following the beast' so to speak, rather than trying to stick to rigid plans dictated by one single teacher or supervisor.

To be able to try out an experimental course like this, I had to take some risks and trust my PhD students without losing oversight as the course was my responsibility. One of the biggest problems was that not all the master's students were happy at all times as some teams really struggled, the workload was heavy, and we spent very little time in formal classroom teaching, asking students to do their readings independently instead. This was different from what they were used to from their previous courses. Here, the PhD students facilitating the course with me were needed, as together we were able to be available to master's students, guide their work, and listen to their concerns when necessary.

Ultimately, such an endeavor is about learning how technology and the dynamic requirements of work enable each other while at the same time meeting the learning standards set out for both MSc and doctoral students. For MSc students the work in GVTs is something they need to learn to succeed. The role of technology is a rather minor one and we can rely on the current generation to find the appropriate tools that can facilitate coordination, knowledge exchange, decision-making and communication across many borders and very different institutional settings; our students were located in Finland, Russia, Latvia and Estonia. At the same time, we try also to challenge the students to use non-traditional ways of reporting. For instance, instead of asking for written reports to summarize the consulting cases, we require them to develop 7-minute video presentations directed to a client, which we upload to a YouTube channel which is visible to all.

This is how we build opportunities for our students to develop important skills (for example, how to animate a presentation and bring team members who have never met face-to-face into it). At the same time, our PhD students in the multinational teaching team have to rely heavily on technology to make coordination and data collection work. The chosen technologies vary to some extent in comparison to MSc students, with more reliance on email instead of Skype for instance, but otherwise technology is understood as an enabler and as means to raise productivity in, for instance, data collection and even applied in collective sensemaking when it comes to theorizing.

Technological prowess, however, might also be a particular feature of the Finnish context. Finland has been leading in establishing mobile communication (1970s), video conferencing (1980s) and internet banking (1990s) early, partly because of the size of the country and low population density. One could argue that the perceived enabling benefits of technology have been higher than resistance to change. Therefore, we see many new technologies adopted early on throughout most demographic groups, which might also favor the inclusion of technology as an important instrument to conduct work.

In general, individuals in our PhD program have a lot of freedom to design their research. This way of working can create anxieties, as writing a dissertation is intellectually very demanding. Here our community comes into the picture – there is always someone to turn to and if the realm of the issues at hand is outside the expertise in our group, PhD candidates are encouraged to consult with members of academia elsewhere autonomously, helping them to expand their personal networks. This way of working may look chaotic from the outside, but dealing with complexity and a multifaceted world in constant flux is what IB is all about. Just like practitioners in the field, we create temporary order out of chaos and with hard work and some sweat, tears as well as laughter, learn to muddle through while increasing our knowledge.

Learning to lead academic teams, to manage international courses, and to conduct meaningful and innovative research in this context are skills I believe are essential to future PhDs no matter where they end up working. Doing it all at once, not being afraid to let go of control, and to cross institutional borders and break age-old educational routines is one way to respond to the efficiency-demands placed on us as multitasking academics, working longer and longer hours, and eager to maintain high motivational levels and our professional integrity.

In my view, this setting effectively represents who we are as a research community and what our identity is. It is more about critical and creative thinking, and about understanding important research phenomena, than being concerned with reinforcing a theoretical research paradigm; it is more about developing pluralism among our students when it comes to different philosophical stances, methodological approaches, and theoretical perspectives than about relying on the well tried and tested ways of working. It also favors the chance to develop radically new insights and theorizing than confirmatory research and hypothesis testing.

Katja's Story

I joined the doctoral program as a 'mature' PhD student after over ten years in various project management roles in a large multinational telecommunications company and over twenty years of globetrotting. In a sense, I was not an 'average' PhD student, as I had already held leadership positions in managing strategic programs and marketing and resource management. My work had already exposed me heavily to virtual collaboration tools and teamwork over distance, although I felt I had not developed any strong answers to the question of how to build successful teams. Rather to the contrary, I wanted to study virtual collaboration in my PhD project to deepen my personal understanding of the phenomenon.

I had conducted my university studies in North America. With my rather broad life experience and good understanding of the Finnish culture, I had some ideas and expectations about doctoral education before beginning. Many surprises were in store. The first was the level of autonomy expected and freedom given, which was very different from the more hierarchical settings I was accustomed to. For instance, as an entry requirement, I was required to write a fully independent research proposal on a relevant topic in the field of IB. This was challenging for a practicing professional with no previous exposure to academic work, even though my chosen field (GVTs) as a phenomenon was more than familiar to me from a practitioner point of view. A study plan for approval was required – a preliminary schedule for courses and seminars I was planning to attend, and a financial plan for completing my dissertation. Undertaking this required thinking through my plan carefully, finding out about local, national and international courses and meeting multiple members of our community to sort through the many options and to understand how the program was structured. Once accepted into the program, the second surprise was the interest in our rather small department to develop teaching and conduct research in unconventional and experimental ways, as my previous understanding of the academic world was that it was quite rigid, formal and hierarchical.

PhD candidates like me are often worried about their future careers in a world where academic education is suffering from inflation and public funding to universities is being axed. It does not help that while doctoral education tends to be research focused, for a career in academia, pedagogical experience is necessary. Further, any international job inside or outside academia requires knowledge in program management, and the capability to collaborate with international peers, as well as entrepreneurial skills as many career paths are no longer nested within institutions but increasingly driven by individuals.

In my first year, when Peter invited me and another new doctoral candidate to join him to develop an advanced course on international strategy, I first thought the risks were too high. The course was new and underdeveloped, we were supposed to cooperate with a large number of teachers and students in three other countries and the students were expected to build working virtual communication routines with people they had never met before to work on complex projects. Peter's question 'Think about it, what can go wrong that we cannot do something about?' This made me think more positively and we all jumped in enthusiastically. I think this enthusiasm and a sentiment of genuine care we had for students and their learning helped us carry through our own mistakes, conflicts and the daunting workload we all had to somehow negotiate with our families and other projects. During this course, I worked about 70–80 hours per week (not unlike our colleagues in many consultancies we simulated when project hours peak), but the amount of learning and the empirical material gathered made it worth the effort.

There is also the pedagogical question of how to teach IB in a classroom setting inside four walls when the life of a successful IB practitioner requires contextual sensitivity, capability to adjust ad hoc and to deal with different others located in different countries whom one often does not know personally, to make quick decisions, and to integrate different streams of often incomplete information. 'Is it even possible to teach such skills in a meaningful way in a university setting by academic staff with often little exposure to field work?' This was one of my silent doubts as we started out, and for social reasons of courtesy and consideration, these types of thoughts are not easy to express. I still vividly remember when I was a fresh graduate and got my first job as a marketing manager at Ericsson Inc. in Canada. I felt lost in the expectation of getting projects with very concrete outputs like material for a trade show or a demo system going with a team based in Stockholm and Dallas. I felt my graduate IB and marketing degree was of little use at that terrifying starting point of what gradually became my business career. After three iterations of the course, my answer to this question is affirmative.

Due to my professional background in virtual project management, I was already familiar with facilitating collaboration. While this experience was helpful, I was far from being 'done' with learning and each year in the course my learning continued. In my role as a researcher, I could finally focus on understanding teamwork instead of fighting fires, managing project deliverables and solving human resources issues caused by teams in a business firm.

Our course ambitiously aims to address all doctoral learning goals from research to teaching to academic program management and communication. The nature of this huge effort was collective as we created and shaped the course together while it was running. Many misunderstandings surfaced which we then had to resolve to the best of our ability, mostly at a distance. One example was that students at one location were getting half the credits our own students were for the same effort, leading to an 'unequal pay for the same work' type of situation. While we were not able to address this fully, we could find workarounds, and could at least have a better understanding of why some people were dissatisfied and show them we cared by promising to fix the problem for the next cohort. A problem we could not solve was the unequal workload between the teachers – us. The focal team in Finland ended up doing most of the work as the others took what we thought was a more laid back attitude. Many student teams were complaining about similar problems so it was easy for us to sympathize with them as we tried to find solutions and identified causes to this problem as course instructors and team members.

With time, we started to tell the students upfront to try to detect negative team dynamics and to take action if unreflective free-riding happened. There were also challenges to find the right mix of digital applications for the whole team to use. In some locations, the internet connection was not good or people's access was limited, so asynchronous communication in chat groups, or OneDrive or Dropbox, worked better than live chat. Often, we saw that some student team members spontaneously taught their team-mates how to use certain applications. Better teams took responsibility to make sure members had needed skills, and that the team's self-designed communication toolbox helped the team function and achieve its goals. Finding an optimal mix of applications and schedules for meetings and project deliverables was typically a matter of constant adjustment.

In our team, my colleague, the other PhD student involved, took the application bridge builder role and made sure all the teachers understood how we should use Dropbox, what the WhatsApp group was for, and when we should just pick up the phone and call. In all this, we did have some internal conflicts. For instance, one night when I was working on another task, my fellow PhD student kept on sending text messages, WhatsApp alerts, Skype prompts and emails about what she considered an urgent matter and, exhausted, I ended up losing my self-control and blew up. It took some time to solve this, but we both managed with our work despite significant tension (it was just less fun for some time) and we relied mostly on virtual means for interpersonal communication and avoided meeting each other.

We exerted significant effort online (for example, Facebook, emails) and in ad hoc encounters to take the pulse of the student teams and other teachers. Despite the *Teaching Manual* Peter had written, based on our sketchy plans to help us stay aligned, we continuously adjusted the course along the way. For instance, early on students from one location had problems that were likely due to their inferior English skills. We openly discussed this not so uncommon real-life problem with the participants and encouraged the teams to find ways to circumvent this situation. This included considering different language skills in dividing tasks, favoring easier-to-follow written communication formats such as Google Docs or chats, and using meeting minutes to recap important team decisions. I also adjusted my research question along the way to follow the phenomenon and made modifications to our data collection to include ethnographic data.

The course instructors established our rhythm and kept adjusting it as our understanding of good virtual teamwork deepened. I also became more reflective about how student communication needs to be handled:

formal matters via email, more delicate ones via chat or other social media, and personal matters in person or over the phone (and if not possible, great caution is called for). Communication via social media can be tremendously helpful to create closer ties with students and to better understand student learning and challenges they go through. If applied well and thoughtfully, technology can help create better teacher–student trust and more nuanced interaction than traditional classroom interaction alone, and ultimately better teaching and learning outcomes.

Observing students interact in a large number of teams brought depth and breadth to my research that became a mix of a social experiment, auto-ethnography and longitudinal case study, a new sort of methodology all together. Mirroring what students were going through, we (the teachers) also formed a GVT struggling with a complex and stressful project, which made me more sensitive to the phenomenon itself.

As I write these lines, my dissertation on sensemaking on well-performing global teams has just been published and Peter and I have a number of research projects drawing on this course both when it comes to pedagogy and GVTs. As I move forward to a new job, three other PhD students take turns in leading and further developing the course, collecting research data, and learning practical academic skills needed in the job market. Our experiences have inspired us to think to the future beyond the student setting. One idea is to take the concepts we have developed, test and further improve them in collaboration with companies as tools to improve modern teamwork. Another one is to package the course in a way that could be reusable in other contexts by other coaches, teachers and mentors responsible for facilitating learning what it is like to become an IB practitioner. When it comes to technology, I learned that it is best not to think of it as something that automatically should solve problems. Instead, it should be actively adapted and worked with over time to facilitate communication, enable collaboration and build bridges over distances. Each team is different and their situation changes over time as teams learn and go through both external and internal changes.

CONCLUDING THOUGHTS

Leaders in IB are often described as heroes, great strategists, and visionaries. We read biographies and get inspiration from the likes of Steve Jobs of Apple, Louis V. Gerstner of IBM, and Ingvar Kamprad of IKEA. The reality of IB is much less fixed and heroic in nature. More than anything, IB leaders may need tenacity, courage, competence, confidence and capability to tolerate ambiguity and to sort out challenges that surface every day and that are often hard to predict and control. One of us once asked a C-level executive at a telecom equipment provider how she managed to do her work in the constant chaos of the industry and in an organization that was known to be rather rigid due to its history as a publicly owned company. She answered that she just did things she believed in despite how difficult it was to enact change or make an elephant dance to a new tune. She did her homework to stay informed, extended work hours when needed, mobilized people the best she could, and tackled problems upfront, often made mistakes and then did the best she could to fix them.

This storyline is different from the image of the superheroes of IB. But just like most other practitioner accounts, it does not make explicit the challenges that a virtual, dispersed work environment comes with, maybe because the virtual environment is so ubiquitous that communication, or rather, *communicating*, is not always something people are explicitly mindful about. Sophisticated technology alone does not solve human problems when it comes to collaboration. A similar pattern can be seen in higher education where the likes of mass online courses are developed, and the use of modern technologies has become in many cases the master as an end in itself rather than placing it where it fits better: as a servant to enable collaboration, purposeful human reflection and a support for learning. We find it dubious that, in our efforts to refresh our study programs, so much thought is often given to technology and so little to the important question of how to put it to meaningful use.

Our learning platform for PhD and master's students aims to develop both basic professional and leadership skills needed to tackle a complex, unpredictable and increasingly digital world to learn to generate meaningful academic research to better understand important aspects of international organizations. They need to learn to work in GVTs that any international firm ultimately depends on. In our work and practice, we try to acknowledge that transformation and modernization are needed both inside the academic field of IB and business education, and work from within to make changes and inspire others.

One important insight is that for the new generations, technology is no longer a tool to learn, to teach, or to harness for a specific purpose, educational or other, but rather a platform on which a significant part of people's lives takes place and depends. This requires a change in our mindsets about how to study and understand such contemporary phenomena as globalization and virtual teamwork. In our school, we have chosen to take an experimental approach to facilitate PhD learning of both teaching and academic project management skills, while doing doctoral research in a virtual environment. We have also taken a leadership position in our region to allow our students to explore the phenomenon of strategy work using virtual means of communication and modern technology from a practice-perspective, to better prepare our graduates for the challenges they face once their degrees are completed.

REFERENCES

Alvesson, M., Y. Gabriel and R. Paulsen (2017). *Return to Meaning: A Social Science with Something to Say*. Oxford: Oxford University Press.

Arum, R. and J. Roksa (2011). *Academically Adrift: Limited Learning on College Campuses*. Chicago, IL: University of Chicago Press.

Bennis, W.G. and J. O'Toole (2005). How business schools lost their way. *Harvard Business Review*, **83**(5), 96–104.

Brett, J., K. Behfar and M.C. Kern (2006). Managing multicultural teams. *Harvard Business Review*, **84**, 84–91.

Chiravuri, A., D. Nazareth and K. Ramamurthy (2011). Cognitive conflict and consensus generation in virtual teams during knowledge capture: Comparative effectiveness of techniques. *Journal of Management Information Systems*, **28**(1), 311–50.

Delios, A. (2017). The death and rebirth (?) of international business research. *Journal of Management Studies*, **54**(3), 391–7.

Einola, K. (2017). Making sense of successful global teams. Doctoral dissertation: Turku School of Economics.

Gibson, C.B. and J.L. Gibbs (2006). Unpacking the concept of virtuality: The effects of geographic dispersion, electronic dependence, dynamic structure and national diversity on team innovation. *Administrative Science Quarterly*, **51**, 451–95.

Gilson, L.L., M.T. Maynard, N.C.J. Young, M. Vartiainen and M. Hakonen (2015). Virtual teams research: 10 years, 10 themes, and 10 opportunities. *Journal of Management*, **41**(5), 1313–37.

Hallett, R. (2016). The most innovative country in the world takes top spot again. 2 November. Accessed at https://www.weforum.org/agenda/2016/11/the-most-innovative-countries-in-the-world/.

Hertel, G., S. Geister and U. Konradt (2005). Managing virtual teams: A review of current empirical research. *Human Resource Management Review*, **15**(1), 69–95.

Hsu, A. et al. (2016). *2016 Environmental Performance Index*. New Haven, CT: Yale University. Accessed at http://epi2016.yale.edu/sites/default/files/2016EPI_Full_Report_opt.pdf.

Hull, C.L. (1930). Simple trial and error learning: A study in psychological theory. *Psychological Review*, **37**(3), 241–56.

Jarvenpaa, S.L. and D.E. Leidner (1998). Communication and trust in global virtual teams. *Journal of Computer-Mediated Communication*, **3**(4).

Jonsen, K., M.L. Maznevski and S.C. Davison (2012). Global virtual team dynamics and effectiveness. In G. Stahl, I. Bjorkman and S. Morris (eds), *Handbook of Research in International HR Management* (pp. 363–92). Cheltenham, UK and Northampton, MA, USA: Edward Elgar Publishing.

McDonald, D. (2017). *The Golden Passport: Harvard Business School, the Limits of Capitalism, and the Moral Failure of the MBA Elite*. New York, NY: HarperBusiness.

Messner, J.J. and N. Haken (2016). Fragile States Index 2016 – Annual Report. Accessed at http://fundforpeace.org/fsi/2016/06/27/fragile-states-index-2016-annual-report.

Mockaitis, A.I., E.L. Rose and P. Zettinig (2009). The determinants of trust in multicultural global virtual teams. *Academy of Management Proceedings*, **2009**(1), 1–6.

Mockaitis, A.I., E.L. Rose and P. Zettinig (2012). The power of individual cultural values in global virtual teams. *International Journal of Cross Cultural Management*, **12**(2), 193–210.

Peñarroja, V., V. Orengo, A. Zornoza and A. Hernández (2013). The effects of virtuality level on task-related collaborative behaviors: The mediating role of team trust. *Computers in Human Behavior*, **29**(3), 967–74.

Sosna, M., R.N. Trevinyo-Rodríguez and S.R. Velamuri (2010). Business model innovation through trial-and-error learning: The Naturhouse case. *Long Range Planning*, **43**(2–3), 383–407.

The disposable academic (2010). *The Economist*. Accessed at https://www.economist.com/news/christmas-specials/17723223-why-doing-phd-often-waste-time-disposable-academic.

The Global Competitiveness Report 2015–2016 (n.d.). Accessed at http://reports.weforum.org/global-competitiveness-report-2015-2016/country-highlights/.

Townsend, A.M., S.M. DeMarie and A.R. Hendrickson (1998). Virtual teams: Technology and the workplace of the future. *The Academy of Management Executive*, **12**(3), 17–29.

Vaara, E. and R. Whittington (2012). Strategy-as-practice: Taking social practices seriously. *Academy of Management Annals*, **6**(1), 285–336.

'Welcome to study in Finland' (2017). Accessed at http://www.studyinfinland.fi/destination_finland.

Zander, L., C.L. Butler, A.I. Mockaitis, K. Herbert, J. Lauring, K. Mäkelä and P. Zettinig (2015). Team-based global organizations: The future of global organizing. In R. van Tulder, A. Verbeke and R. Drogendijk (eds), *The Future of Global Organizing* (pp. 227–43). Bingley: Emerald Group Publishing.

Zander, L., A.I. Mockaitis and C.L. Butler (2012). Leading global teams. *Journal of World Business*, **47**(4), 592–603.

Zander, L., P. Zettinig and K. Mäkelä (2013). Leading global virtual teams to success. *Organizational Dynamics*, **42**(3 SI), 228–37.

Zettinig, P. and Z. Vincze (2008). Developing the international business curriculum: Results and implications of a Delphi study on the futures of teaching and learning in international business. *Journal of Teaching in International Business*, **19**(2), 109–41.

Zettinig, P. and Z. Vincze (2011). The domain of international business: Futures and future relevance of international business. *Thunderbird International Business Review*, **53**(3), 337–49.

13. E-mentoring in a technology mediated world: implications for doctoral leadership education

Sean Robinson

Although scholars contend that mentoring encompasses a myriad of definitions and perspectives (for example, Allen and Eby, 2010; Bierema and Merriam, 2002), most agree that it is both a process and a relationship (Williams and Kim, 2011; Wright-Harp and Cole, 2008). While definitions range from sponsor to coach, to the more classical image of a mentor who oversees all aspects of a protégé's development, Zey's (1984) definition speaks to the true functions of a mentor as someone 'who oversees the career and development of another person, usually a junior, through teaching, counseling, providing psychological support, protecting, and at times promoting or sponsoring' (p. 7).

Due in large part to the ubiquitous forms of technology in our work and personal lives, new mentoring opportunities in the 21st century have been created beyond email, and include social media platforms, instant messaging, and videoconferencing tools such as Facebook, LinkedIn, Google Hangouts, Skype, Facetime, WhatsApp, and numerous others. All of these tools can be used to capitalize on the boundarylessness and egalitarian aspects of Bierema and Merriam's (2002) notion of e-mentoring. The purpose of this chapter is to explore the role of mentoring within online doctoral leadership education, with attention directed to the benefits and role of e-mentoring as a way to help aspiring leaders (doctoral students) develop the necessary skills and mindset needed for effective leadership. Given the shifting landscape of communication processes, coupled with the exponentially changing world of computers and technology that now encompasses smartphones, tablets and various apps, including social media platforms available on them, considering the role of e-mentoring for leadership development within doctoral education is both timely and necessary.

According to Jacobi (1991), student–faculty mentoring exemplifies what in doctoral education is considered the apprenticeship model. Since this type of interaction provides a means of learning beyond the classroom, it is regarded as a necessary part of the student's educational experience. In this context, the faculty member imparts knowledge, provides support, and offers guidance on both academic and non-academic issues (Pascarella, 1980). The mentoring relationship can thus help a student develop a sense of belonging within the institution as well as the discipline (Austin, 2002), in addition to providing guidance for those aspiring to an academic career. Many faculty in doctoral education promote the benefits and importance of mentoring as a core component of the educational experience. Henry Ellis's (1992) widely read piece is still representative of the thinking among educators who engage in a mentoring relationship at this level:

> I am convinced that the success of graduate education depends on a student–faculty relationship based on integrity, trust, and support. I believe that quality graduate programs have some sort of faculty mentor system in which students can obtain advice, counseling, and helpful direction in their training.... Good mentoring represents one of the important factors in graduate training, fosters long term competence, and promotes effectiveness for both scientists and professionals. (p. 575)

In her groundbreaking book *Mentoring at Work: Developmental Relationships in Organizational Life*, Kathy Kram (1985) outlines two important functions of the mentor, career-related and psychosocial; these aspects are just as important in doctoral education as in the business world. Career functions aid in the career development of protégés, while psychosocial functions enhance a protégé's sense of competence and identity. In effect, career development functions assist the protégé in career advancement not only while in a graduate program but in post-graduation early career stages, whereas the psychosocial functions help a protégé's personal development by relating to them on a personal level.

Career-related functions involve particular activities that aid in career development and advancement, and include sponsorship, exposure and visibility, coaching, protection and challenging assignments. *Psychosocial functions* are more personal aspects and include role modeling, acceptance and confirmation, counseling and friendship. Unlike the career functions which are more dependent on the mentor's ability to create opportunities for the protégé, psychosocial functions depend upon the relationship between the mentor and the protégé.

Considering the prevalence of technology-driven education leads one to raise questions about the processes and outcomes of mentoring within such an environment. One particular discipline in which mentoring can have a profound impact is that of doctoral leadership programs, which, along with more traditional leadership and management programs, have been at the forefront of innovation in shifting the mode of delivery from face-to-face into the world of virtual and online programs and curricula. Technology developments and the use of technology-mediated communications are changing the way faculty and students interact, and are a natural extension of the way mentors and protégés interact (Smith and Israel, 2010). Bierema and Merriam (2002) define this as *e-mentoring*: 'a computer mediated, mutually beneficial relationship between the mentor and a protégé which provides learning, advising, encouraging, promoting, and modeling, that is often boundaryless, egalitarian, and qualitatively different than traditional face-to-face mentoring' (p. 214). Single and Single (2005) maintain e-mentoring offers individuals the same instrumental, informational, psychosocial and career benefits as those engaged in traditional face-to-face mentoring programs. However, the benefits of such technology-mediated mentoring allow such a relationship to develop and to be maintained without the geographical, spatial or time constraints typically found in face-to-face mentoring relationships.

Developments in online and virtual education in the past several decades offer a myriad of options for both formal and informal learning opportunities, including the manner in which mentoring relationships are developed and maintained. Eli Noam of Columbia University believed that the internet would pave a difficult road ahead for traditional academic institutions when he proclaimed in a 1995 *Science* article that 'as one connects in new ways [the internet], one also disconnects the old ways' (p. 247). More than two decades later, online, virtual learning has become an important element in higher education, showing how this arena has in fact moved from old ways of teaching to new ways of learning. According to the 2017 *Survey of Online Learning* conducted by Elaine Allen and Jeff Seaman, in the fall of 2015 over 6 million college students in the US, representing approximately 30 percent of college students, were taking courses via distance education, with 14 percent (2.9 million) taking all their courses at a distance and 16 percent (3.1 million) taking some, but not all, courses at a distance. While 29 percent of undergraduates were taking at least one class via distance education, 34 percent of graduate students were enrolled in distance education courses during the fall of 2015, with 8 percent taking at least part of their programs online and at a distance, but 26 percent taking all of their classes in this format. Graduate students were twice as likely to be taking all of their courses via distance education, compared with undergraduates. These are not inconsequential numbers for graduate programs. Before continuing the discussion of mentoring within doctoral leadership education, a brief overview of the tenets of leadership development is necessary.

LEADERSHIP DEVELOPMENT

One element of organizational success is effective leadership. Leadership remains the top human capital concern and the largest 'readiness gap' according to Loew and Garr (2014). Researchers have documented the outcomes associated with successful leadership, including higher levels of individual commitment (for example, Chen, 2004), satisfaction (for example, Fuller and Patterson, 1996), effort (for example, Bass, 1999), effectiveness (for example, Bass, 1985; Lowe et al., 1996), and team outcomes (for example, Burke et al., 2006). Furthermore, leadership development is often a focus of many organizations relative to attracting and retaining individuals at all levels within an organization. In 2013, companies spent $15.5 billion on leadership programs (Loew and Garr, 2014). Yet, according to Barbara Kellerman and Jeffrey Pfeffer (as cited by Bersin et al., 2016), the leadership world continues to be dominated by stories, myths and fads, often promoting superficial solutions that appear effective but fail to address the issue of helping leaders to learn and that do not deliver measurable impact and results. Fully 89 percent of executives who participated in the research by Bersin et al. rated the need to strengthen, reengineer and improve organizational leadership as an important priority. The traditional pyramid-shaped leadership development model is simply not producing leaders fast enough to keep up with the demands of business and the pace of change.

Bersin and his associates suggest that organizations need to raise the bar in terms of rigor, evidence, and more structured and scientific approaches to identifying, assessing and developing leaders, and that this process needs to start earlier in leaders' careers. Adding to this complexity of leadership development is that the entire concept of leadership is being radically redefined. The whole notion of 'positional leadership' – that people become leaders by virtue of their power or position – is being challenged. Leaders are instead being asked to inspire team loyalty through their expertise, vision and judgment. This broad span of control demands leaders who are skilled coaches and mentors – not strictly supervisors – with the ability to attract, inspire and retain great people.

Since leadership development is dependent upon a particular context, a one-size-fits-all approach to leadership development is unrealistic. Successful leadership development depends more on interpersonal competencies than on particular technical skills or knowledge. In fact, leadership is generally considered the ability to influence others directly or indirectly within different contexts. As Day (2000) and Yukl (2006) have both discussed, leadership development takes two forms: training or individualized development activities.

Training is primarily conducted in seminars, classes, workshops, or formal degree programs. Regarding actual degree programs, organizations are increasingly aligning tuition assistance with their employee development and talent management strategies. Lamoureux (2012) found that 86 percent of 300 companies surveyed have aligned tuition assistance with their talent management strategies, up from 49 percent in 2009; 71 percent of the US organizations surveyed offer tuition assistance to their employees. It is also worth noting that organizations are spending on average $5000 per employee when they participate in a formal, degree-oriented leadership development program, which is just under the allowable federal tax threshold.

In contrast to more formalized training, individualized activities are more often geared to preparing individuals for their current or future leadership roles, and involve experiential activities and reflection focused on particular knowledge or skills; coaching and mentoring are the two primary forms of such individual developmental and experiential activities. As already mentioned, a mentor is an expert who provides wisdom and guidance based on their own experience. Mentoring may include advising, counseling and coaching. Coaching, in contrast, focuses on an individual's setting and reaching their own objectives. The International Coach Federation's (n.d.) formal definition of coaching is:

> partnering with clients in a thought-provoking and creative process that inspires them to maximize their personal and professional potential, which is particularly important in today's uncertain and complex environment. Coaches honor the client as the expert in his or her life and work and believe every client is creative, resourceful and whole. (International Coach Federation, para. 1)

While mentoring and coaching are different types of activity, coaching often occurs as part of mentoring and is more skill focused. Mentoring and coaching provide opportunities for both mentor and protégé to reflect on prior experiences, and to use such reflections and revelations as key learning opportunities in exactly the manner Kolb (1984) believes experiential learning activities should occur. Bersin et al. (2016) contend that organizations are increasingly using both coaching and mentoring as part of their leadership development strategies and initiatives due to their potential to help leaders reflect on their experiences and create new learning opportunities.

According to Kolb (1984), experientially-based learning usually involves reflecting upon some particular experience, gaining different perspectives about that experience, gaining insight about what occurred, and then extrapolating that learning into a new situation. Feedback from others helps the reflection process in which others act as a sounding board facilitating learning within this context. This is where mentors, and by extension coaches, can provide additional value to individuals engaged in leadership development activities, through their guidance, feedback and support. In fact, previous organizational research on mentoring has demonstrated its overall positive impact on individuals within an organization (Allen et al., 2004).

In providing an understanding of leadership development, it is imperative that graduate students within leadership programs appreciate the reality of lifelong learning and understand what it entails. Faculty can ensure that students know how to think and learn critically, thus helping to prepare students for their leadership development journey. Although more formal in nature, degree programs should also work to develop students' inter- and intra-personal skills, which are essential for leadership development; this can occur through reflection activities, simulations and other hands-on activities, training in systems thinking and learning styles, and understanding the role of language for leaders (Day, 2000). Finally, students would probably benefit if faculty focused on leadership praxis, that is, moving theories of leadership into the practice of leadership.

MENTORING AS LEADERSHIP DEVELOPMENT

Although mentoring as a form of leadership development is recognized as a complex process, there is agreement that mentoring seems to benefit leaders in significant ways including: reduced feelings of isolation, increased job satisfaction, role socialization, improved leadership skills, professional development, and leadership-capacity building (Browne-Ferrigno and Muth, 2004; Fagan and Walter, 1982; Scandura et al., 1996; Stott and Walker, 1992).

One reason that mentoring can be successful with developing leaders is that it can be viewed as a model based on relational learning that is helpful in co-creating a learning environment (Beattie, 2002). Thus, mentoring can be seen as a holistic and fluid concept that attends to professional, career, psychosocial and personal development (Clutterbuck, 2001; Kram, 1983; Parsloe and Wray, 2000). Beech and Brockbank (1999) suggest two main purposes of mentoring within an organizational context. The first role of the mentor is helping the protégé understand how the organization operates at a cultural and political level. The second role is more psychosocial and includes role modeling, offering personal support, providing feedback to increase the confidence and self-awareness of the protégé, and helping them create and refine a professional identity, especially as it relates to what it means to be a leader.

Holding such a holistic view of the mentor's role as attending to institutional, professional and personal needs and perspectives can also be reflected in key characteristics defining the nature of the mentoring relationship. For example, from an organizational perspective, Townley (1994) views the mentoring relationship as a social relationship where the mentor works to socialize the protégé into the culture of an organization. In addition, McDougall and Beattie (1997) suggest that from a professional angle, mentoring offers a confidential space that enables a protégé to test out new ideas and look at issues from a fresh perspective in a safe and non-judgmental environment. Given this idea of mentoring within the workplace, a number of scholars and practitioners have touted the importance of mentorship in promoting leader development (for example, London, 2002; McCauley and Van Velsor, 2004) and further research suggests that mentorship can lead to behavioral, attitudinal and performance change in general (for example, Eby et al., 2008; Gentry et al., 2008).

According to Lord and Hall (2005) and Avolio (2011), leadership programs and interventions in the earlier stages of one's career impact both the protégé's ideas about leadership and their self-concept, both of which are needed for developing, organizing and carrying out future leadership skills as well as what it means to earn the title *Doctor in Leadership*. Consequently, to the extent that viewing oneself as a leader is part of one's early identity development, the schemas and beliefs created as part of that identity become a framework for incorporating ongoing leadership experiences and feedback (Hannah et al., 2009; Lord and Hall, 2005). Therefore, it stands to reason that mentoring as a specific leadership intervention focused specifically on developing aspects of a protégé's leader identity, and included as part of a doctoral student's leadership program would be an important complement to both coursework and field experiences, particularly during the early stages of leader development.

DeRue and Ashford (2010) suggested that leaders' identity development occurs through various social interactions, including performing leadership behaviors in front of others or by others naming certain behaviors as 'leadership'. Individuals 'claim' leadership through stepping up and attempting to influence others. Others then 'grant' leadership through affirming and supporting that leader's attempts. Through this reciprocal process, individuals begin to see themselves as capable leaders, reinforcing a leader identity. Mentors can serve similar functions, operating as experienced role models offering external acknowledgment of leadership behaviors, serving to reinforce particular ideas, beliefs and schemas about what it means to be a leader. A primary role of mentors is to provide psychosocial support to protégés, helping them to understand their behaviors and drivers through serving as a sounding board or a mirror, helping to interpret or reframe thoughts and actions, while also serving as a source of validation for the protégé (Kram, 1985). As suggested by DeRue and Ashford (2010), for one's identity as a leader to solidify, others must endorse that identity; thus, a mentor can often serve to reinforce and shape a protégé's identity in a non-judgmental manner. Given the nature and purpose of a mentoring relationship, protégés might be more likely to explore their leadership identity and behaviors in this safe, non-threatening manner. The regular, ongoing exploration of identity, cognitions, beliefs, and what it means to be a leader and to hold the title of Doctor may serve to increase both self-esteem and self-efficacy of the aspiring leader, particularly if it is done in conjunction within a more formalized, knowledge-building academic arena.

Leader efficacy can be further developed through role modeling or vicarious learning, where individuals observe leaders successfully perform-ing similar tasks, or where protégés are encouraged to cognitively envision and work through their own leadership decisions and actions (Stajkovic and Luthans, 1998). Drawing on work by Scandura (1998) and Payne and Huffman (2005), it stands to reason therefore that mentorship relation-ships work in part because of the role modeling exhibited by the mentor to the protégé, which can influence the protégé's development of leader effi-cacy beliefs. Thus, while mentoring has several purposes, a primary benefit can be that of having the mentor serve as a role model, offering vicarious, experiential learning experiences, and walking protégés through prior or future leadership actions, using key theories and information presented during their academic coursework as a foundation. These types of learning moments can help protégés develop needed aspects of successful leader-ship behaviors and performances (Kram, 1985; Phillips-Jones, 1982).

Finally, as noted by Bandura (1997), an individual's self-efficacy devel-opment often occurs through social persuasion, which is often present in a strong mentoring relationship (Kram, 1985; Phillips-Jones, 1982). Such a relationship might also exist between a doctoral student and his or her dissertation supervisor or program advisor. Even when feedback to an aspiring leader is negative (for example, discussing an incident of poor per-formance), mentors can engage the protégé in thinking through feedback in a positive manner, highlighting what was learned and how feedback can then be used to enhance future performance (Berson et al., 2001; Garland and Adkinson, 1987).

E-MENTORING IN DOCTORAL EDUCATION

As educational institutions and organizations realize that online and distance education programs can be effective in addressing work-specific skills and knowledge related to leadership development, there is simply not enough time during in-person or online class meetings with faculty members to also meet the individual leadership development needs of students. Many businesses and organizations who have partnered with online graduate leadership programs have discovered that mentoring can improve the effectiveness of distance training and education (Jossi, 1997). They recognize that mentoring can address interpersonal and cognitive needs of individuals; e-mentoring in a technology-mediated environment is the 21st-century extension of this, given the available technological tools and resources.

According to Muilenburg and Berge (2005), despite having the technology at hand, success in formal online programs may still be hampered if faculty are not well trained or prepared, there are issues with the course materials, motivation waxes and wanes, poor time management exists, or overall interactions within the online courses are limited. There is often a high dropout rate from online programs if classes are not delivered effectively, if the faculty's training or style are not conducive to creating an appropriate learning environment online, if there is insufficient feedback, or if there is poor course design (McKenzie et al., 2006; Muirhead and Betz, 2002; Williams et al., 2012). While there have been many suggestions on how to overcome these and other barriers, e-mentoring is being used by more organizations as an effective way to mitigate many or all of these potential problems. While mentoring, and as an extension e-mentoring, may include actual instruction, it supports much of what is known about learning, including the socially constructed nature of learning and the importance of situated learning (Kerka, 1998).

There is evidence that face-to-face mentoring is positively associated with doctoral student outcomes, including: satisfaction; scholarly activities, such as publications or presentations; research interest; and time to degree. Researchers have found that mentored doctoral students were significantly more likely to have scholarly products, such as published articles or conference presentations (for example, Cronan-Hillix et al., 1986; Nettles and Millett, 2006), and to have a greater interest in research (Kahn, 2001), than students who had no mentors. Paglis et al. (2006) contend that mentored students were significantly more productive and had higher self-efficacy than those who were not mentored.

In more recent research, Lunsford (2012) corroborated prior research showing that the effect of mentoring support on student outcomes was positive. According to Lunsford, psychosocial mentoring was significantly related to satisfaction with a student's advisor, while career mentoring was significantly related to publications, presentations and degree progress. Furthermore, when examining the interaction effects of psychosocial and career support significantly, Lunsford showed a positive interaction influencing satisfaction with one's advisor; in this case the main, primary effects of psychosocial and career mentoring dropped out as significant predictors. It appears that having a personal relationship with an advisor creates a situation where a student is more likely to take their career advice and report being more satisfied with their advisor. These results suggest that the interactive effect of psychosocial and career mentoring, and not just psychosocial mentoring, have an impact on ratings of advisor satisfaction. However, psychosocial and career mentoring did not interact for the objective outcomes, publications, presentations and degree progress – this was strictly a result of career mentoring alone. It may be that these two types of mentoring operate independently for some student outcomes, a counterintuitive but important finding.

Given that graduate faculty are responsible for shepherding students through their academic programs, including research and writing activities, inducting them into the intellectual community, introducing them to professional networks, and often launching their academic career – all elements of both the psychosocial and career functions of mentoring – it is no wonder that students' satisfaction with their doctoral experience hinges on a high degree of satisfaction, support and engagement with their faculty (Forehand, 2008). Despite the fact that mentoring by faculty is conspicuously absent or lacking for graduate students (Yob and Crawford, 2012), mentoring has been identified by the Council of Graduate Schools (2008) as one of six key factors leading to doctoral degree completion. It must be noted that there may be differences in the role of mentoring for traditional PhD versus professional doctorates, and while each has slightly different program outcomes and learning modalities, both present opportunities for faculty to support terminal degree students through their mentoring.

When mentors are used to support online graduate students' academic program, they are in a position to assess protégés' learning needs, and then offer one-on-one assistance in key areas where leadership skills or knowledge seem most appropriate, tapping directly into the career functions of mentoring. As problems or areas of interest are identified, e-mentors can work with students to offer feedback, explore issues, encourage active reflection, propose additional learning activities, or strategize solutions to challenges (McKenzie et al., 2006). E-mentors can serve as a guide for both the academic program and a protégé's workplace, helping to translate formal learning into practical application (Owens, 2006). Furthermore, e-mentors can offer to help mediate the flow of learning, provide actual case scenarios, share experiences, and in some ways reduce the sense of isolation many online students feel (Falconer, 2006). Thus, within online doctoral leadership programs, e-mentoring career-functions can look and feel different from how they are in other disciplines such as the natural sciences, or in more traditional face-to-face relationships.

In e-mentoring relationships, the distance factor can create a space where participants are able to express themselves more freely than in face-to-face communication. This often provides a more honest, open and reflective learning environment where, in addition to the course topics and mastering particular skills, mentoring pairs can explore their values, feelings and objectives differently than when sitting in the same room, where there is often added pressure to respond immediately. In this way, the psychosocial functions of mentors, namely creating trust and building a relationship, constitute a different process as well. More than in classroom situations or synchronous online teaching venues, using the virtual medium of asynchronous communication, e-mentors can create a reflective learning environment where, in addition to the subject matter, both mentor and protégé can discuss and explore their values, feelings and objectives more deeply and reflectively and over a longer period of time (Headlam-Wells et al., 2005). By operating more as teaching partners than as authority figures in this virtual social environment, e-mentors can also minimize status barriers.

Of course, as with any type of instruction, interaction or communication, there are challenges specific to a mentoring relationship. Funding the effort, finding mentors, matching them with appropriate students, getting a dedicated amount of their time, and continuing to support the program can take an enormous amount of initial administration and effort for the graduate program and its faculty. In the case of e-mentoring, if the technology, software or apps are too complex and difficult to navigate, protégés find they need more training to use them, or if they are unfamiliar with the ways and means of communicating online or with social media apps, they will not reap the full benefits of the mentorship relationship. Fluency in using social media apps and in navigating online communication systems is a vital skill, and the tools and processes involved are not always intuitive and may require additional planning, training and support. A structured practice period might be useful early on in such an online relationship (for example, requiring a weekly posting format and time).

A number of studies have shown the effectiveness of mentoring programs and that they really do support and sustain online training and education programs (for example, Headlam-Wells et al., 2005; Kumar and Coe, 2017; Kumar and Johnson, 2017). According to the literature, protégés in this arena have reported increased job satisfaction, improved career readiness and outcomes, increased dissertation support, and increased moral and psychological support. However, the benefits for protégés are not always equal. While it is clear that e-mentoring can level the playing field by providing flexibility and easy access to those who might otherwise be excluded due to gender, race, ethnicity, disability or geography, faculty, programs, administrators and mentors themselves must remember that there is a 'digital divide' and participants that have online access both at work and at home have a clear advantage over those who do not.

For those that do have the privilege of mentoring doctoral students, a number of key elements are worth noting that tap into both the psychosocial and the career functions discussed earlier. First, it is important for the mentor to offer increasing mutuality and reciprocity. Mentoring should not be a one-way relationship. Research suggests that while graduate students are appreciative of the emotional support and encouragement from mentors, they are likely to rate mutuality higher than other aspects of the relationship (Johnson, 2007; 2008). Furthermore, they are more likely to expect and appreciate relationships characterized as both transformational and reciprocal (Johnson, 2014). Progressive mutuality might involve sharing personal and professional challenges, discussing one's career trajectory or aspirations, sharing stories of success and failure, and in general becoming more friendly over time. The gradual shift towards friendship shows a protégé that the mentor values their relationship, sees them as a colleague, and trusts the protégé's judgment.

The second element for mentors to keep in mind is that mentoring should occur in different contexts. Mentoring should happen beyond the classroom and office settings. Mentors should seek to model and guide a protégé into the disciplinary network outside the academic department. This could include enlisting them as collaborators on research and writing projects, including them as peer reviewers, inviting them to attend professional meetings and conferences and introducing them to others in the field, including them as guest speakers, and empowering them to carry out various independent, professionally oriented tasks. Those doctoral students who have expressed an interest in an academic career should have additional opportunities to grow and develop as researchers, writers, teachers and novice members of their broader academic community.

In contrast to undergraduate settings where the mentor's task might be to help a student realize that one's major could in fact lead to a fulfilling career, a graduate student's mentor's task is to instill a sense of professionalism, which is the third aspect important for mentors to understand. A graduate student becomes socialized into a discipline over the course of their academic tenure, assimilating the values, beliefs, attitudes and expectations of the disciplinary culture. It is necessary for the mentor to find ways to foster an attitude of personal responsibility regarding one's career and chosen path. A successfully socialized protégé develops pride in their discipline and profession, and is committed to behaving ethically and morally.

Finally, mentors must actively sponsor a protégé for further training as well as postgraduate employment. For many mentors, this occurs for years after a student has graduated. Mentors should be highly invested in the careers of their protégés, and endeavor to support them throughout their journey. It is highly likely that the protégé will need strong support, guidance, advice, insider information, and requisite letters of recommendation towards the end of their academic program and into the early phase of their career. Faculty might consider creating and cultivating social media profiles for the specific purposes of networking with doctoral students, connecting them to professional networks, keeping them updated (for example, articles, jobs, grant and conference opportunities), and providing a dedicated messaging platform for interaction (for example, LinkedIn, Twitter). This is where a career-long commitment to the protégé is often called upon. Effective mentorship throughout a protégé's academic studies and into early career should not be taken lightly. Given the increasing demands placed upon program faculty, outside mentors should be utilized whenever possible to support the professional identity development of students. For doctoral students in a leadership program, mentoring should not be viewed merely as a way to get students through a degree program; mentoring instead should be approached as a process to develop a new generation of leaders.

PERSONAL CASE STUDY

I would like to offer my own experiences with e-mentoring. In the spirit of transparency, I should add that in addition to being a faculty member in a leadership program, I am also a certified professional coach. As mentioned earlier in this chapter, coaching can be a key part of the mentoring relationship. In most of my mentoring relationships with my students, I do assume the 'coach' role, more than the 'expert mentor' role. Taking this stance allows me to move the relationship from a purely educative one to one that is both educative and productive, where I am able to focus both on the goals of my protégé (the *what*) as well as personal issues, challenges and development (the *who*). The crux of the mentoring relationship then provides the opportunity to consider the strategies for *how* to support and guide my protégé towards their individual goals.

Using one of my current protégés, Chris (a pseudonym), I provide a sketch of what mentoring for leadership development with a doctoral student might look like in practice; over the course of our relationship we have engaged in both traditional face-to-face interactions as well as those mediated by technology. Chris is a 32-year-old, Black male, works as a mid-level university administrator at a large public research university and aspires to be the president of a minority serving institution within the next 15 years. I have known Chris for six years, and we have had a solid, formal mentoring relationship for the past three years, beginning with his entrance into our PhD program. For the first half of the program, Chris was in at least one of my courses every term, so we had regular encounters, mostly of an academic nature. We did meet at least once every 2–3 months off campus for face-to-face mentoring sessions, where we could debrief experiences and analyze or process current challenges or situations Chris was facing. In between our regular mentoring sessions, generally every other week, I would often engage with Chris through email, instant messages (via WhatsApp and Facebook messenger), Google Hangouts and Facetime about relevant leadership-oriented topics from one of our classes and how he was translating that knowledge into practice. For example, in my organizational theory course, we use Bolman and Deal's (2013) four frames (structural, human resources, political, and cultural) to analyze the behavior of individuals, teams, and organizations as a whole.

During each section of the course surrounding individual frames, I would ask Chris what he noticed in his role as a leader, what new insights he had about things or people on campus from that frame, and what he might be doing differently because of his new knowledge. Through a series of strategic questions via text or email, I could probe his thinking and gauge his own development as a leader. This asynchronous exchange would allow him time to reflect and for me to push his thinking deeper, sometimes suggesting specific activities for him to try in his workplace. Often one or both of us would also send each other articles relevant to our class from either a major newspaper such as the *Wall Street Journal*, InsideHigherEd.com, or the *Chronicle of Higher Education*, with comments and questions about the article and its relationship to course material. These exchanges provided further discussions about translating theory into practice, and for engaging Chris in deeper meaning-making conversations about his own leadership development (for example: What would you do in that situation, and why? How does this fit into your personal identity as a leader?).

These same types of exchanges happened throughout other courses as well, including ones on leadership theory, administration and governance, legal issues, and organizational culture and change management. The uses of technology in our relationship allowed for constant give and take, and many times provided the opportunity for almost immediate feedback or check-ins. Unlike in more traditional face-to-face mentoring relationships, the various forms of technology we used helped to remove barriers of time and place as I became Chris's partner in his success as a leader, and as a doctoral student.

During our quarterly face-to-face mentoring sessions, I generally took a coaching approach by letting him set the agenda at first, which often included questions and concerns about possible research topics, how to make the most of his academic experiences so they supported his career goals, possible conferences to attend and present at, and finally onto specific issues and challenges he was seeing and experiencing on campus. Since we were on the same campus for the first two years, I could offer my own perspectives on things as well, and act more of a mentor to offer advice and guidance based on my own experiences and insider knowledge. When he moved to a new campus, my direct experience was useful as a frame for him, but we were able to use that as a springboard for him to conceptualize and analyze issues from his point of view on his campus. And in the weeks following our face-to-face time, we once again turned to various forms of technology to continue the conversation in both synchronous and asynchronous fashion. Throughout this process, I was able to attend to both the psychosocial and career aspects that Kram (1985) described. And our conversations were certainly what Kolb (1984) described as experientially-based learning.

Chris is both a high performing doctoral student, and a high achieving, but young, leader. Chris is more comfortable than most doctoral students in that role, but still has much to learn on his leadership journey. As I continue to work with Chris, the focus of our mentoring and coaching entails not just his academic experiences, but includes helping him develop a set of key leadership skill sets: leading people (inspiration and execution), leading relationships (influence and collaboration), organizational leadership (vision and acumen), and entrepreneurial leadership (talent development and driving change) (O'Leonard, 2014). These are the capabilities that all leaders require regardless of their culture, organization, or situation. As an aspiring college president, these are the skills that will serve Chris now and in the future.

CONCLUSION

When a mentor provides support, challenge, encouragement and nurturance, the career and psychosocial functions as described by Kram (1985) together create a safe environment in which the protégé can learn and take risks. Kram suggested that the greater the number and depth of functions by the mentor, the more beneficial the relationship will be to the protégé. Waldeck et al. (1997) believe that 'taken together, these personal and professional tools assist in the career advancement of protégés' (p. 89). But as Ragins and Cotton (1999) contend, mentoring is not an all or nothing phenomenon; a mentor may address any number of the specific domains within a specific function.

The benefits of a mentoring relationship clearly suggest that it is an activity that should be undertaken by all doctoral students, and that faculty should want to encourage this type of work with students to ensure their success, engagement and retention. Yet much of the research on the prevalence of mentoring indicates that only 50–60 percent of students have been mentored in graduate school (Atkinson et al., 1991; Clark et al., 2000; Fallow and Johnson, 2000; Smith and Davidson, 1992). While it is a given that mentoring relationships take time, most institutions do not have a formal system in place for graduate students or faculty to develop such working relationships.

Graduate leadership programs stand in a unique position to be able to offer mentoring opportunities for their students focused specifically on developing their capacity as leaders. As graduate programs become more technologically driven, providing academic programs in distance and virtual spaces, e-mentoring offered as part of their programs can serve more students, and work to move students further and faster along the leadership development continuum than they might otherwise without a mentor. In the end, organizations, educational institutions, students or protégés, and mentors all benefit.

REFERENCES

Allen, I.E. and J. Seaman (2017). *Digital Learning Compass: Distance Education Enrollment Report 2017*. Babson Survey Research Group. Accessed at https://www.onlinelearningsurvey.com/highered.html.

Allen, T.D. and L.T. Eby (2010). *The Blackwell Handbook of Mentoring*. Oxford: Wiley-Blackwell.

Allen, T.D., L.T. Eby, M.L. Poteet, E. Lentz and L. Lima (2004). Career benefits associated with mentoring for protégés: A meta-analysis. *Journal of Applied Psychology*, **89**(1), 127–36.

Atkinson, D.R., H. Neville and A. Casas (1991). The mentorship of ethnic minorities in professional psychology. *Professional Psychology: Research and Practice*, **22**, 336–8.

Austin, A.E. (2002). Preparing the next generation of faculty: Graduate school as socialization to the academic career. *Journal of Higher Education*, **73**(1), 94–122.

Avolio, B.J. (2011). *Full Range Leadership Development*. Thousand Oaks, CA: Sage.

Bandura, A. (1997). *Self-efficacy: The Exercise of Control.* New York, NY: W.H. Freeman.

Bass, B.M. (1985). *Leadership and Performance Beyond Expectations.* New York, NY: Free Press.

Bass, B.M. (1999). Two decades of research and development in transformational leadership. *European Journal of Work and Organizational Psychology*, **8**(1), 9–32.

Beattie, R.S. (2002). Developmental managers: Line managers as facilitators of workplace learning in voluntary organizations. Unpublished doctoral dissertation. University of Glasgow, Scotland.

Beech, N. and A. Brockbank (1999). Power/knowledge and psychosocial dynamics in mentoring. *Management Learning*, **30**(1), 7–25.

Bersin, J., J. Geller, N. Wakefield and B. Walsh (2016). *Global Human Capital Trends 2016.* Oakland, CA: Deloitte. Accessed at https://www2.deloitte.com/content/dam/Deloitte/global/Documents/HumanCapital/gx-dup-global-human-capital-trends-2016.pdf.

Berson, Y., B. Shamir, B.J. Avolio and M. Popper (2001). The relationship between vision, strength, leadership style, and context. *Leadership Quarterly*, **12**, 53–73.

Bierema, L.L. and S.B. Merriam (2002). E-mentoring: Using computer mediated communications to enhance the mentoring process. *Innovation in Higher Education*, **26**(3), 211–20.

Bolman, L.G. and T.E. Deal (2013). *Reframing Organizations: Artistry, Choice, and Leadership* (5th edn). San Francisco, CA: Jossey-Bass.

Browne-Ferrigno, T. and R. Muth (2004). Leadership mentoring in clinical practice: Role socialization, professional development and capacity building. *Educational Administration Quarterly*, **40**(4), 468–94.

Burke, C.S., K.C. Stagl, C. Klein, G.F. Goodwin, E. Salas and S.M. Halpin (2006). What type of leadership behaviors are functional in teams? A meta-analysis. *The Leadership Quarterly*, **17**(3), 288–307.

Chen, L.Y. (2004). Examining the effect of organization culture and leadership behaviors on organizational commitment, job satisfaction, and job performance at small and middle-sized firms of Taiwan. *Journal of American Academy of Business*, **5**(1), 432–8.

Clark, R.A., S.L. Harden and W.B. Johnson (2000). Mentor relationships in clinical psychology doctoral training: Results of a national survey. *Teaching of Psychology*, **27**, 262–8.

Clutterbuck, D. (2001). *Everyone Needs a Mentor: Fostering Talent at Work* (3rd edn). London: Chartered Institute of Personnel and Development.

Council of Graduate Schools (2008). PhD Completion Project. Accessed at http://www.cgsnet.org.

Cronan-Hillix, T., L.K. Gensheimer, W.A. Cronan-Hillix and W.S. Davidson (1986). Students' views of mentors in psychology graduate training. *Teaching of Psychology*, **13**(3), 123–7.

Day, D.V. (2000). Leadership development: A review in context. *The Leadership Quarterly*, **11**(4), 581–613.

DeRue, D.S. and S.J. Ashford (2010). Who will lead and who will follow? A social process of leadership identity construction in organizations. *Academy of Management Review*, **35**, 627–47.

Eby, L.T., T.D. Allen, S.C. Evans, T. Ng and D.L. Dubois (2008). Does mentoring matter? A multidisciplinary meta-analysis comparing mentored and non-mentored individuals. *Journal of Vocational Behavior*, **72**, 254–67.

Ellis, H.C. (1992). Graduate education in psychology: Past, present, and future. *American Psychologist*, **47**, 570–76.

Fagan, M. and G. Walter (1982), Mentoring among teachers. *Journal of Educational Research*, **76**(2), 113–17.

Falconer, L. (2006). Organizational learning, tacit information, and e-learning: A review, *The Learning Organization*, **13**(20), 140–51.

Fallow, G.O. and W.B. Johnson (2000). Mentor relationships in secular and religious professional psychology programs. *Journal of Psychology and Christianity*, **19**, 363–76.

Forehand, R.L. (2008). The art and science of mentoring in psychology: A necessary practice to ensure our future. *American Psychologist*, **63**, 744–55.

Fuller, J.B. and C.E.P. Patterson (1996). A quantitative review of research on charismatic leadership. *Psychological Reports*, **78**(1), 271–87.

Garland, H. and J.H. Adkinson (1987). Standards, persuasion, and performance: A test of cognitive mediation theory. *Group and Organizational Management*, **12**, 208–20.

Gentry, W.A., T.J. Weber and G. Sadri (2008). Examining career related mentoring and managerial performance across cultures: A multilevel analysis. *Journal of Vocational Behavior*, **72**, 241–53.

Hannah, S.T., R.L. Woolfolk and R.G. Lord (2009). Leader self-structure: A framework for positive leadership. *Journal of Organizational Behavior*, **30**, 269–90.

Headlam-Wells, J., J. Gosland and J. Craig (2005). There's magic in the web: E-mentoring for women's career development. *Career Development International*, **10**(6/7), 444–59.

International Coach Federation (n.d.). What is professional coaching? Accessed at https://www.coachfederation.org/need/.

Jacobi, M. (1991). Mentoring and undergraduate success: A literature review. *Review of Educational Research*, **61**, 505–32.

Johnson, W.B. (2007). Transformational supervision: When supervisors mentor. *Professional Psychology: Research and Practice*, **38**, 259–67.

Johnson, W.B. (2008). Are advocacy, mutuality, and evaluation incompatible mentoring functions? *Mentoring and Tutoring: Partnership in Learning*, **16**, 31–44.

Johnson, W.B. (2014). Mentoring in psychology education and training: A mentoring relationship continuum model. In W.B. Johnson and N.J. Kaslow (eds), *The Oxford Handbook of Education and Training in Professional Psychology* (pp. 272–90). New York: Oxford University Press.

Jossi, F. (1997). Mentoring in changing times. *Training*, **34**(8), 50–54.

Kahn, J.H. (2001). Predicting the scholarly activity of counseling psychology students: A refinement and extension. *Journal of Counseling Psychology*, **48**(3), 344–54.

Kerka, S. (1998). *New Perspectives on Mentoring*. Columbus, OH: ERIC Clearinghouse on Adult, Career and Vocational Education.

Kolb, D.A. (1984). *Experiential Learning: Experience as the Source of Learning and Development*. Englewood Cliffs, NJ: Prentice-Hall.

Kram, K.E. (1983), Phases of the mentor relationship. *Academy of Management Journal*, **26**, 608–25.

Kram, K.E. (1985). *Mentoring at Work: Developmental Relationships in Organizational Life*. Glenview, IL: Scott Foresman.

Kumar, S. and C. Coe (2017). Mentoring and student support in online doctoral programs. *American Journal of Distance Education*, **31**(2), 128–42.

Kumar, S. and M. Johnson (2017). Mentoring doctoral students online: Mentor strategies and challenges. *Mentoring & Tutoring: Partnership in Learning*, **25**(2), 202–22.

Lamoureux, K. (2012). *Tuition Assistance Programs: Best Practices for Maximizing a Key Talent Investment*. Oakland, CA: Bersin & Associates.

Loew, L. and S.S. Garr (2014). *Benchmarks and Trends in U.S. Leadership Development*. Oakland, CA: Bersin & Associates.

London, M. (2002). *Leadership Development: Paths to Self-Insight and Professional Growth*. Mahwah, NJ: Erlbaum.

Lord, R.G. and R.J. Hall (2005). Identity, deep structure and the development of leadership skills. *Leadership Quarterly*, **16**, 591–615.

Lowe, K.B., K.G. Kroeck and N. Sivasubramanian (1996). Effectiveness correlates of transformational and transactional leadership: A meta-analytic review of the MLQ literature. *Leadership Quarterly*, **7**(3), 385–425.

Lunsford, L. (2012). Doctoral advising or mentoring? Effects on student outcomes. *Mentoring & Tutoring: Partnership in Learning*, **20**(2), 251–70.

McCauley, C.D. and E. Van Velsor (eds) (2004). *Handbook of Leadership Development* (2nd edn). San Francisco, CA: Jossey-Bass.

McDougall, M. and R.S. Beattie (1997). Peer mentoring at work. *Management Learning*, **28**(4), 423–37.

McKenzie, B.K., B.C. Özkan and K. Layton (2006). Tips for administrators in promoting distance programs using peer mentoring. *Online Journal of Distance Learning Administration*, **9**(2).

Muilenburg, L.Y. and Z.L. Berge (2005). Student barriers to online learning: A factor analytic study, *Distance Education: An International Journal*, **26**(1), 29–48.

Muirhead, B. and M. Betz (2002). Faculty training at an online university. *USDLA Journal*, **16**(1), 99–103.

Nettles, M.T. and C.M. Millett (2006). *Three Magic Letters: Getting to Ph.D.* Baltimore, MD: Johns Hopkins University Press.

Noam, E. (1995). What then is the role of the university? *Science*, **13**, 247.

O'Leonard, K. (2014). Universal leadership competencies: Does one size fit all? Oakland, CA: Bersin & Associates.

Owens, D.M. (2006). Virtual mentoring. *HR Magazine*, **51**(3), 105–107.

Paglis, L.L., S.G. Green and T.N. Bauer (2006). Does adviser mentoring add value? A longitudinal study of mentoring and doctoral student outcomes. *Research in Higher Education*, **47**(4), 451–76.

Parsloe, E. and M. Wray (2000). *Coaching and Mentoring: Practical Methods to Improve Learning*. London: Kogan Page.

Pascarella, E. (1980). Student faculty informal contact and college outcomes. *Review of Educational Research*, **50**, 545–95.

Payne, S.C. and A.H. Huffman (2005). A longitudinal examination of the influence of mentoring on organizational commitment and turnover. *Academy of Management Journal*, **48**, 158–68.

Phillips-Jones, L. (1982). *Mentors and Protégés*. New York, NY: Arbor House.

Ragins, B.R. and J.L. Cotton (1999). Mentor functions and outcomes: A comparison of men and women in formal and informal mentoring relationships. *Journal of Applied Psychology*, **84**, 529–50.

Scandura, T. (1998). Dysfunctional mentoring relationships and outcomes. *Journal of Management*, **24**, 449–67.

Scandura, T.A., M.J. Tejeda, W.B. Werther and M.J. Lankau (1996). Perspectives on mentoring. *Leadership and Organization Development Journal*, **17**(3), 50–57.

Single, P.B. and R.M. Single (2005). E-mentoring for social equity: Review of research to inform program development. *Mentoring and Tutoring*, **13**(2), 301–20.

Smith, E.P. and W.S. Davidson (1992). Mentoring and the development of African American graduate students. *Journal of College Student Development*, **33**, 531–9.

Smith, S.J. and M. Israel (2010). E-mentoring: Enhancing special education teacher induction. *Journal of Special Education Leadership*, **23**(1), 30–40.

Stajkovic, A.D. and F. Luthans (1998). Self-efficacy and work-related performance: A meta-analysis. *Psychological Bulletin*, **124**(2), 240–61.

Stott, K. and A. Walker (1992). Developing school leaders through mentoring: A Singapore perspective. *School Organization*, **12**(2), 153–65.

Townley, B. (1994), *Reframing Human Resource Management: Power, Ethics and the Subject at Work*. London: Sage.

Waldeck, J.H., V.O. Orrego, T.G. Plax and P. Kearney (1997). Graduate student/faculty mentoring relationships: Who gets mentored, how it happens, and to what end. *Communication Quarterly*, **45**, 93–109.

Williams, S.L. and J. Kim (2011). E-mentoring in online course projects: Description of an e-mentoring scheme. *International Journal of Evidence Based Coaching & Mentoring*, **9**(2), 80–95.

Williams, S., J. Sunderman and J. Kim (2012). E-mentoring in an online course: Benefits and challenges to e-mentors. *International Journal of Evidence Based Coaching & Mentoring*, **10**(1), 109–23.

Wright-Harp, W. and P.A. Cole (2008). A mentoring model for enhancing success in graduate education. *Contemporary Issues in Communication Science and Disorders*, **35**, 4–16.

Yob, I. and L. Crawford (2012). Conceptual framework for mentoring doctoral students. *Higher Learning Research Communication*, **2**, 34–47.

Yukl, G. (2006). *Leadership in Organizations*. Upper Saddle River, NJ: Pearson Education.

Zey, M.G. (1984). *The Mentor Connection*. Homewood, IL: Dow-Jones Irwin.

Index